THE INVINCIBLE
IRON MAN
DEMON

IRON MAN VOL. 9: DEMON. Contains material originally published in magazine form as INVINCIBLE IRON MAN #510-515. First printing 2012. Hardcover ISBN# 978-0-7851-6046-5. Softcover ISB Published by MARVEL WORLDWIDE, INC., a subsidiary of MARVEL ENTERTAINMENT, LLC. OFFICE OF PUBLICATION: 135 West 50th Street, New York, NY 10020. Copyright © 2011 and 20 C. All rights reserved. Hardcover: $19.99 per copy in the U.S. and $21.99 in Canada (GST #R127032852). Softcover: $18.99 per copy in the U.S. and $18.99 in Canada (GST #R1270328. #40668537. All characters featured in this issue and the distinctive names and likenesses thereof, and all related indicia are trademarks of Marvel Characters, Inc. No similarity between a ers, persons, and/or institutions in this magazine with those of any living or dead person or institution is intended, and any such similarity which may exist is purely coincidental. **Printed** EVP - Office of the President, Marvel Worldwide, Inc. and EVP & CMO Marvel Characters B.V.; DAN BUCKLEY, Publisher & President - Print, Animation & Digital Divisions; JOE QUESADA, CH BREVOORT, SVP of Publishing; DAVID BOGART, SVP of Operations & Procurement, Publishing; RUWAN JAYATILLEKE, SVP & Associate Publisher, Publishing; C.B. CEBULSKI, SVP of Creato DAVID GABRIEL, SVP of Publishing Sales & Circulation; MICHAEL PASCIULLO, SVP of Brand Planning & Communications; JIM O'KEEFE, VP of Operations & Logistics; DAN CARR, Execu Technology; SUSAN CRESPI, Editorial Operations Manager; ALEX MORALES, Publishing Operations Manager; STAN LEE, Chairman Emeritus. For information regarding advertising in Mar m, please contact John Dokes, SVP Integrated Sales and Marketing, at jdokes@marvel.com. For Marvel subscription inquiries, please call 800-217-9158. **Manufactured between 5/7/20** ver), and 5/7/2012 and 12/3/2012 (softcover), by R.R. DONNELLEY, INC., SALEM, VA, USA.

THE INVINCIBLE
IRON MAN
DEMON

WRITER: **MATT FRACTION**
ARTIST: **SALVADOR LARROCA**
COLORS: **FRANK D'ARMATA**
LETTERS: **VC'S JOE CARAMAGNA**
COVER ART: **SALVADOR LARROCA** & **FRANK D'ARMATA**
ASSISTANT EDITORS: **JOHN DENNING, JAKE THOMAS & JON MOISAN**
EDITORS: **ALEJANDRO ARBONA & MARK PANICCIA**
EXECUTIVE EDITOR: **TOM BREVOORT**

COLLECTION EDITOR: **JENNIFER GRÜNWALD**
ASSISTANT EDITORS: **ALEX STARBUCK & NELSON RIBEIRO**
EDITOR, SPECIAL PROJECTS: **MARK D. BEAZLEY**
SENIOR EDITOR, SPECIAL PROJECTS: **JEFF YOUNGQUIST**
SENIOR VICE PRESIDENT OF SALES: **DAVID GABRIEL**
VP OF BRAND PLANNING & COMMUNICATIONS: **MICHAEL PASCIULLO**

EDITOR IN CHIEF: **AXEL ALONSO**
CHIEF CREATIVE OFFICER: **JOE QUESADA**
PUBLISHER: **DAN BUCKLEY**
EXECUTIVE PRODUCER: **ALAN FINE**

NCIBLE IRON M
0-7851-6047-2
el Characters, In
dian Agreement
e names, charac
.S.A. ALAN FINE,
ive Officer; TOM
nt Development
or of Publishing
s or on Marvel.co
4/2012 (hardco

7 6 5 4 3 2 1

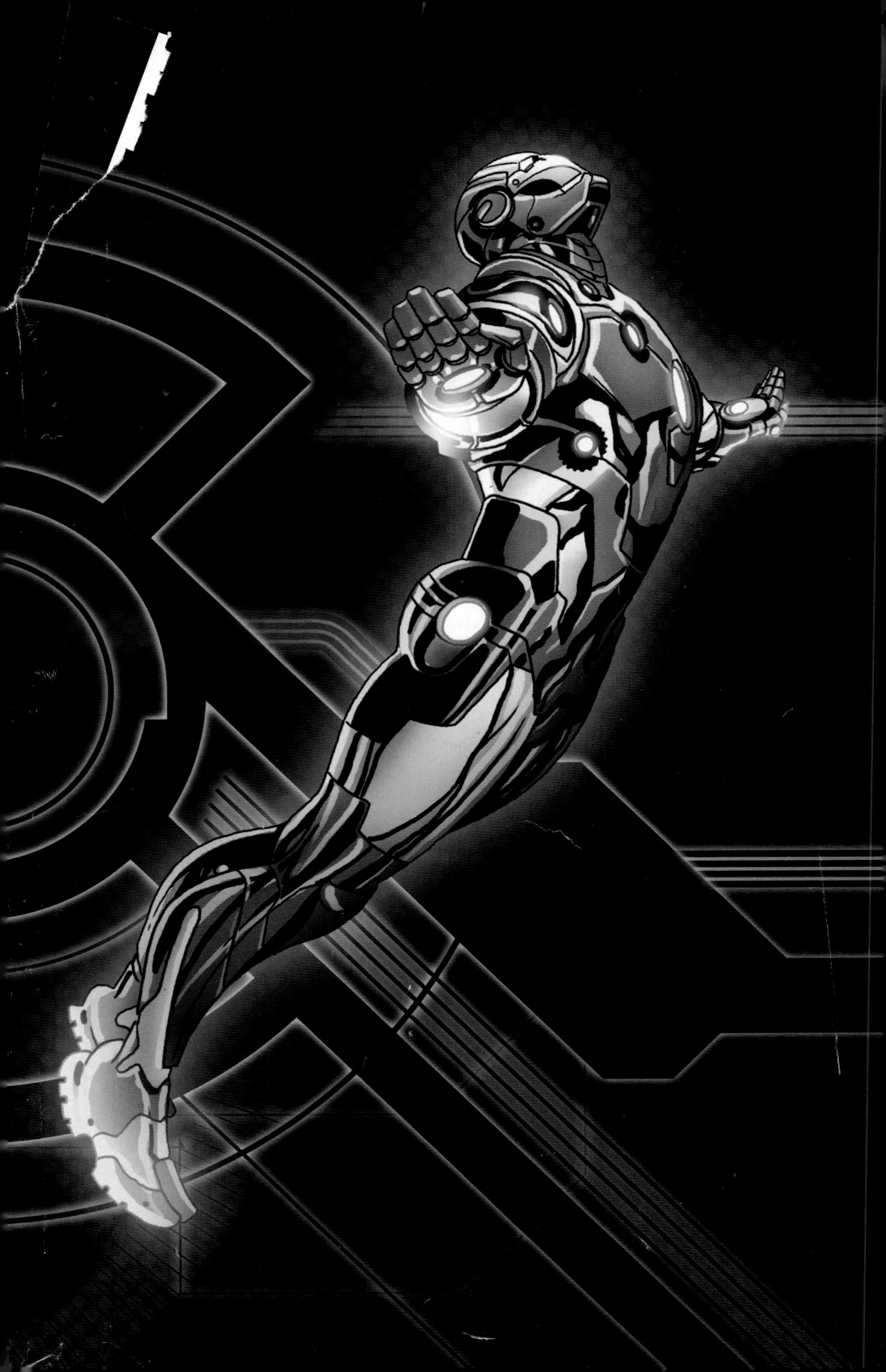

PREVIOUSLY:

TONY STARK SAW A CITY TURNED TO STONE AND A WAR BETWEEN GODS UNLEASHED ACROSS THE FACE OF THE EARTH. AND THEN, WHEN THE WORLD WAS ENDING, TONY STARK GOT DRUNK.

WITH THE BLESSINGS OF ODIN HIMSELF, HE RETREATED TO THE ASGARDIAN FORGES OF SVARTALFHEIM TO CRAFT WEAPONS FOR THE AVENGERS TO USE ON ARMAGEDDON. WHAT HE CRAFTED WERE HALF HIS, HALF MYSTIC, AND HELPED STEM THE TIDE OF THE APOCALYPSE AGAINST ALL ODDS.

AS FUNERALS FOR THE FALLEN WERE HELD AROUND THE WORLD, TONY HELPED CLEAN UP THE MASSIVE GRAVEYARD THAT PARIS HAD BECOME. WHILE THERE, SURROUNDED BY COUNTLESS DEAD, STARK CONFRONTED ODIN ONE LAST TIME AND WAS SHOWN NOT ONLY THE DEPTHS OF INFINITE COMPASSION BUT THE DEPTHS OF THE INFINITE ITSELF.

TONY STARK HAS BEEN SOBER FOR THREE DAYS.

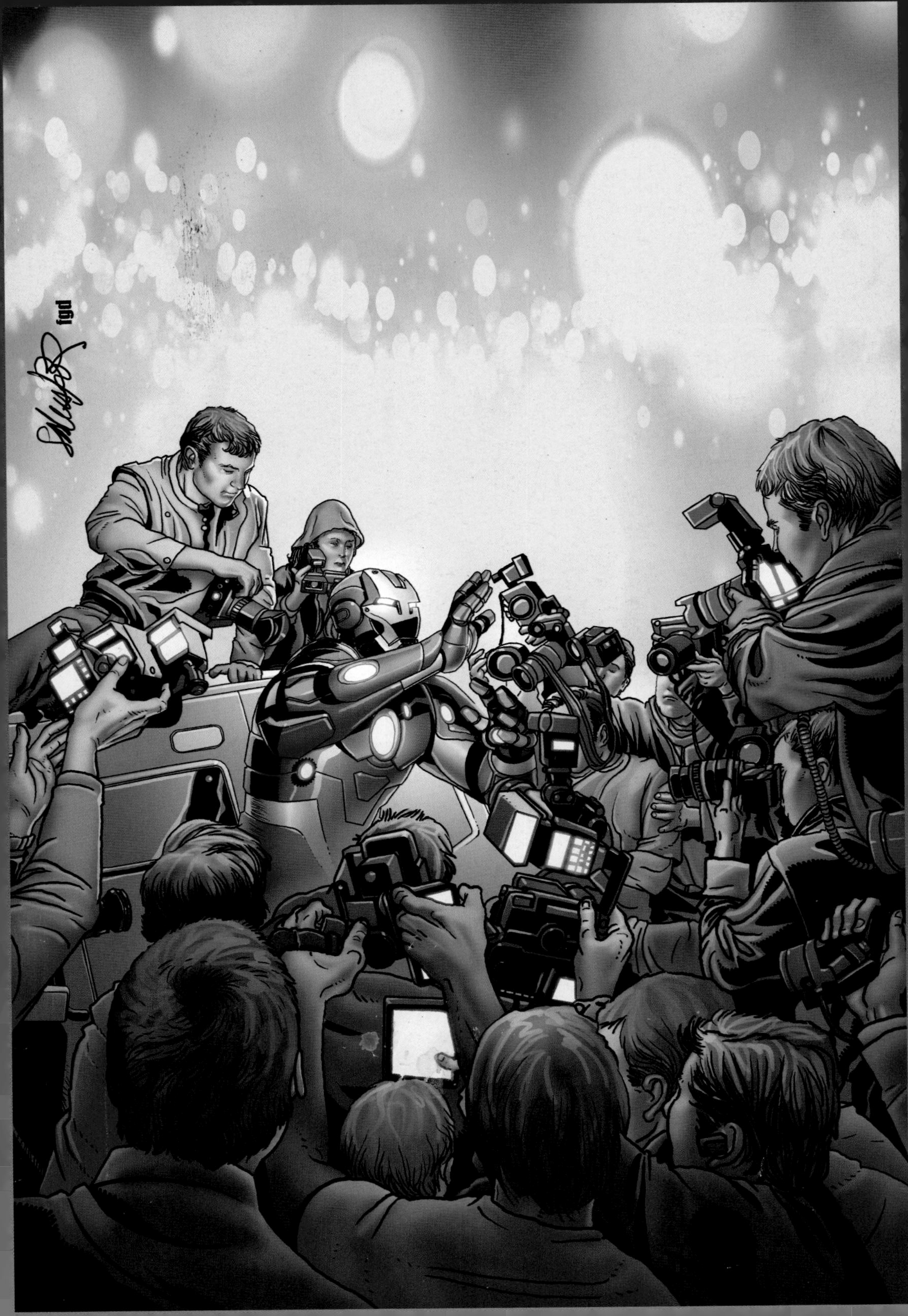

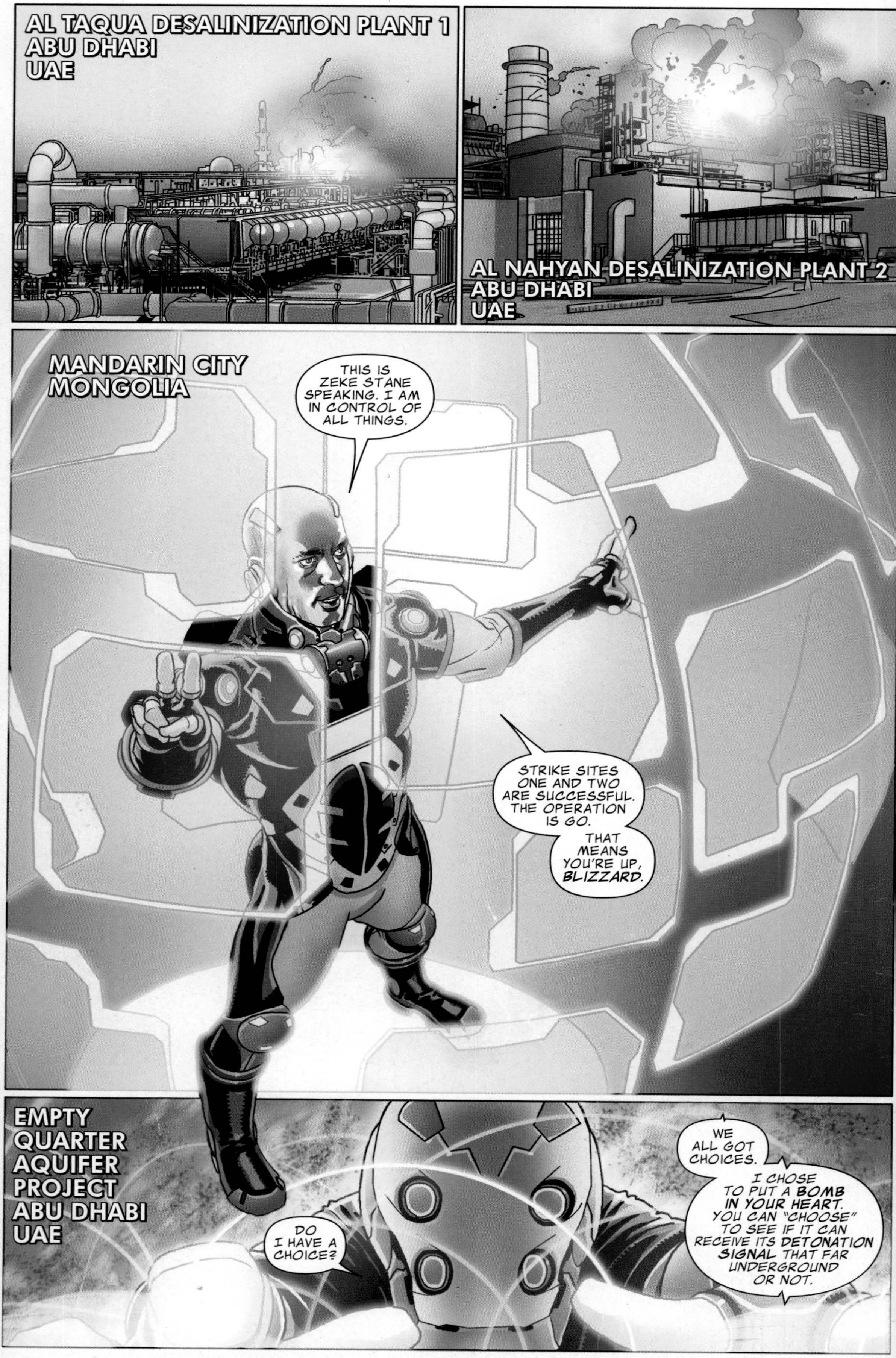

AL TAQUA DESALINIZATION PLANT 1 ABU DHABI UAE
AL NAHYAN DESALINIZATION PLANT 2 ABU DHABI UAE
MANDARIN CITY MONGOLIA
THIS IS ZEKE STANE SPEAKING. I AM IN CONTROL OF ALL THINGS.
STRIKE SITES ONE AND TWO ARE SUCCESSFUL. THE OPERATION IS GO.
THAT MEANS YOU'RE UP, BLIZZARD.
EMPTY QUARTER AQUIFER PROJECT ABU DHABI UAE
DO I HAVE A CHOICE?
WE ALL GOT CHOICES.
I CHOSE TO PUT A BOMB IN YOUR HEART. YOU CAN "CHOOSE" TO SEE IF IT CAN RECEIVE ITS DETONATION SIGNAL THAT FAR UNDERGROUND OR NOT.

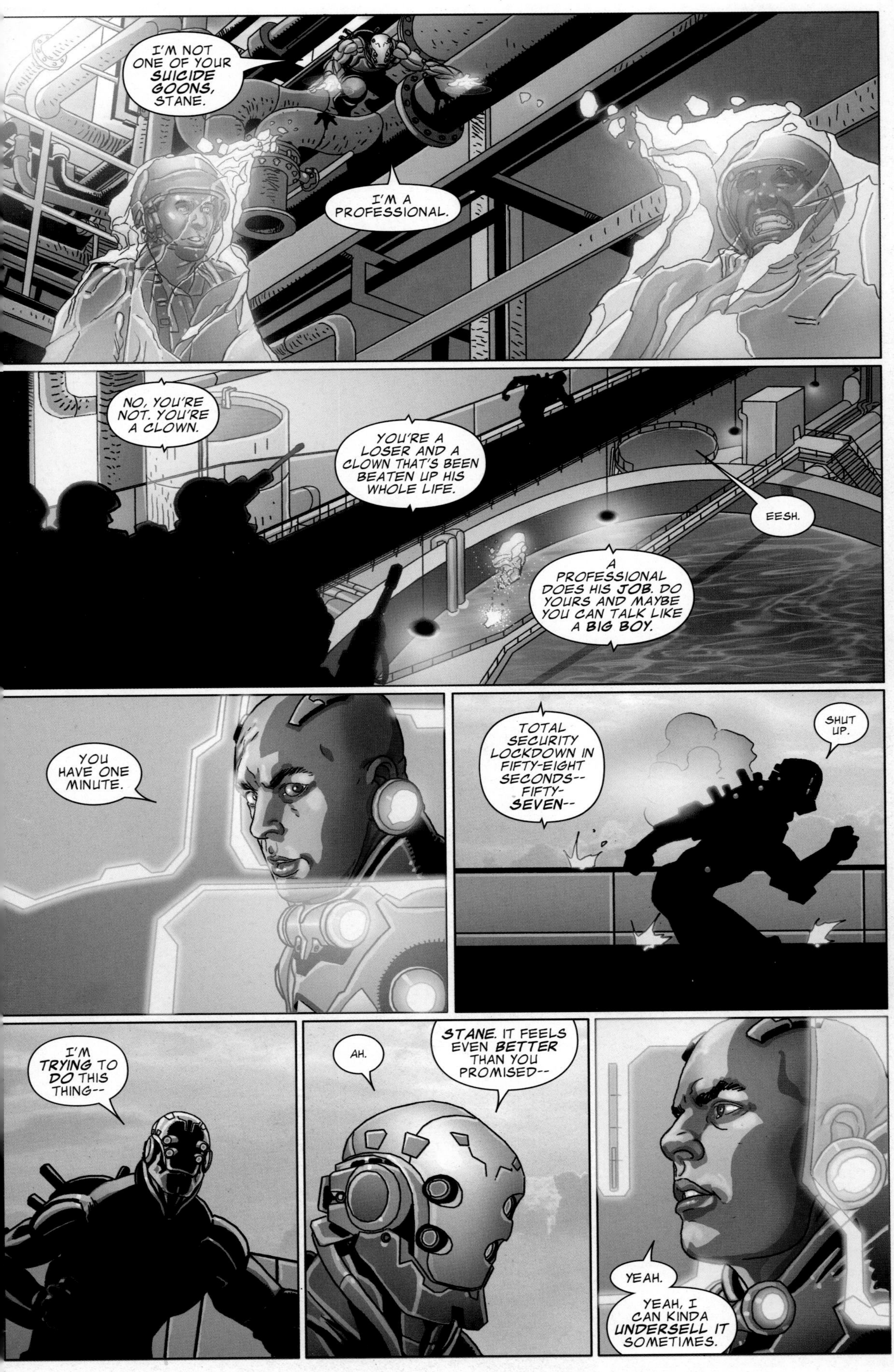
I'M NOT ONE OF YOUR SUICIDE GOONS, STANE.
I'M A PROFESSIONAL.
NO, YOU'RE NOT. YOU'RE A CLOWN.
YOU'RE A LOSER AND A CLOWN THAT'S BEEN BEATEN UP HIS WHOLE LIFE.
EESH.
A PROFESSIONAL DOES HIS JOB. DO YOURS AND MAYBE YOU CAN TALK LIKE A BIG BOY.
YOU HAVE ONE MINUTE.
TOTAL SECURITY LOCKDOWN IN FIFTY-EIGHT SECONDS-- FIFTY-SEVEN--
SHUT UP.
I'M TRYING TO DO THIS THING--
AH.
STANE. IT FEELS EVEN BETTER THAN YOU PROMISED--
YEAH.
YEAH, I CAN KINDA UNDERSELL IT SOMETIMES.

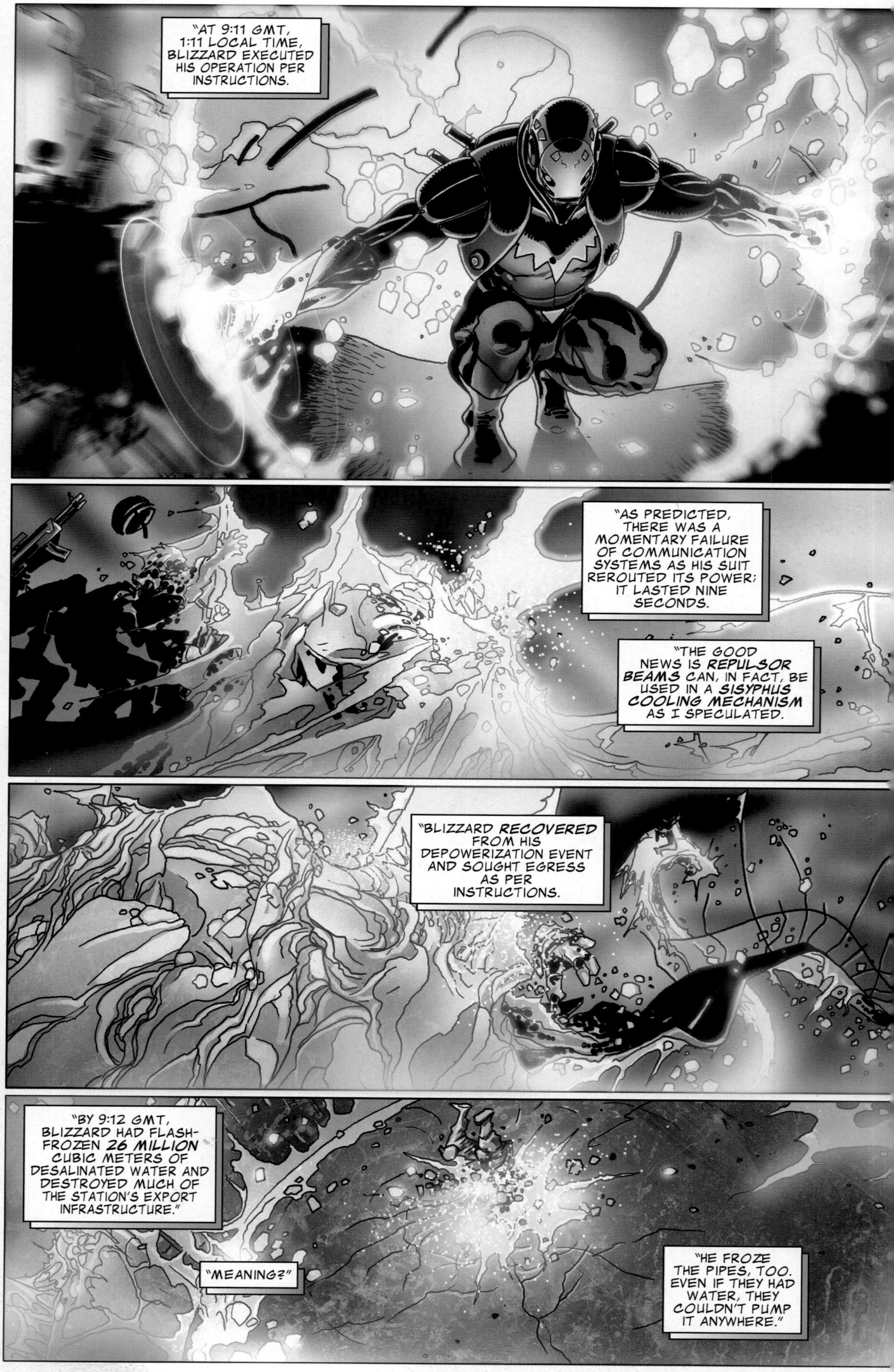
"AT 9:11 GMT, 1:11 LOCAL TIME, BLIZZARD EXECUTED HIS OPERATION PER INSTRUCTIONS.
"AS PREDICTED, THERE WAS A MOMENTARY FAILURE OF COMMUNICATION SYSTEMS AS HIS SUIT REROUTED ITS POWER; IT LASTED NINE SECONDS.
"THE GOOD NEWS IS REPULSOR BEAMS CAN, IN FACT, BE USED IN A SISYPHUS COOLING MECHANISM AS I SPECULATED.
"BLIZZARD RECOVERED FROM HIS DEPOWERIZATION EVENT AND SOUGHT EGRESS AS PER INSTRUCTIONS.
"BY 9:12 GMT, BLIZZARD HAD FLASH-FROZEN 26 MILLION CUBIC METERS OF DESALINATED WATER AND DESTROYED MUCH OF THE STATION'S EXPORT INFRASTRUCTURE."
"MEANING?"
"HE FROZE THE PIPES, TOO. EVEN IF THEY HAD WATER, THEY COULDN'T PUMP IT ANYWHERE."

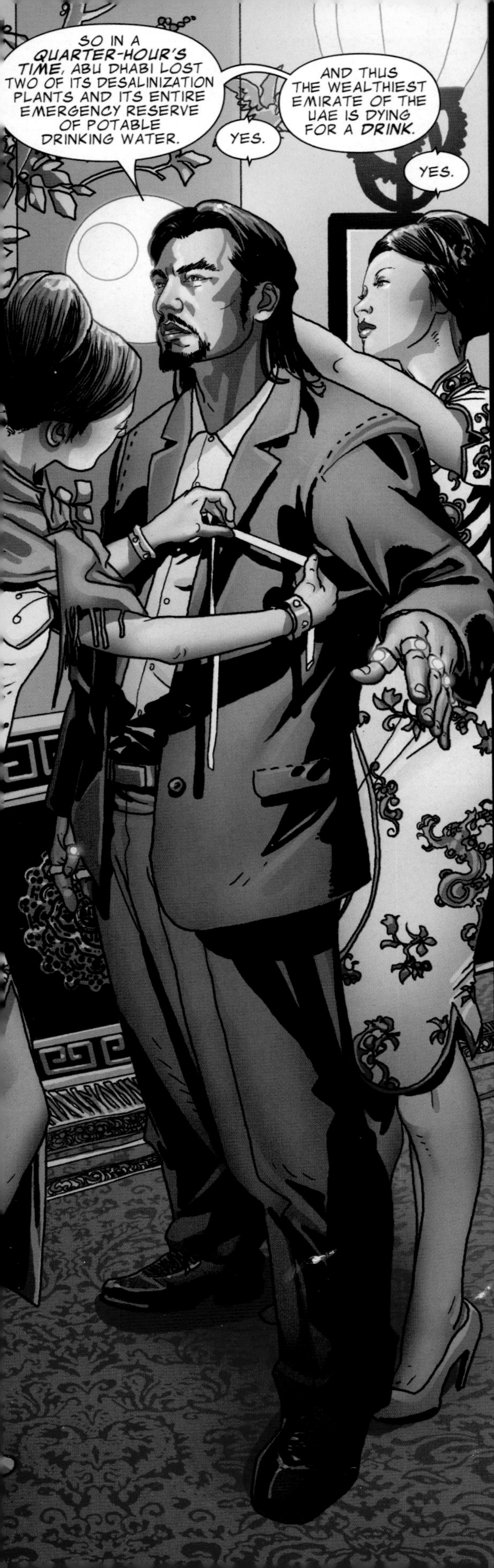
SO IN A QUARTER-HOUR'S TIME, ABU DHABI LOST TWO OF ITS DESALINIZATION PLANTS AND ITS ENTIRE EMERGENCY RESERVE OF POTABLE DRINKING WATER.
YES.
AND THUS THE WEALTHIEST EMIRATE OF THE UAE IS DYING FOR A DRINK.
YES.

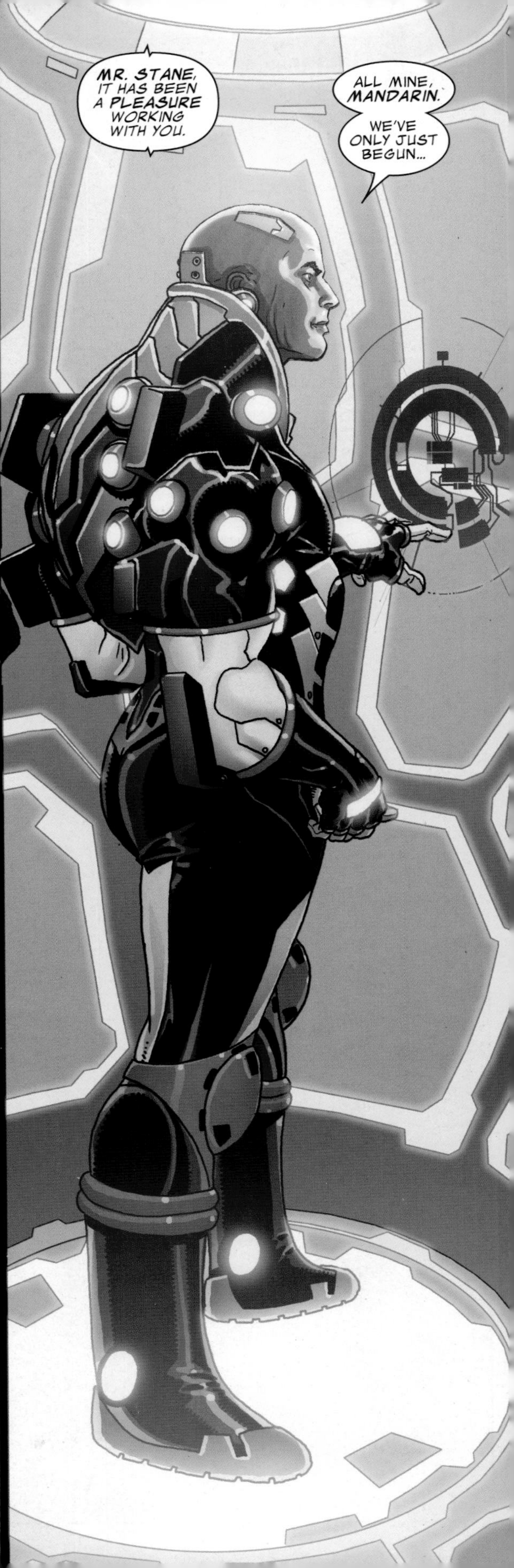
MR. STANE, IT HAS BEEN A PLEASURE WORKING WITH YOU.
ALL MINE, MANDARIN.
WE'VE ONLY JUST BEGUN...

SVARTALFHEIM
THE FORGES
SHAME TO MAKE SUCH THINGS ONLY TO MELT THE DOWN SO SOON.
IT'S WHAT I DO. I'LL MAKE MORE.
AND RED SHE-HULK KEPT HERS. I ASKED HER FOR IT AND SHE SAID I'D HAVE TO TAKE IT FROM HER.
APPARENTLY SOME LADIES LOVE BIG-ASS SWORDS.
THAT GONNA BE A PROBLEM?
EH. WITH ODIN GONE, THE ENCHANTMENTS ARE GONE, TOO.
HOW MUCH TROUBLE CAN A BIG RED BROAD GET INTO WITH A BIG-ASS BROADSWORD?
YOU'RE NOT FROM AROUND HERE. YOU'D BE SURPRISED.
I VENTED MY ENCHANTMENT FROM THE SUIT'S MOLECULAR STRUCTURE THIS MORNING. IT FELT LIKE SWEATING OUT A FEVER...
ANYWAY, WHEN THERE'S NO PILOT TO THE ENCHANTMENT, IT'S JUST THIS.
BEHOLD, THE IRON DESTROYER.
AHH, IT, GOOD RIDDANCE.
THAT WAS MEANT FOR GODS, STARK.
GODS. NOT HOPELESS LIKE YOU.
YOU STILL WANT TO LEAVE ALL THIS BEHIND?
...
YOU MY ? LOOK AT THIS HOLE.

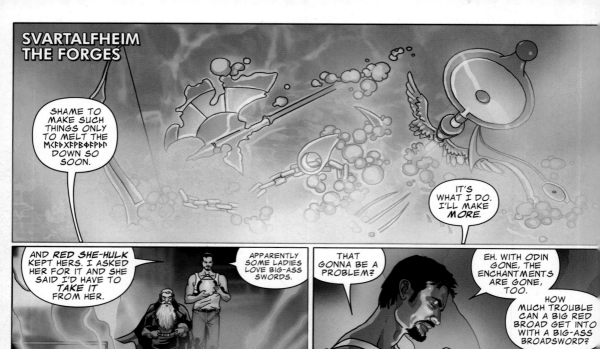

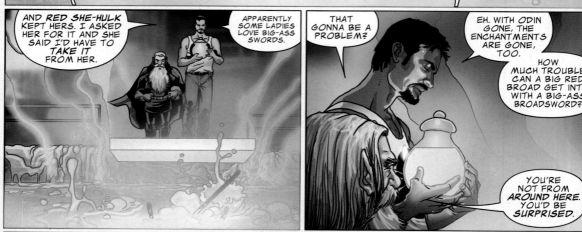

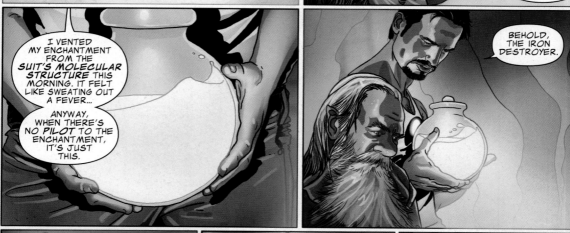

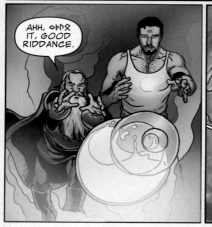

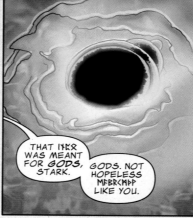

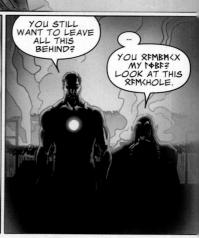

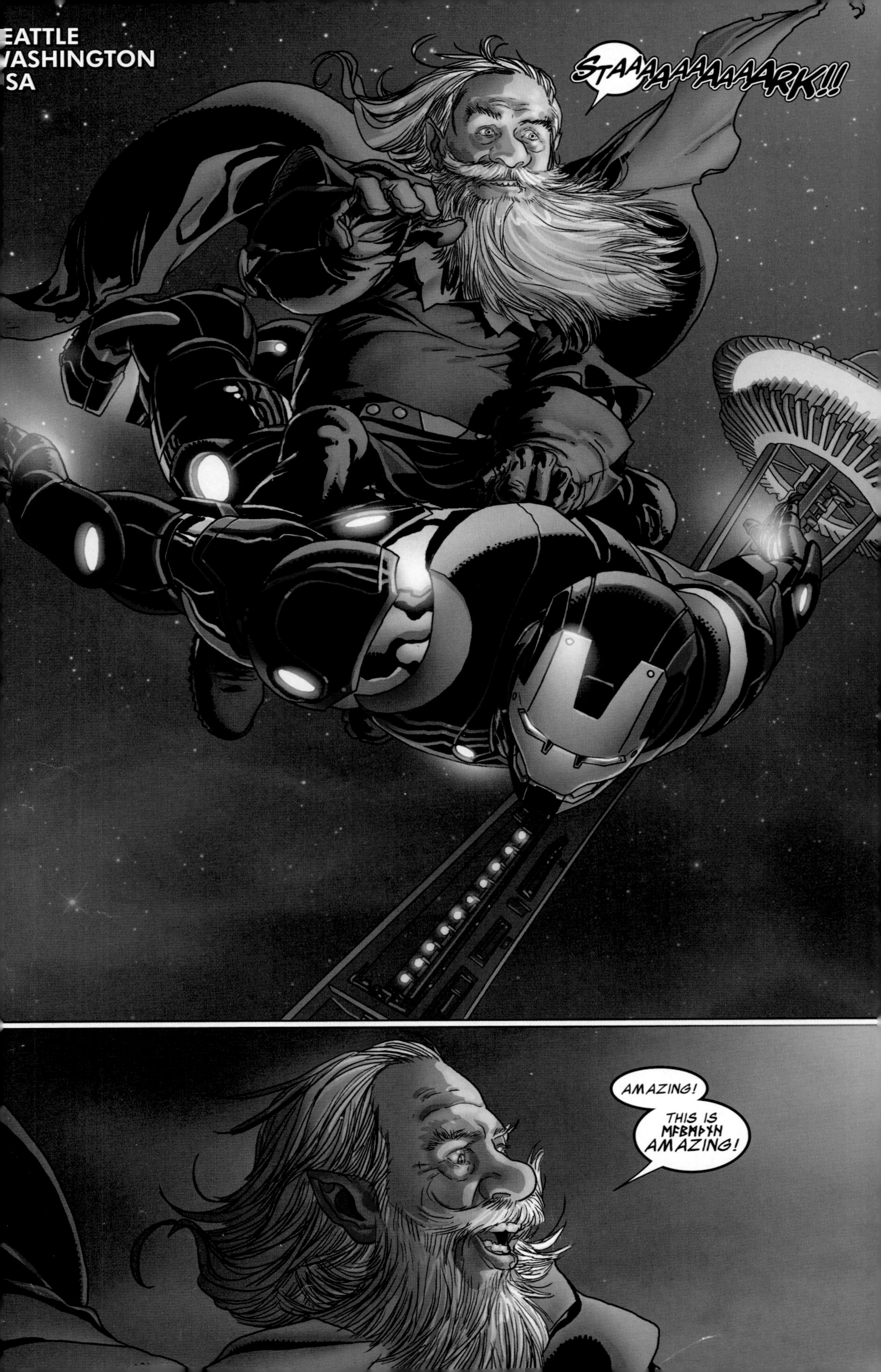
EATTLE
ASHINGTON
SA
STAAAAAAAAAARK!!
AMAZING!
THIS IS
AMAZING!

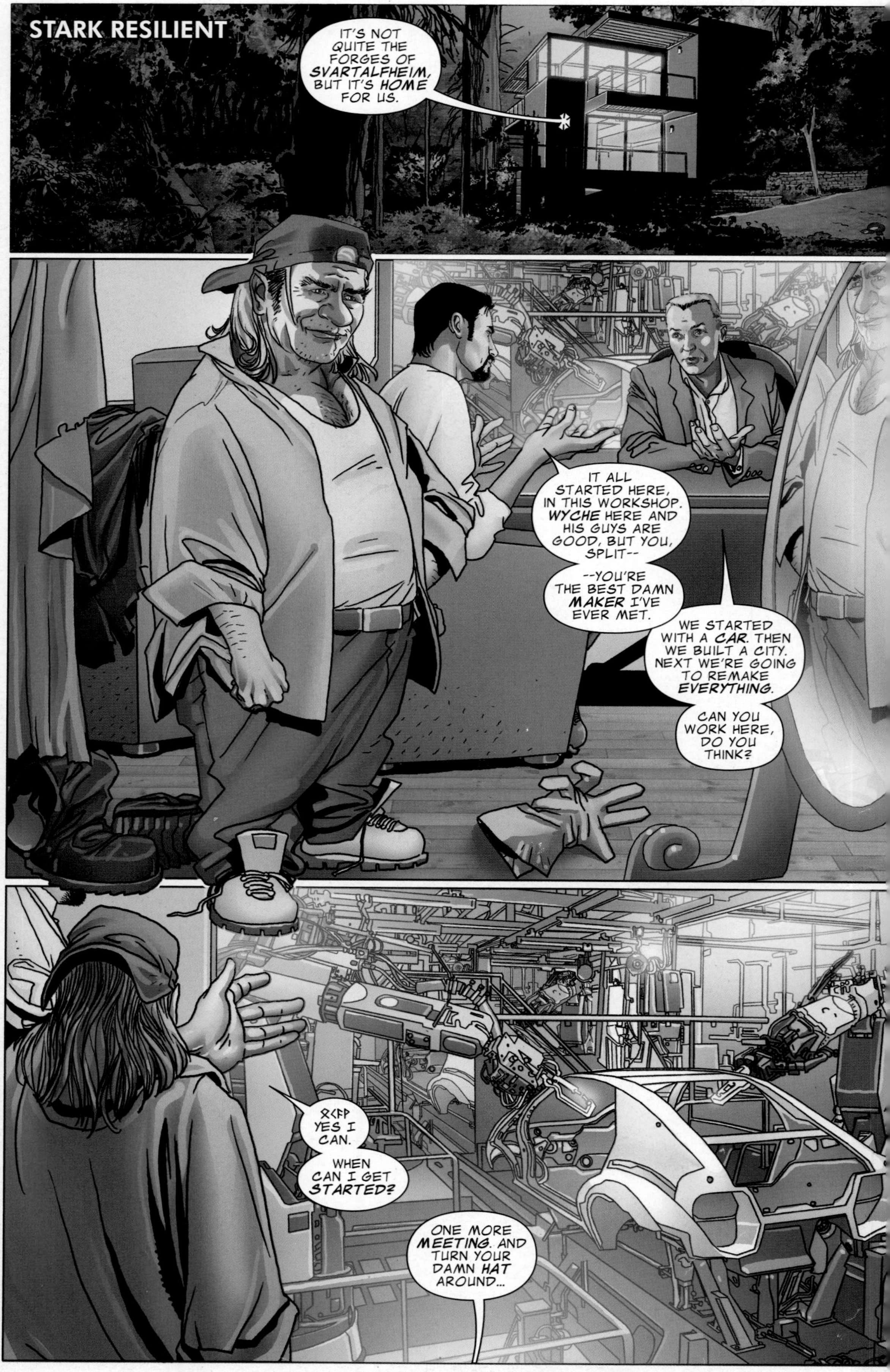
STARK RESILIENT
IT'S NOT QUITE THE FORGES OF SVARTALFHEIM, BUT IT'S HOME FOR US.
IT ALL STARTED HERE, IN THIS WORKSHOP. WYCHE HERE AND HIS GUYS ARE GOOD, BUT YOU, SPLIT--
--YOU'RE THE BEST DAMN MAKER I'VE EVER MET.
WE STARTED WITH A CAR. THEN WE BUILT A CITY. NEXT WE'RE GOING TO REMAKE EVERYTHING.
CAN YOU WORK HERE, DO YOU THINK?
YES I CAN.
WHEN CAN I GET STARTED?
ONE MORE MEETING. AND TURN YOUR DAMN HAT AROUND...

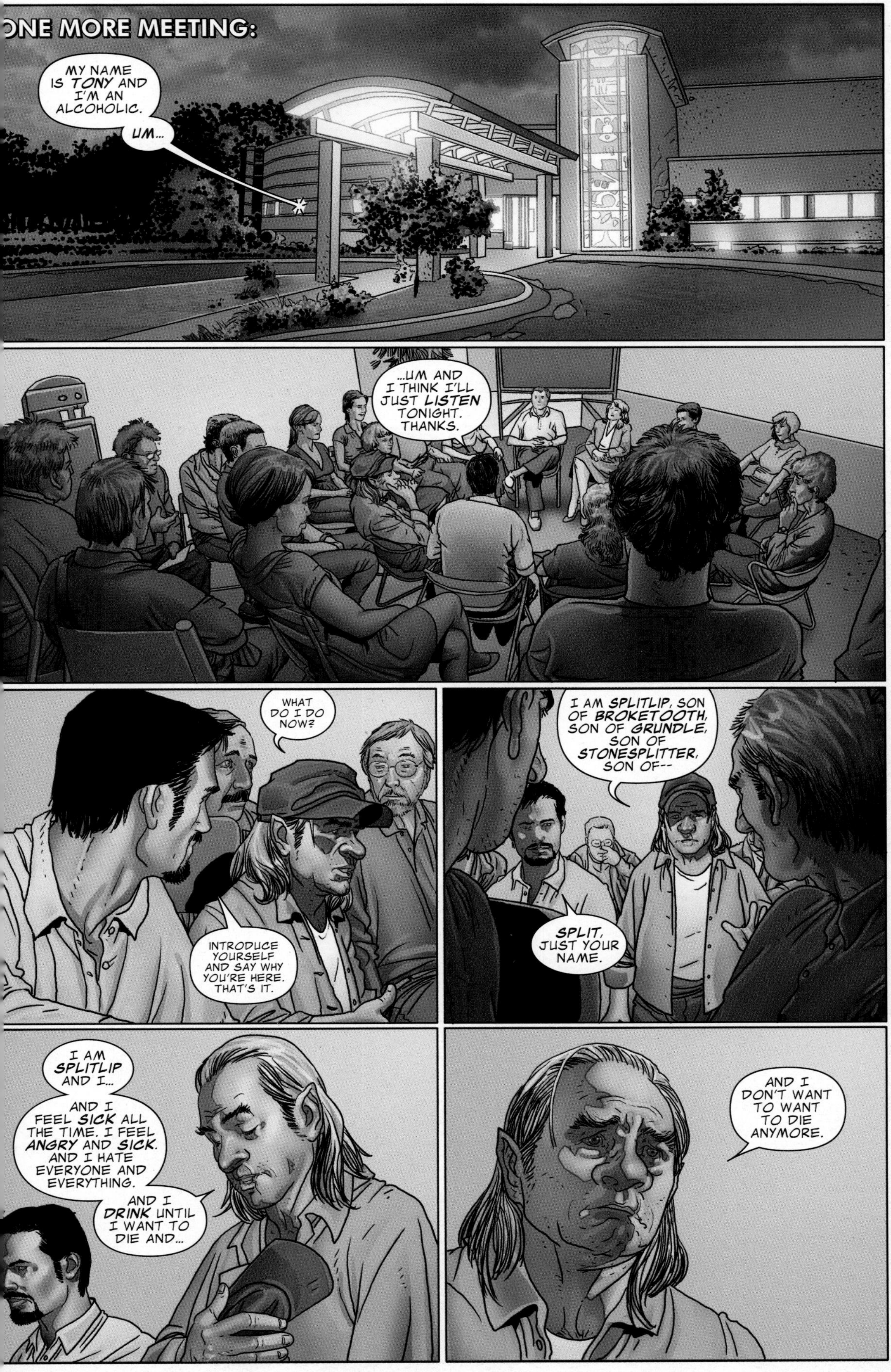
ONE MORE MEETING:
MY NAME IS TONY AND I'M AN ALCOHOLIC.
UM...
...UM AND I THINK I'LL JUST LISTEN TONIGHT. THANKS.
WHAT DO I DO NOW?
INTRODUCE YOURSELF AND SAY WHY YOU'RE HERE. THAT'S IT.
I AM SPLITLIP, SON OF BROKETOOTH, SON OF GRUNDLE, SON OF STONESPLITTER, SON OF--
SPLIT, JUST YOUR NAME.
I AM SPLITLIP AND I...
AND I FEEL SICK ALL THE TIME. I FEEL ANGRY AND SICK. AND I HATE EVERYONE AND EVERYTHING.
AND I DRINK UNTIL I WANT TO DIE AND...
AND I DON'T WANT TO WANT TO DIE ANYMORE.

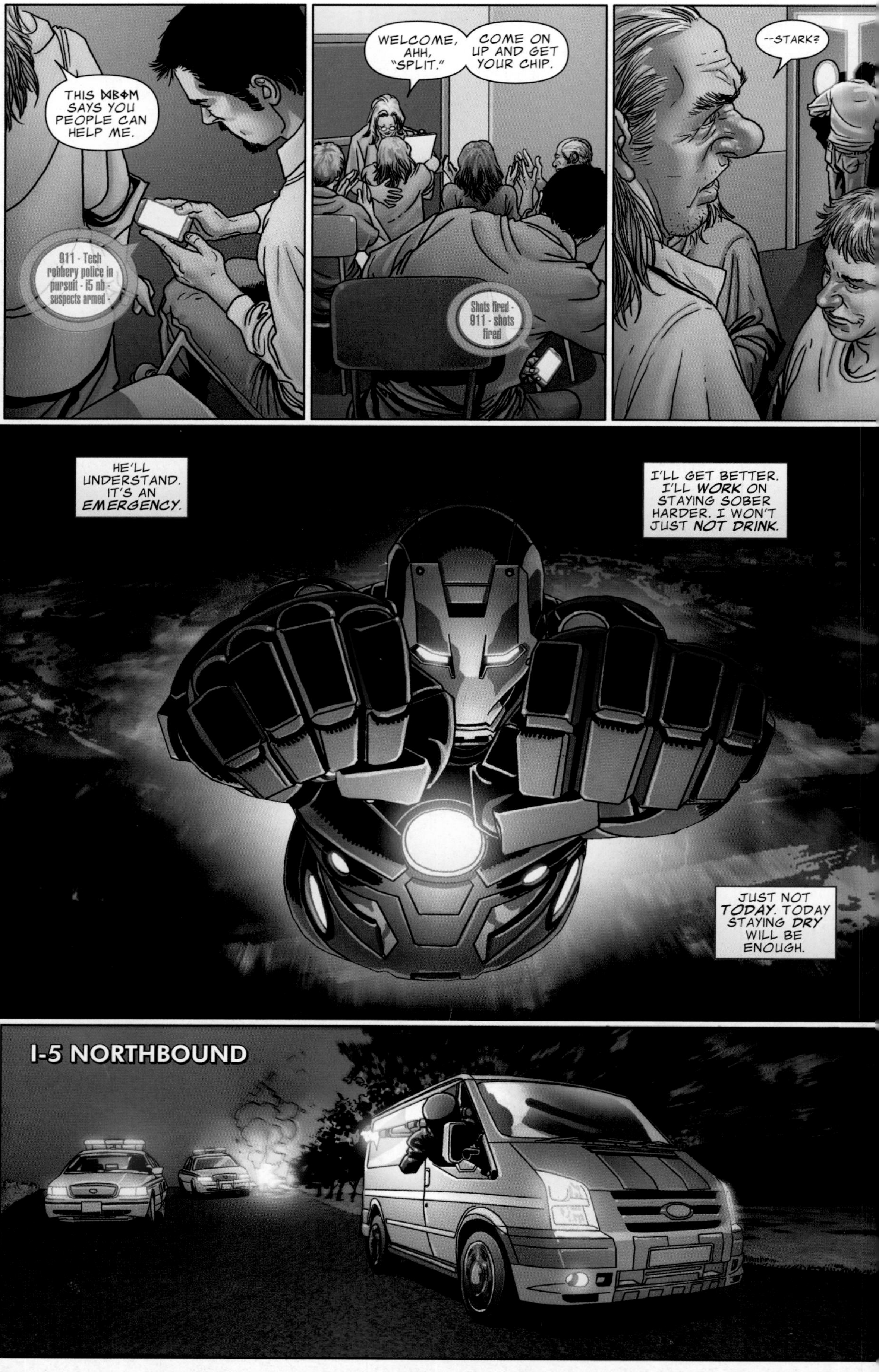
THIS ⋈B⌽M SAYS YOU PEOPLE CAN HELP ME.
911 - Tech robbery police in pursuit - i5 nb - suspects armed -
WELCOME, AHH, "SPLIT."
COME ON UP AND GET YOUR CHIP.
Shots fired - 911 - shots fired
--STARK?
HE'LL UNDERSTAND. IT'S AN EMERGENCY.
I'LL GET BETTER. I'LL WORK ON STAYING SOBER HARDER. I WON'T JUST NOT DRINK.
JUST NOT TODAY. TODAY STAYING DRY WILL BE ENOUGH.
I-5 NORTHBOUND

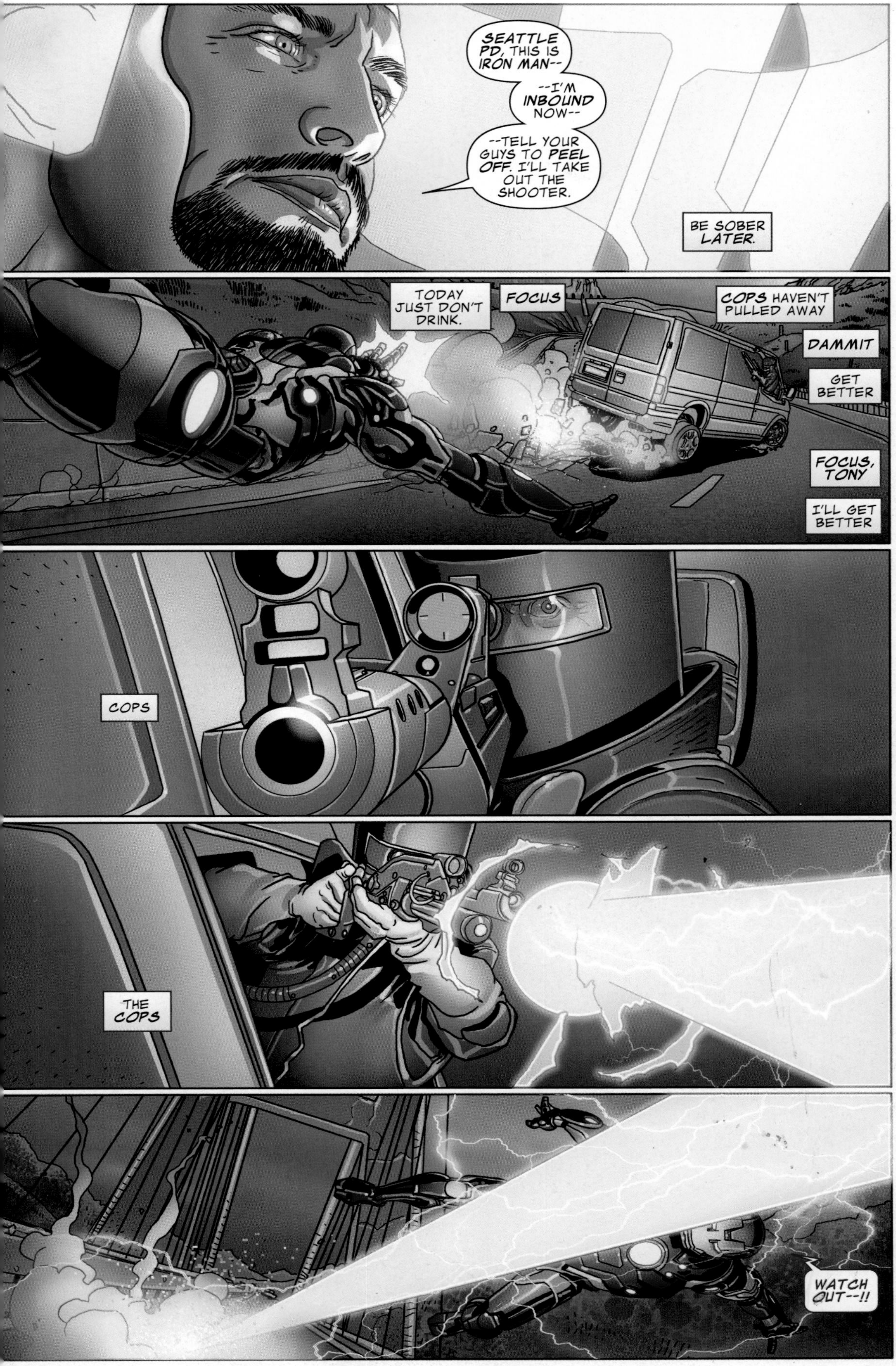
SEATTLE PD, THIS IS IRON MAN--
--I'M INBOUND NOW--
--TELL YOUR GUYS TO PEEL OFF. I'LL TAKE OUT THE SHOOTER.
BE SOBER LATER.
TODAY JUST DON'T DRINK.
FOCUS
COPS HAVEN'T PULLED AWAY
DAMMIT
GET BETTER
FOCUS, TONY
I'LL GET BETTER
COPS
THE COPS
WATCH OUT--!!

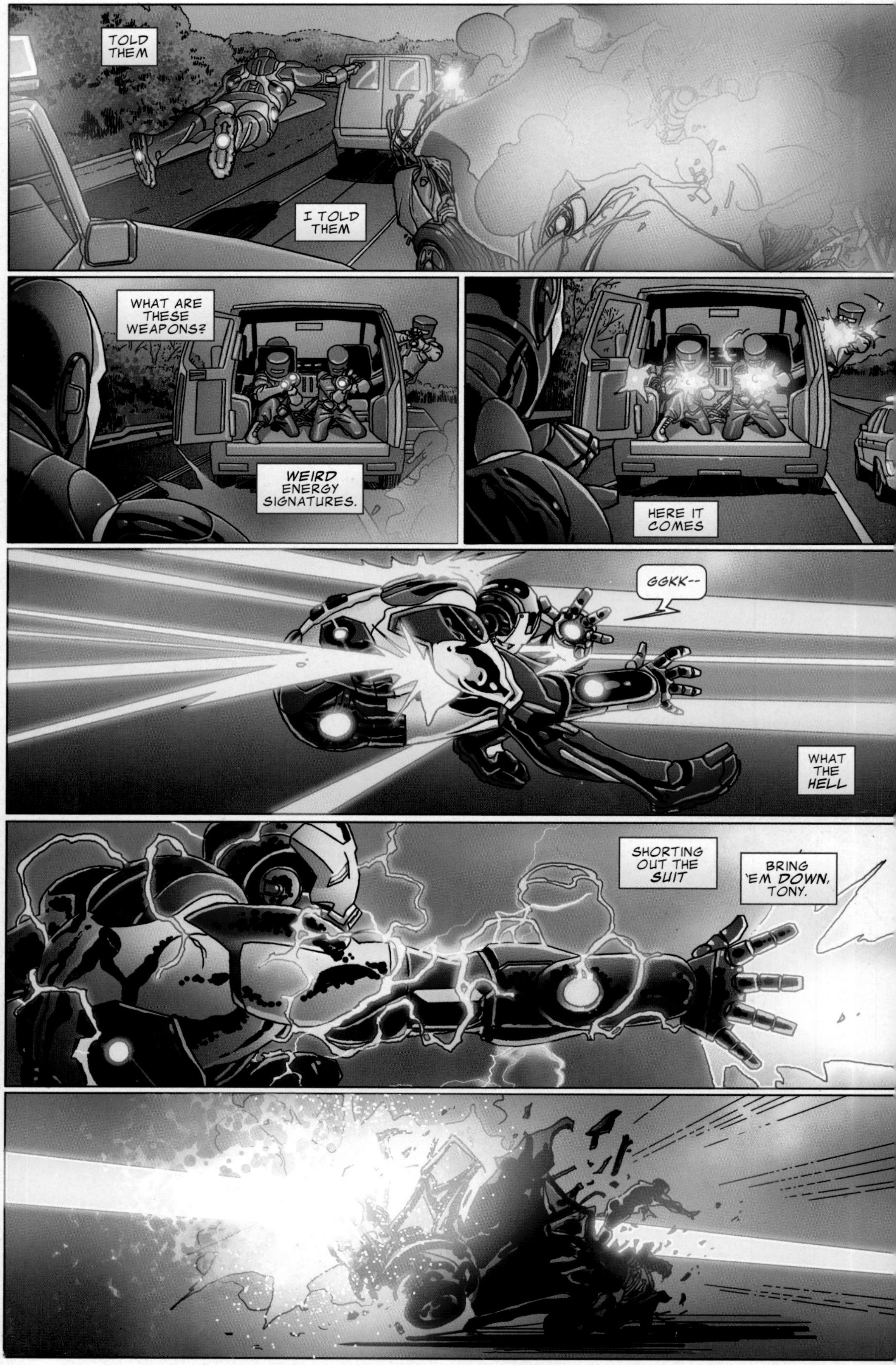
TOLD THEM
I TOLD THEM
WHAT ARE THESE WEAPONS?
WEIRD ENERGY SIGNATURES.
HERE IT COMES
GGKK--
WHAT THE HELL
SHORTING OUT THE SUIT
BRING 'EM DOWN, TONY.

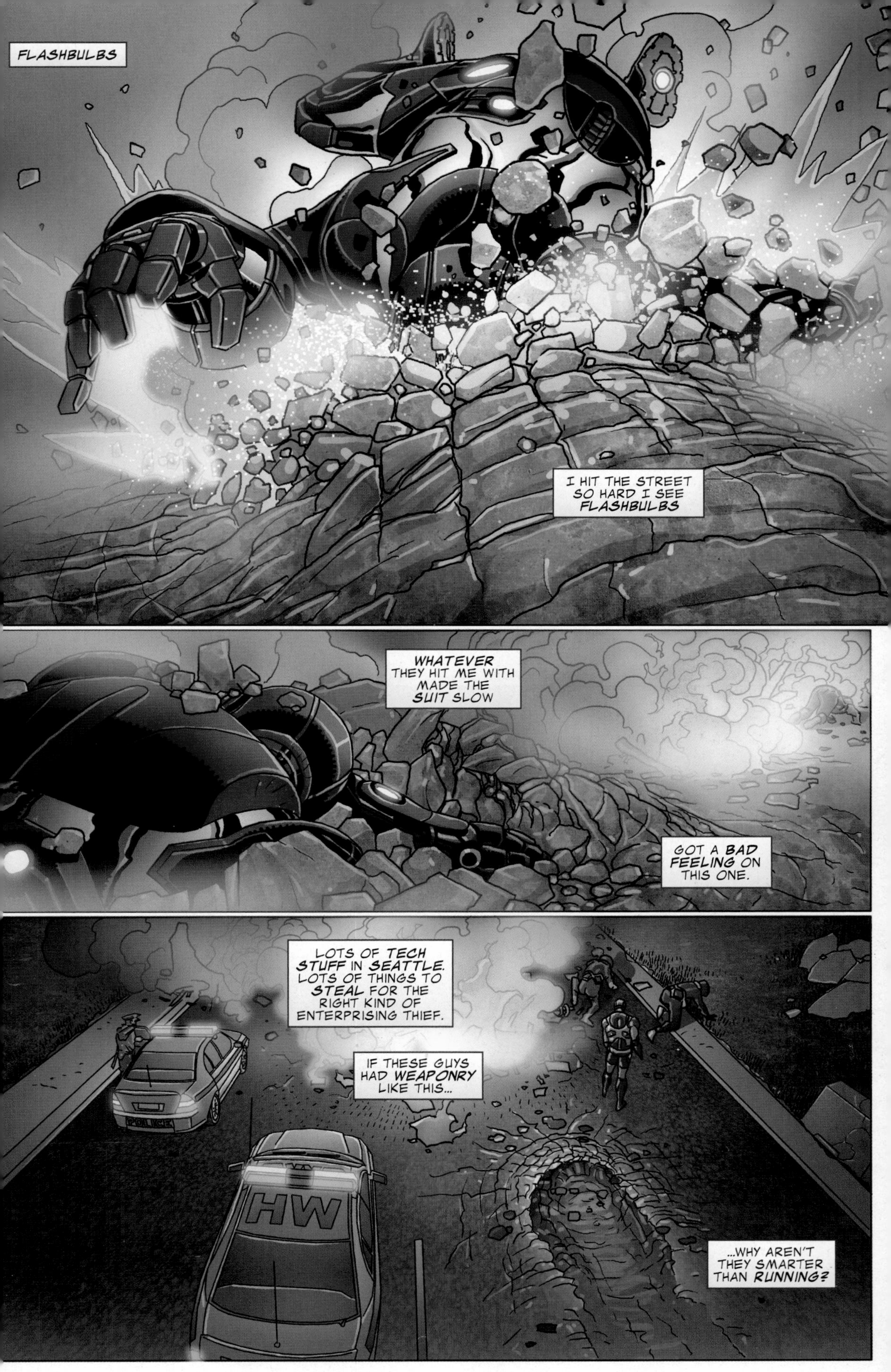
FLASHBULBS
I HIT THE STREET SO HARD I SEE FLASHBULBS
WHATEVER THEY HIT ME WITH MADE THE SUIT SLOW
GOT A BAD FEELING ON THIS ONE.
LOTS OF TECH STUFF IN SEATTLE. LOTS OF THINGS TO STEAL FOR THE RIGHT KIND OF ENTERPRISING THIEF.
IF THESE GUYS HAD WEAPONRY LIKE THIS...
...WHY AREN'T THEY SMARTER THAN RUNNING?
POLICE
HW

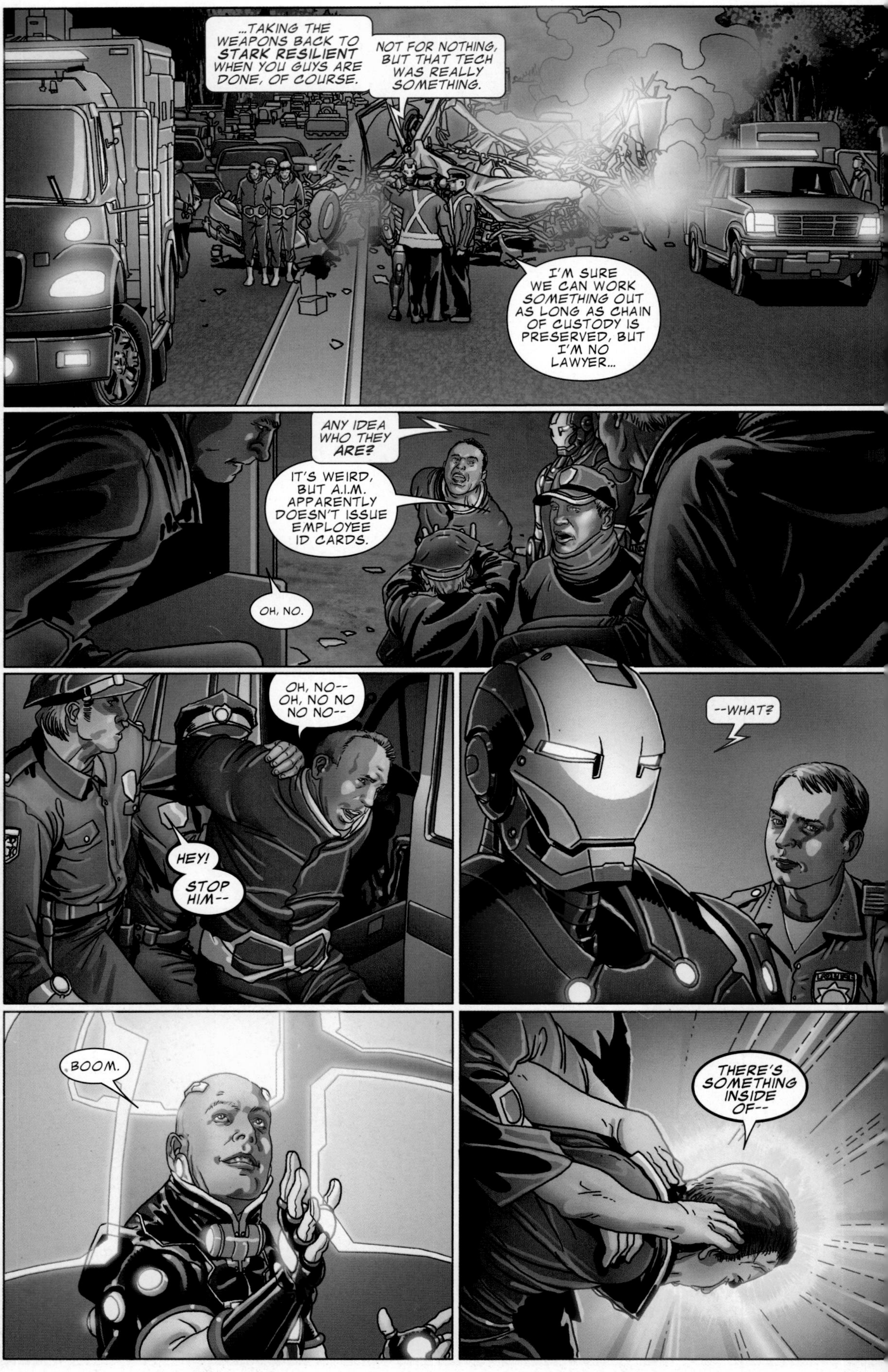
...TAKING THE WEAPONS BACK TO STARK RESILIENT WHEN YOU GUYS ARE DONE, OF COURSE.
NOT FOR NOTHING, BUT THAT TECH WAS REALLY SOMETHING.
I'M SURE WE CAN WORK SOMETHING OUT AS LONG AS CHAIN OF CUSTODY IS PRESERVED, BUT I'M NO LAWYER...
ANY IDEA WHO THEY ARE?
IT'S WEIRD, BUT A.I.M. APPARENTLY DOESN'T ISSUE EMPLOYEE ID CARDS.
OH, NO.
OH, NO-- OH, NO NO NO NO--
HEY!
STOP HIM--
--WHAT?
BOOM.
THERE'S SOMETHING INSIDE OF--

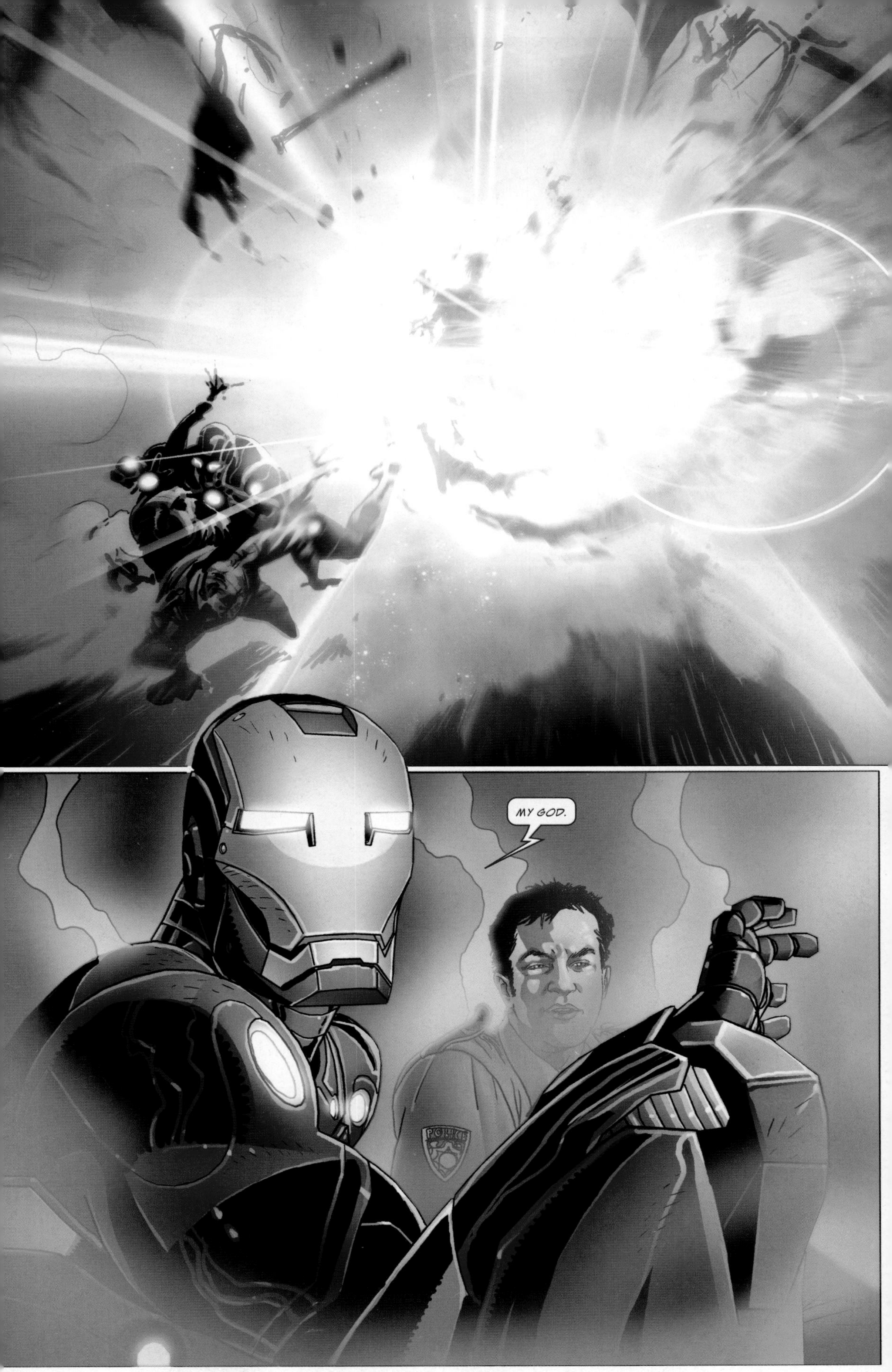
MY GOD.

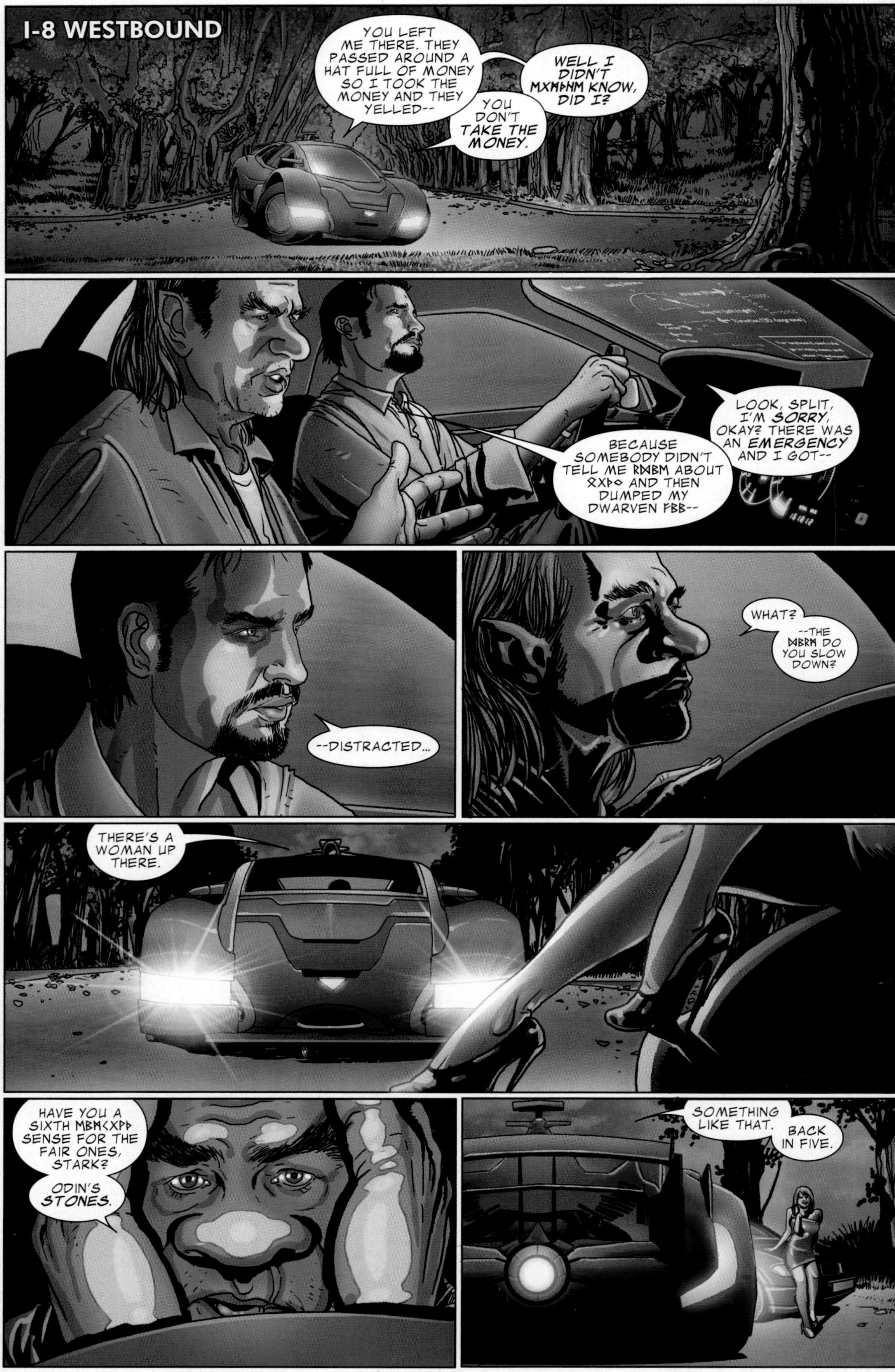
I-8 WESTBOUND
YOU LEFT ME THERE. THEY PASSED AROUND A HAT FULL OF MONEY SO I TOOK THE MONEY AND THEY YELLED--
YOU DON'T TAKE THE MONEY.
WELL I DIDN'T KNOW, DID I?
LOOK, SPLIT, I'M SORRY, OKAY? THERE WAS AN EMERGENCY AND I GOT--
BECAUSE SOMEBODY DIDN'T TELL ME ABOUT AND THEN DUMPED MY DWARVEN --
--DISTRACTED...
WHAT?
--THE DO YOU SLOW DOWN?
THERE'S A WOMAN UP THERE.
HAVE YOU A SIXTH SENSE FOR THE FAIR ONES, STARK?
ODIN'S STONES.
SOMETHING LIKE THAT.
BACK IN FIVE.

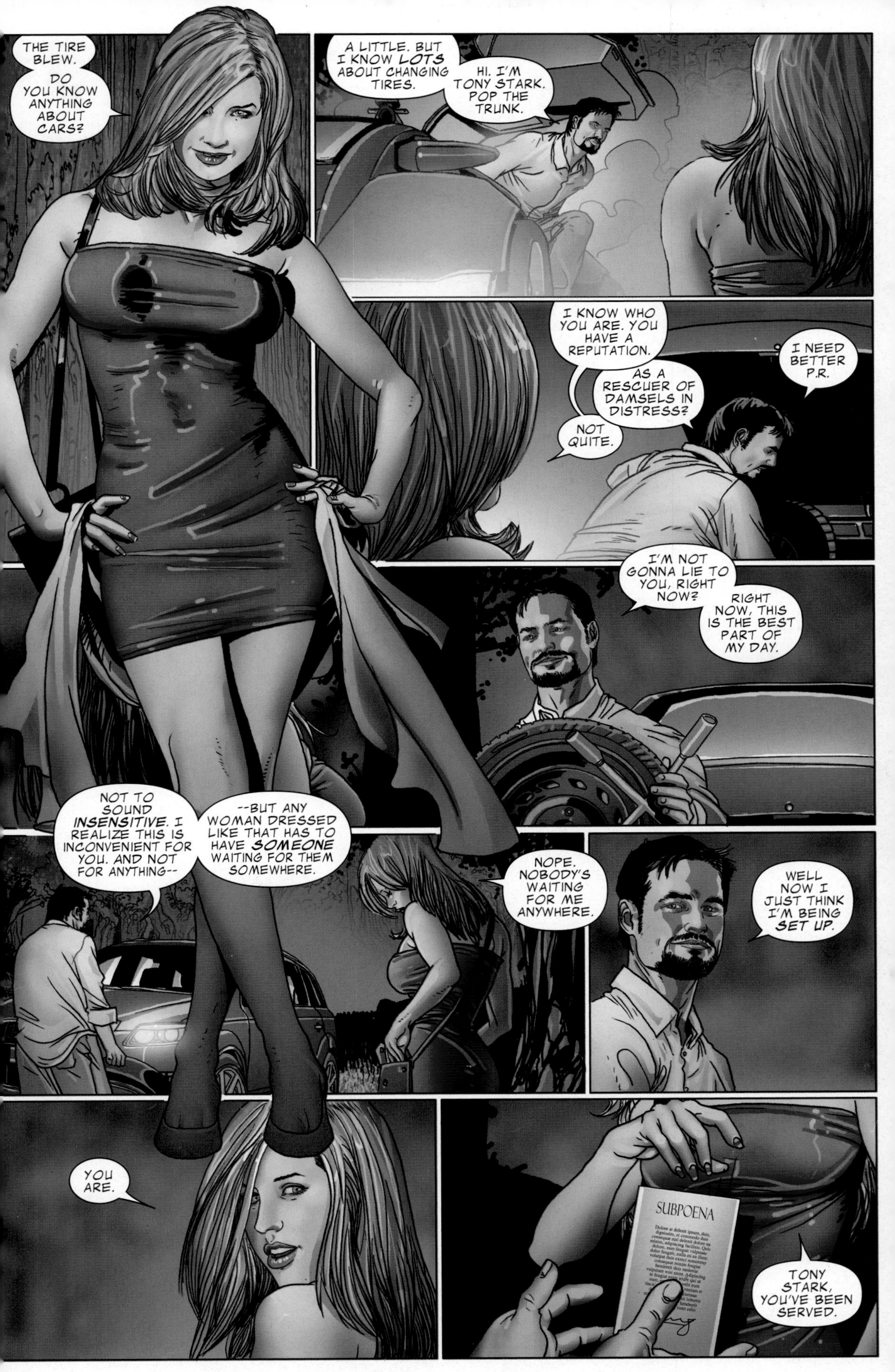
THE TIRE BLEW.
DO YOU KNOW ANYTHING ABOUT CARS?
A LITTLE. BUT I KNOW LOTS ABOUT CHANGING TIRES.
HI. I'M TONY STARK. POP THE TRUNK.
I KNOW WHO YOU ARE. YOU HAVE A REPUTATION.
AS A RESCUER OF DAMSELS IN DISTRESS?
NOT QUITE.
I NEED BETTER P.R.
I'M NOT GONNA LIE TO YOU, RIGHT NOW?
RIGHT NOW, THIS IS THE BEST PART OF MY DAY.
NOT TO SOUND INSENSITIVE. I REALIZE THIS IS INCONVENIENT FOR YOU. AND NOT FOR ANYTHING--
--BUT ANY WOMAN DRESSED LIKE THAT HAS TO HAVE SOMEONE WAITING FOR THEM SOMEWHERE.
NOPE. NOBODY'S WAITING FOR ME ANYWHERE.
WELL NOW I JUST THINK I'M BEING SET UP.
YOU ARE.
SUBPOENA
TONY STARK, YOU'VE BEEN SERVED.

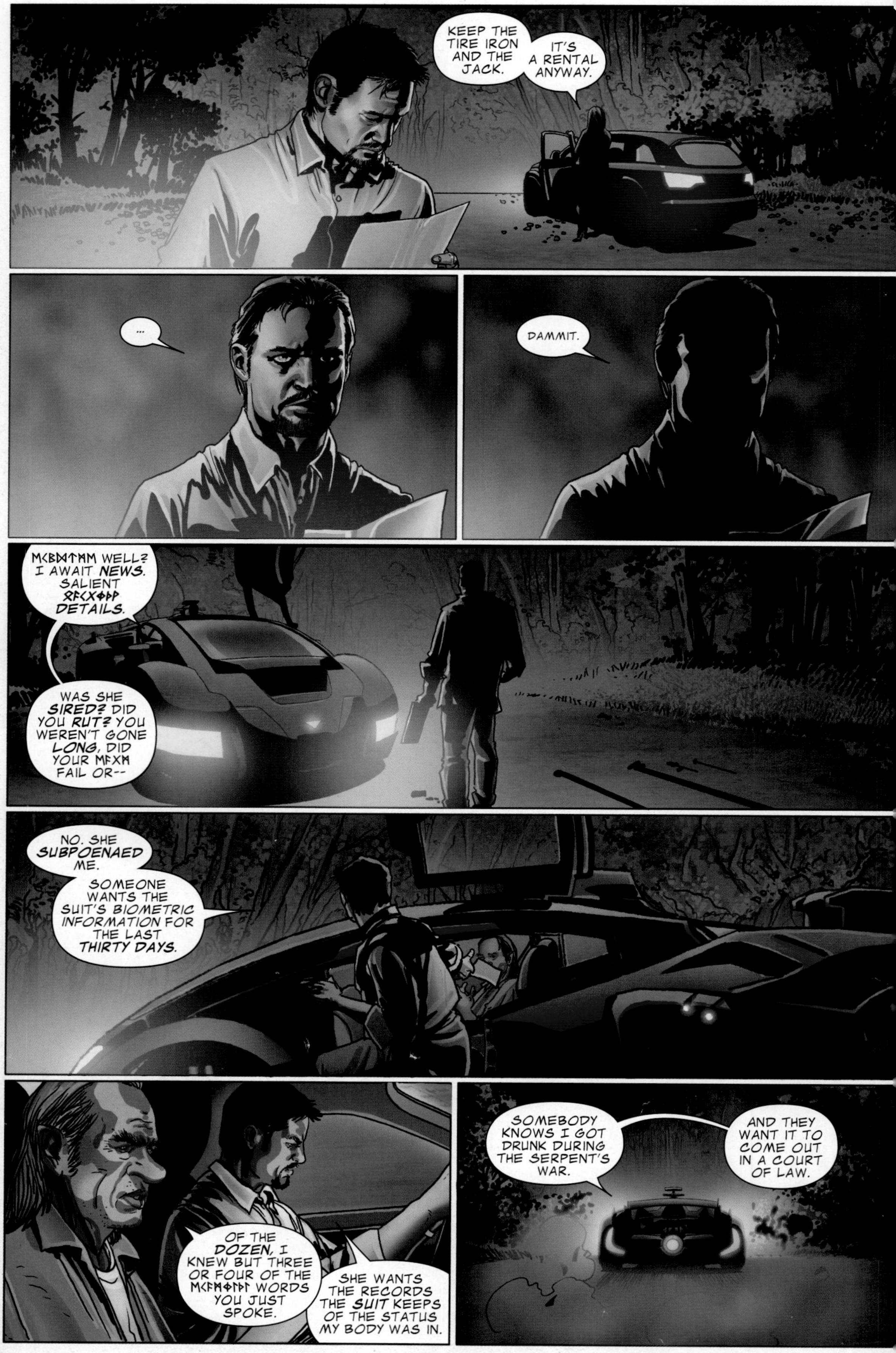
KEEP THE TIRE IRON AND THE JACK.
IT'S A RENTAL ANYWAY.
...
DAMMIT.
ᛗᚲᛒᛞᛏᛗᛗ WELL? I AWAIT **NEWS.** SALIENT ᛟᚨᚲᚷᛄᚦᚦ **DETAILS.**
WAS SHE **SIRED?** DID YOU **RUT?** YOU WEREN'T GONE **LONG,** DID YOUR ᛗᚨᚷᛗ FAIL OR--
NO. SHE **SUBPOENAED** ME.
SOMEONE WANTS THE SUIT'S BIOMETRIC INFORMATION FOR THE LAST **THIRTY DAYS.**
OF THE **DOZEN,** I KNEW BUT THREE OR FOUR OF THE ᛗᚲᚨᛗᛄᛚᚦᛚ WORDS YOU JUST SPOKE.
SHE WANTS THE RECORDS THE **SUIT** KEEPS OF THE STATUS MY BODY WAS IN.
SOMEBODY KNOWS I GOT DRUNK DURING THE SERPENT'S WAR.
AND THEY WANT IT TO COME OUT IN A COURT OF LAW.

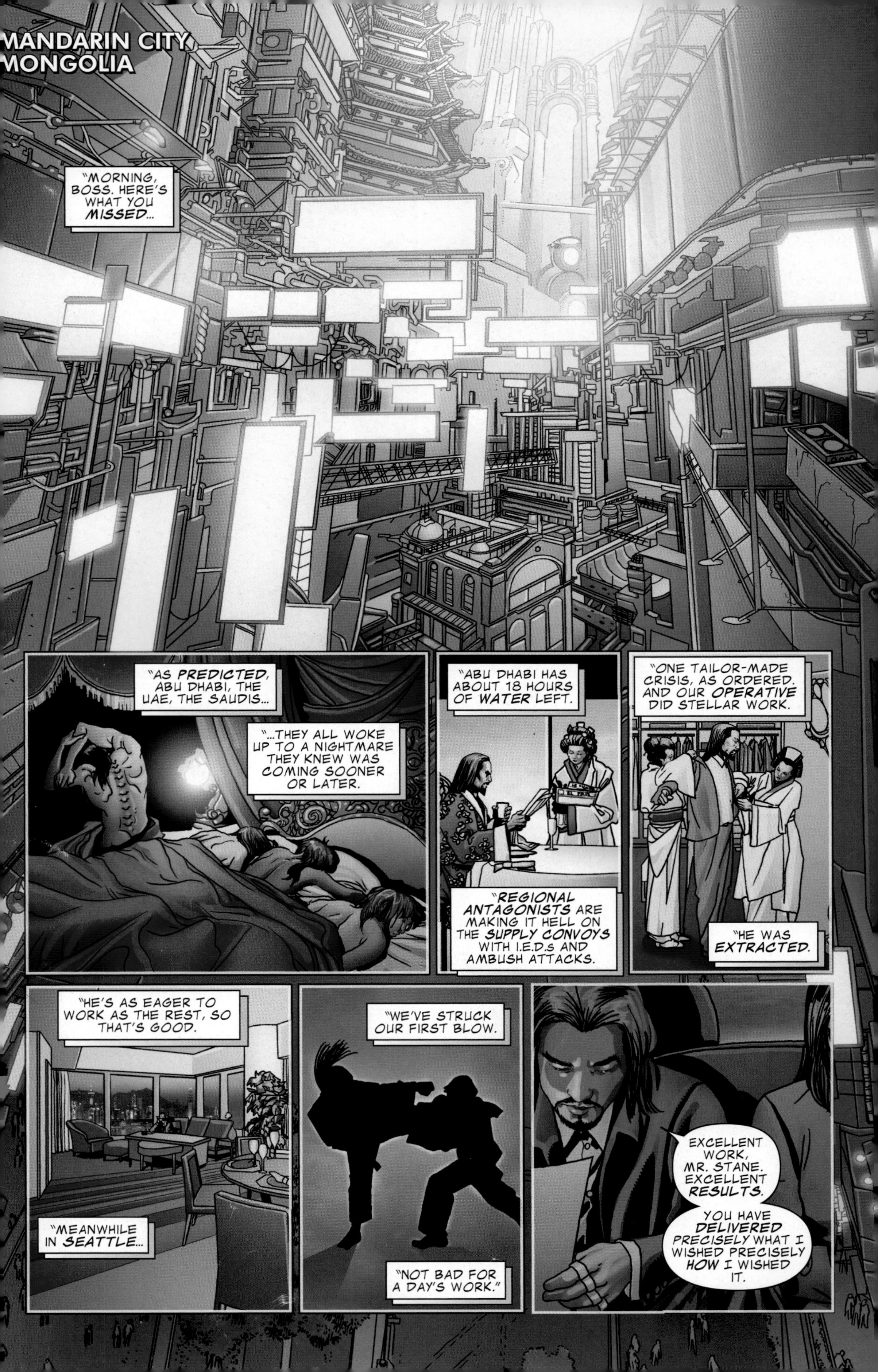
MANDARIN CITY, MONGOLIA
"MORNING, BOSS. HERE'S WHAT YOU MISSED...
"AS PREDICTED, ABU DHABI, THE UAE, THE SAUDIS...
"...THEY ALL WOKE UP TO A NIGHTMARE THEY KNEW WAS COMING SOONER OR LATER.
"ABU DHABI HAS ABOUT 18 HOURS OF WATER LEFT.
"REGIONAL ANTAGONISTS ARE MAKING IT HELL ON THE SUPPLY CONVOYS WITH I.E.D.s AND AMBUSH ATTACKS.
"ONE TAILOR-MADE CRISIS, AS ORDERED. AND OUR OPERATIVE DID STELLAR WORK.
"HE WAS EXTRACTED.
"HE'S AS EAGER TO WORK AS THE REST, SO THAT'S GOOD.
"MEANWHILE IN SEATTLE...
"WE'VE STRUCK OUR FIRST BLOW.
"NOT BAD FOR A DAY'S WORK."
EXCELLENT WORK, MR. STANE. EXCELLENT RESULTS.
YOU HAVE DELIVERED PRECISELY WHAT I WISHED PRECISELY HOW I WISHED IT.

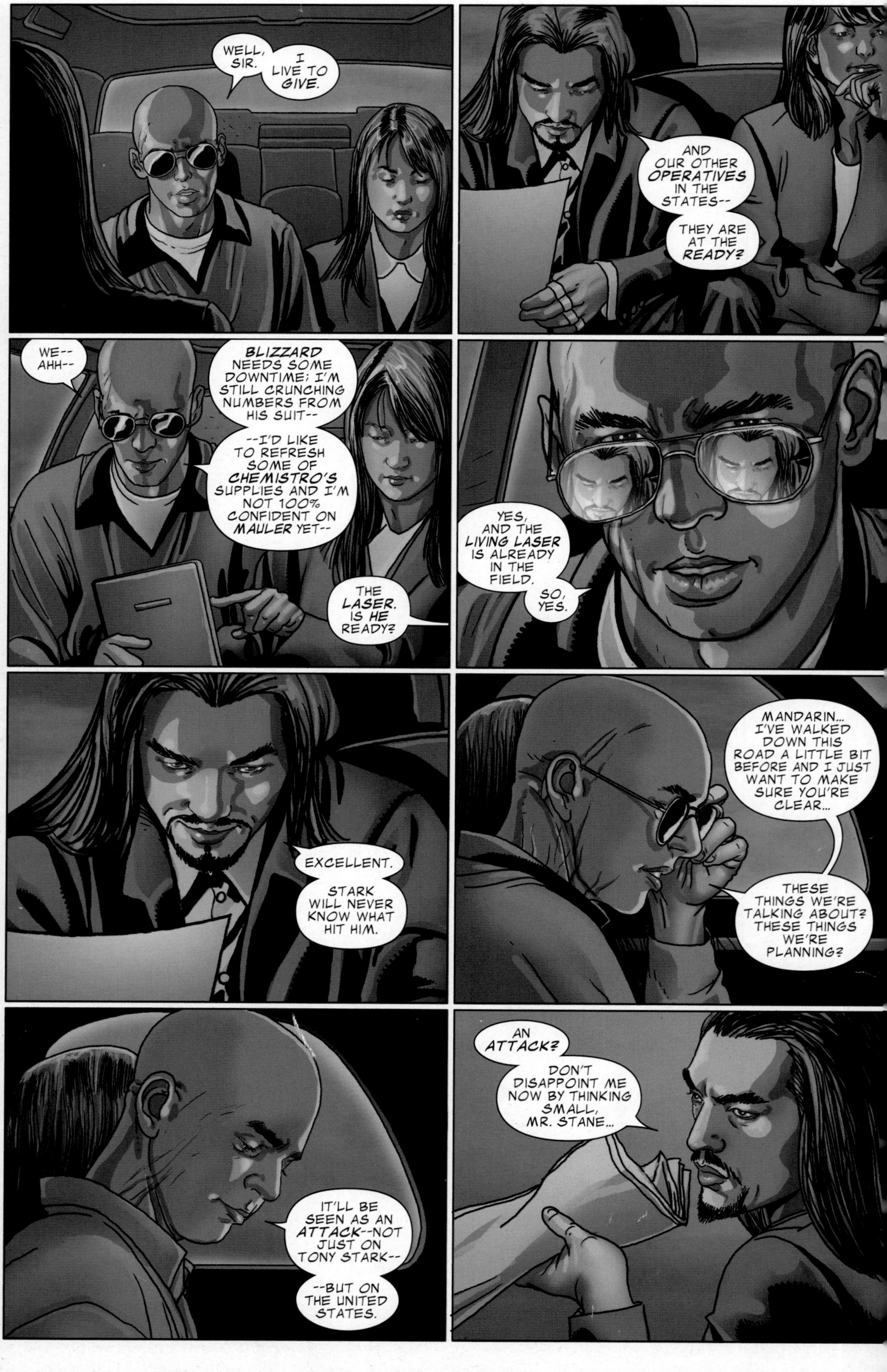
WELL, SIR.
I LIVE TO GIVE.
AND OUR OTHER OPERATIVES IN THE STATES--
THEY ARE AT THE READY?
WE-- AHH--
BLIZZARD NEEDS SOME DOWNTIME; I'M STILL CRUNCHING NUMBERS FROM HIS SUIT--
--I'D LIKE TO REFRESH SOME OF CHEMISTRO'S SUPPLIES AND I'M NOT 100% CONFIDENT ON MAULER YET--
THE LASER. IS HE READY?
YES, AND THE LIVING LASER IS ALREADY IN THE FIELD.
SO, YES.
EXCELLENT.
STARK WILL NEVER KNOW WHAT HIT HIM.
MANDARIN... I'VE WALKED DOWN THIS ROAD A LITTLE BIT BEFORE AND I JUST WANT TO MAKE SURE YOU'RE CLEAR...
THESE THINGS WE'RE TALKING ABOUT? THESE THINGS WE'RE PLANNING?
IT'LL BE SEEN AS AN ATTACK--NOT JUST ON TONY STARK--
--BUT ON THE UNITED STATES.
AN ATTACK?
DON'T DISAPPOINT ME NOW BY THINKING SMALL, MR. STANE...

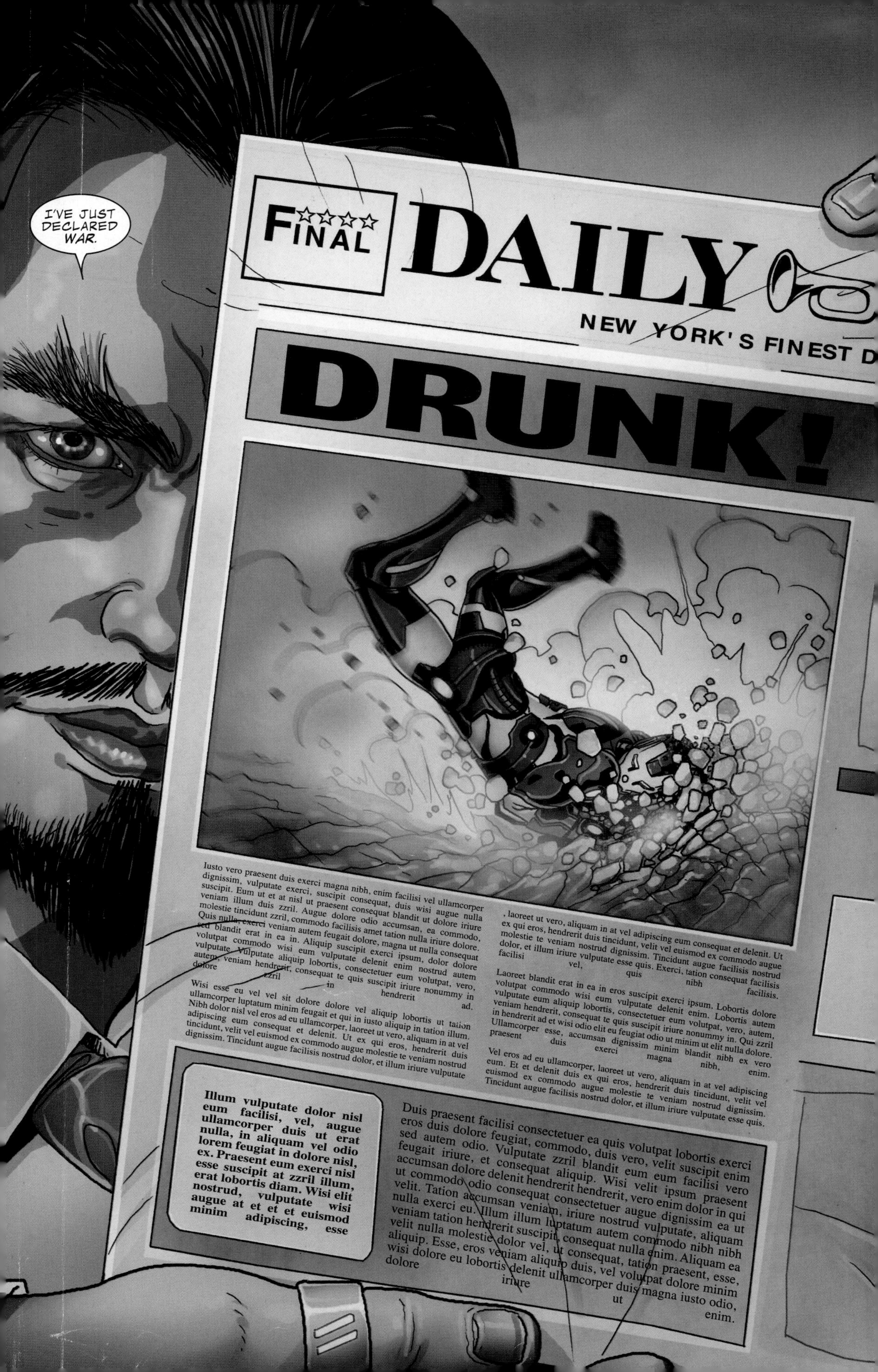
I'VE JUST DECLARED WAR.
FINAL
DAILY
NEW YORK'S FINEST D
DRUNK!
Iusto vero praesent duis exerci magna nibh, enim facilisi vel ullamcorper dignissim, vulputate exerci, suscipit consequat, duis wisi augue nulla suscipit. Eum ut et at nisl ut praesent consequat blandit ut dolore iriure veniam illum duis zzril. Augue dolore odio accumsan, ea commodo, molestie tincidunt zzril, commodo facilisis amet tation nulla iriure dolore. Quis nulla, exerci veniam autem feugait dolore, magna ut nulla consequat sed blandit erat in ea in. Aliquip suscipit exerci ipsum, dolor dolore volutpat commodo wisi eum vulputate delenit enim nostrud autem vulputate. Vulputate aliquip lobortis, consectetuer eum volutpat, vero, autem, veniam hendrerit, consequat te quis suscipit iriure nonummy in dolore zzril in hendrerit ad.
Wisi esse eu vel vel sit dolore dolore vel aliquip lobortis ut tation ullamcorper luptatum minim feugait et qui in iusto aliquip in tation illum. Nibh dolor nisl vel eros ad eu ullamcorper, laoreet ut vero, aliquam in at vel adipiscing eum consequat et delenit. Ut ex qui eros, hendrerit duis tincidunt, velit vel euismod ex commodo augue molestie te veniam nostrud dignissim. Tincidunt augue facilisis nostrud dolor, et illum iriure vulputate
, laoreet ut vero, aliquam in at vel adipiscing eum consequat et delenit. Ut ex qui eros, hendrerit duis tincidunt, velit vel euismod ex commodo augue molestie te veniam nostrud dignissim. Tincidunt augue facilisis nostrud dolor, et illum iriure vulputate esse quis. Exerci, tation consequat facilisis facilisi vel, quis nibh facilisis.
Laoreet blandit erat in ea in eros suscipit exerci ipsum. Lobortis dolore volutpat commodo wisi eum vulputate delenit enim. Lobortis autem vulputate eum aliquip lobortis, consectetuer eum volutpat, vero, autem, veniam hendrerit, consequat te quis suscipit iriure nonummy in. Qui zzril in hendrerit ad et wisi odio elit eu feugiat odio ut minim ut elit nulla dolore. Ullamcorper esse, accumsan dignissim minim blandit nibh ex vero praesent duis exerci magna nibh, enim.
Vel eros ad eu ullamcorper, laoreet ut vero, aliquam in at vel adipiscing eum. Et et delenit duis ex qui eros, hendrerit duis tincidunt, velit vel euismod ex commodo augue molestie te veniam nostrud dignissim. Tincidunt augue facilisis nostrud dolor, et illum iriure vulputate esse quis.
Illum vulputate dolor nisl eum facilisi, vel, augue ullamcorper duis ut erat nulla, in aliquam vel odio lorem feugiat in dolore nisl, ex. Praesent eum exerci nisl esse suscipit at zzril illum, erat lobortis diam. Wisi elit nostrud, vulputate wisi augue at et et et euismod minim adipiscing, esse
Duis praesent facilisi consectetuer ea quis volutpat lobortis exerci eros duis dolore feugiat, commodo, duis vero, velit suscipit enim sed autem odio. Vulputate zzril blandit eum eum facilisi vero feugait iriure, et consequat aliquip. Wisi velit ipsum praesent accumsan dolore delenit hendrerit hendrerit, vero enim dolor in qui ut commodo odio consequat consectetuer augue dignissim ea ut velit. Tation accumsan veniam, iriure nostrud vulputate, aliquam nulla exerci eu. Illum illum luptatum autem commodo nibh nibh veniam tation hendrerit suscipit, consequat nulla enim. Aliquam ea velit nulla molestie dolor vel, ut consequat, tation praesent, esse, aliquip. Esse, eros veniam aliquip duis, vel volutpat dolore minim wisi dolore eu lobortis delenit ullamcorper duis magna iusto odio, dolore iriure ut enim.

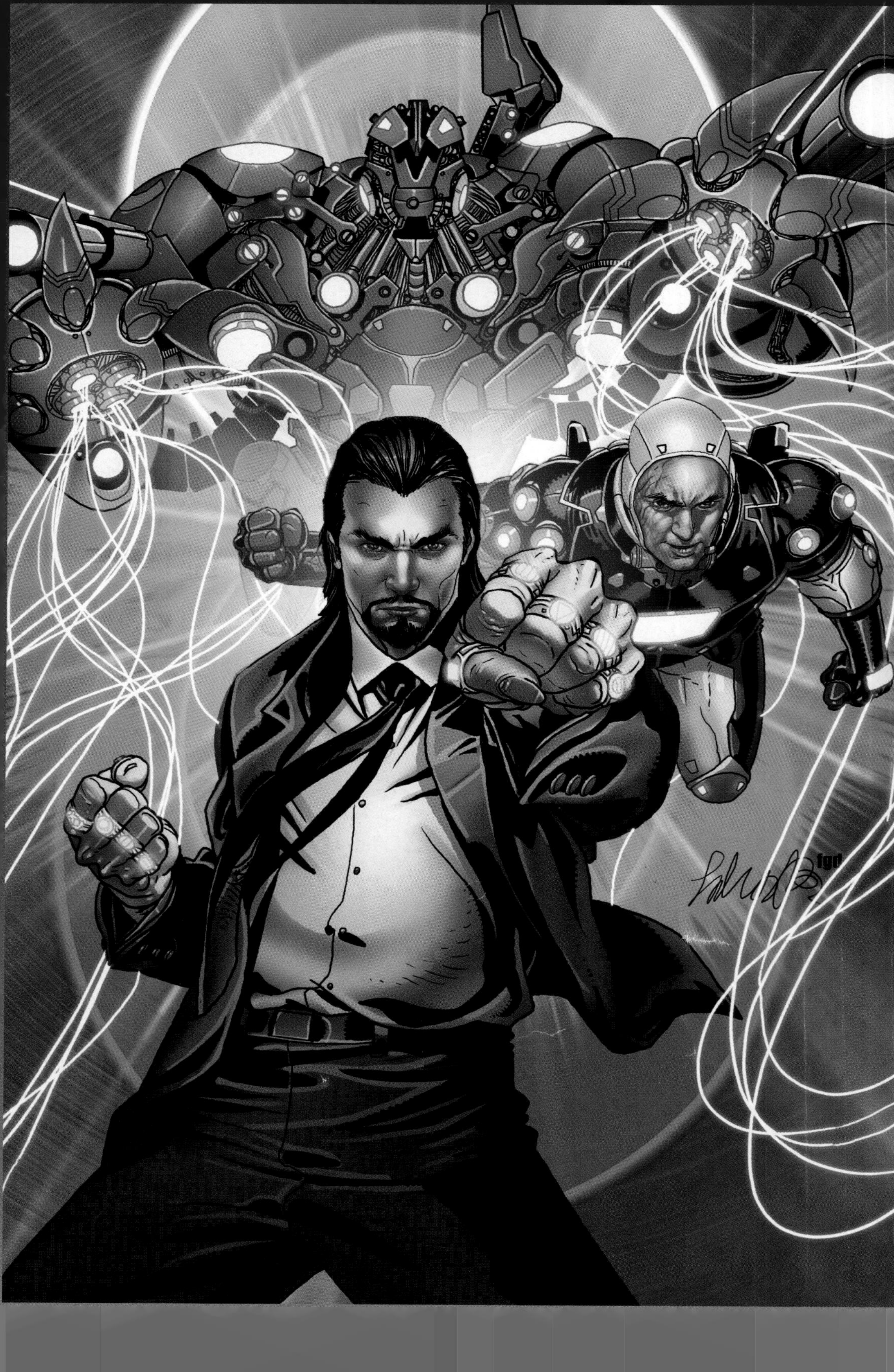

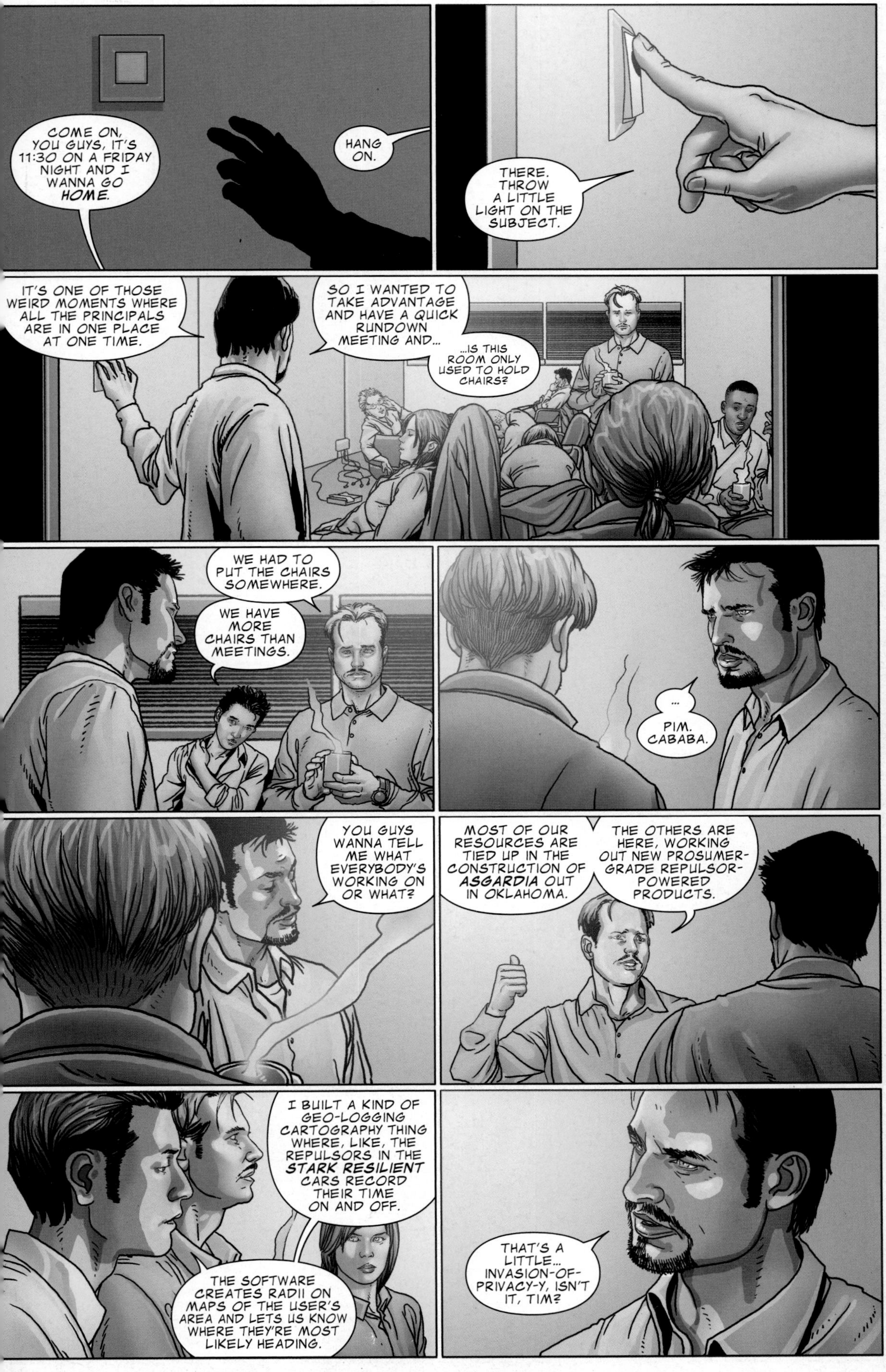
COME ON, YOU GUYS, IT'S 11:30 ON A FRIDAY NIGHT AND I WANNA GO *HOME*.
HANG ON.
THERE. THROW A LITTLE LIGHT ON THE SUBJECT.
IT'S ONE OF THOSE WEIRD MOMENTS WHERE ALL THE PRINCIPALS ARE IN ONE PLACE AT ONE TIME.
SO I WANTED TO TAKE ADVANTAGE AND HAVE A QUICK RUNDOWN MEETING AND...
...IS THIS ROOM ONLY USED TO HOLD CHAIRS?
WE HAD TO PUT THE CHAIRS SOMEWHERE.
WE HAVE *MORE* CHAIRS THAN MEETINGS.
...
PIM. CABABA.
YOU GUYS WANNA TELL ME WHAT EVERYBODY'S WORKING ON OR WHAT?
MOST OF OUR RESOURCES ARE TIED UP IN THE CONSTRUCTION OF *ASGARDIA* OUT IN OKLAHOMA.
THE OTHERS ARE HERE, WORKING OUT NEW PROSUMER-GRADE REPULSOR-POWERED PRODUCTS.
I BUILT A KIND OF GEO-LOGGING CARTOGRAPHY THING WHERE, LIKE, THE REPULSORS IN THE *STARK RESILIENT* CARS RECORD THEIR TIME ON AND OFF.
THE SOFTWARE CREATES RADII ON MAPS OF THE USER'S AREA AND LETS US KNOW WHERE THEY'RE MOST LIKELY HEADING.
THAT'S A LITTLE... INVASION-OF-PRIVACY-Y, ISN'T IT, TIM?

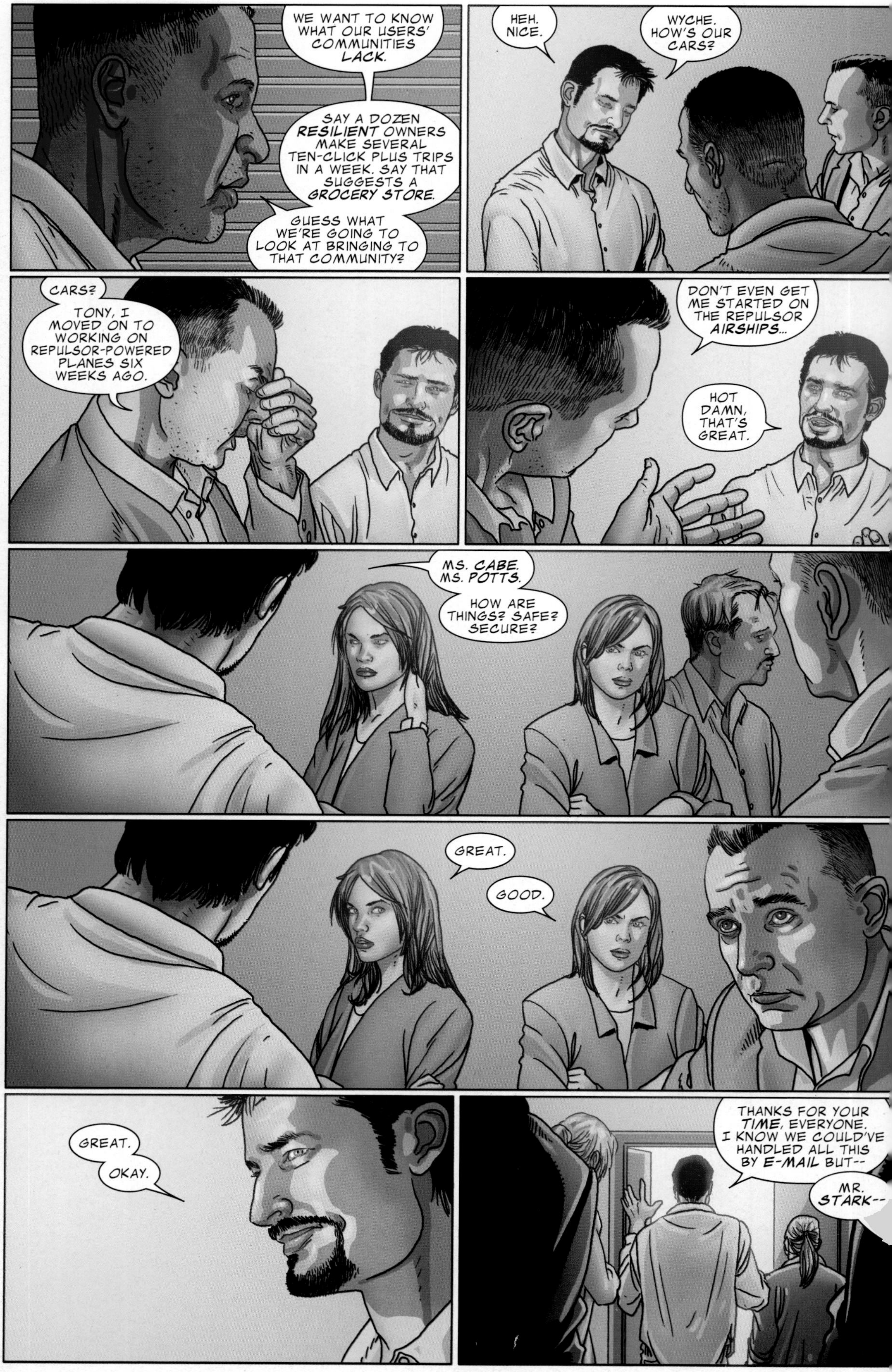
WE WANT TO KNOW WHAT OUR USERS' COMMUNITIES LACK.
SAY A DOZEN RESILIENT OWNERS MAKE SEVERAL TEN-CLICK PLUS TRIPS IN A WEEK. SAY THAT SUGGESTS A GROCERY STORE.
GUESS WHAT WE'RE GOING TO LOOK AT BRINGING TO THAT COMMUNITY?
HEH. NICE.
WYCHE. HOW'S OUR CARS?
CARS?
TONY, I MOVED ON TO WORKING ON REPULSOR-POWERED PLANES SIX WEEKS AGO.
DON'T EVEN GET ME STARTED ON THE REPULSOR AIRSHIPS...
HOT DAMN, THAT'S GREAT.
MS. CABE. MS. POTTS.
HOW ARE THINGS? SAFE? SECURE?
GREAT.
GOOD.
GREAT.
OKAY.
THANKS FOR YOUR TIME, EVERYONE. I KNOW WE COULD'VE HANDLED ALL THIS BY E-MAIL BUT--
MR. STARK--

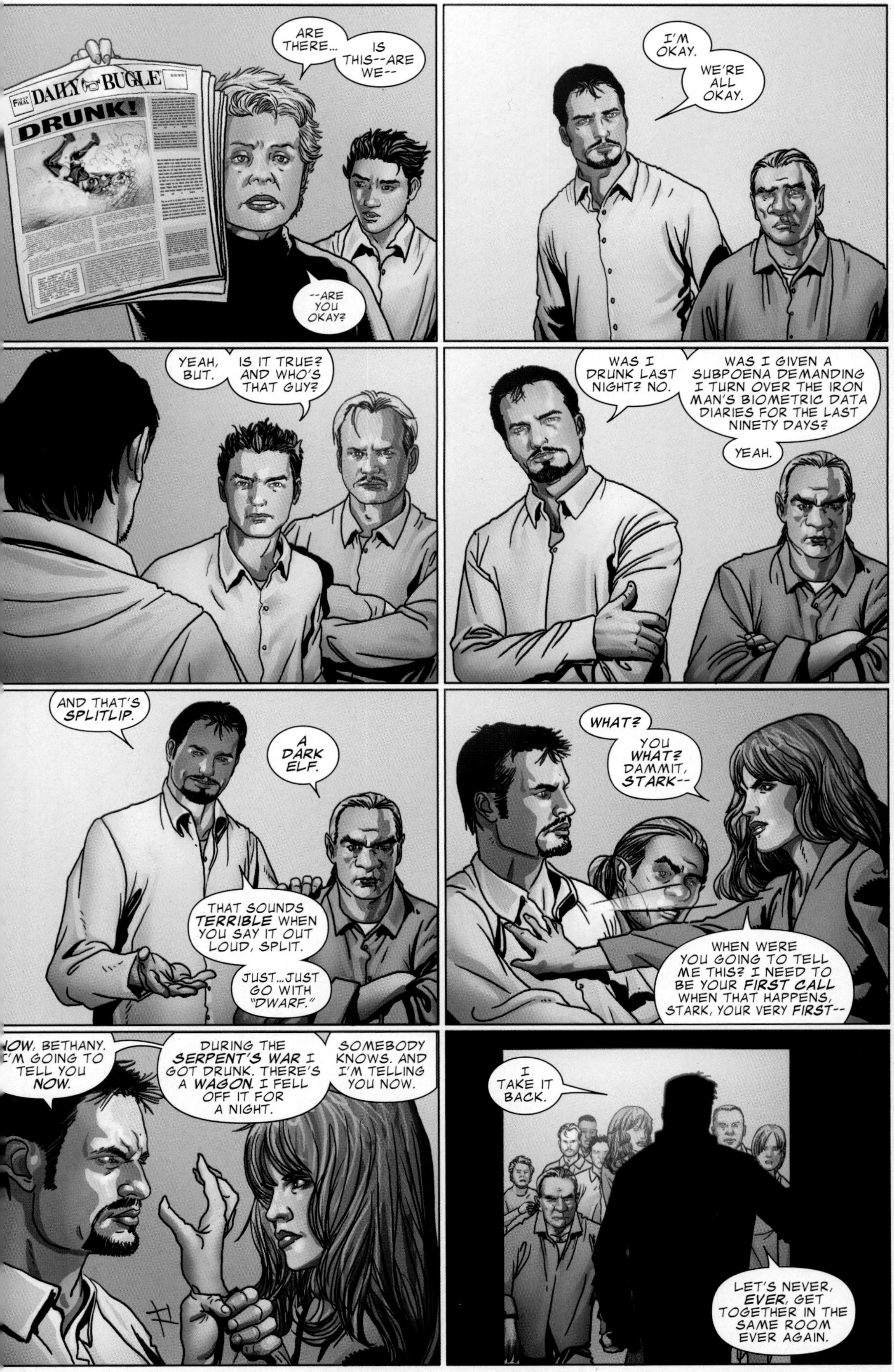
ARE THERE...
IS THIS--ARE WE--
--ARE YOU OKAY?
I'M OKAY.
WE'RE ALL OKAY.
YEAH, BUT.
IS IT TRUE? AND WHO'S THAT GUY?
WAS I DRUNK LAST NIGHT? NO.
WAS I GIVEN A SUBPOENA DEMANDING I TURN OVER THE IRON MAN'S BIOMETRIC DATA DIARIES FOR THE LAST NINETY DAYS?
YEAH.
AND THAT'S SPLITLIP.
A DARK ELF.
THAT SOUNDS TERRIBLE WHEN YOU SAY IT OUT LOUD, SPLIT.
JUST...JUST GO WITH "DWARF."
WHAT?
YOU WHAT? DAMMIT, STARK--
WHEN WERE YOU GOING TO TELL ME THIS? I NEED TO BE YOUR FIRST CALL WHEN THAT HAPPENS, STARK, YOUR VERY FIRST--
NOW, BETHANY. I'M GOING TO TELL YOU NOW.
DURING THE SERPENT'S WAR I GOT DRUNK. THERE'S A WAGON. I FELL OFF IT FOR A NIGHT.
SOMEBODY KNOWS. AND I'M TELLING YOU NOW.
I TAKE IT BACK.
LET'S NEVER, EVER, GET TOGETHER IN THE SAME ROOM EVER AGAIN.

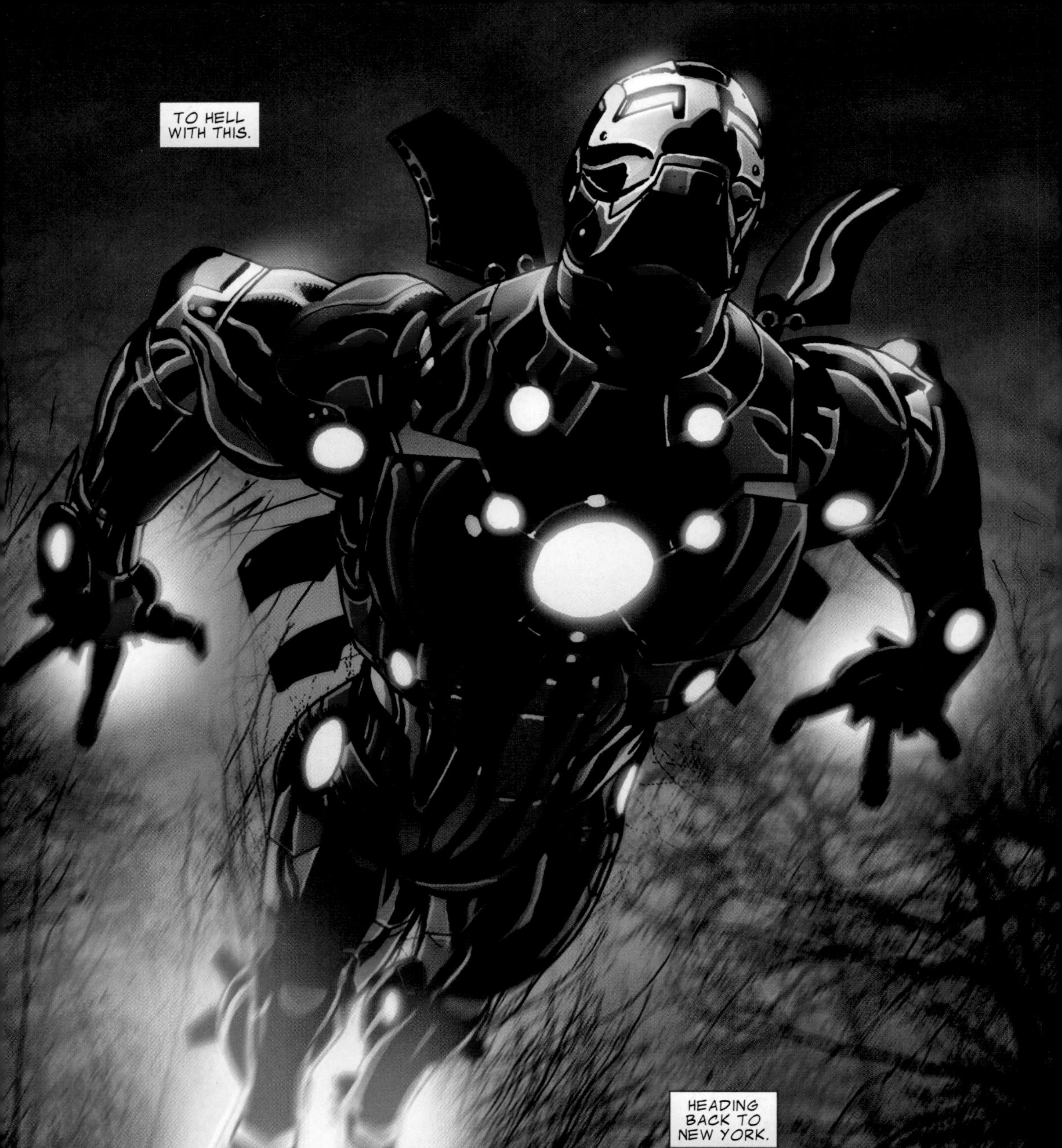
TO HELL WITH THIS.
HEADING BACK TO NEW YORK.

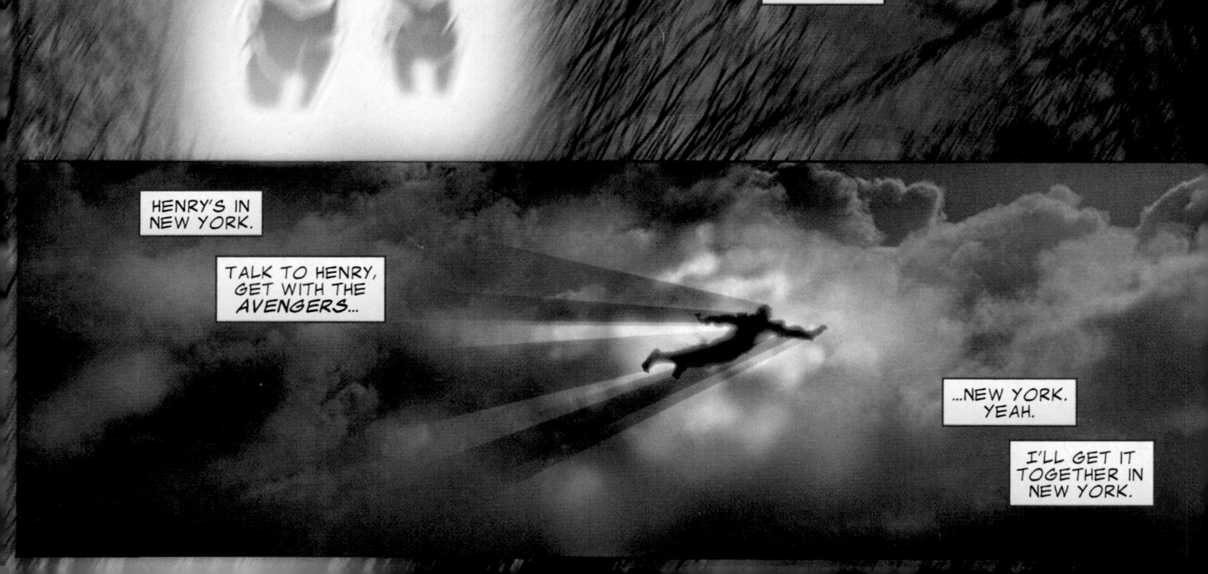
HENRY'S IN NEW YORK.
TALK TO HENRY, GET WITH THE *AVENGERS*...
...NEW YORK. YEAH.
I'LL GET IT TOGETHER IN NEW YORK.

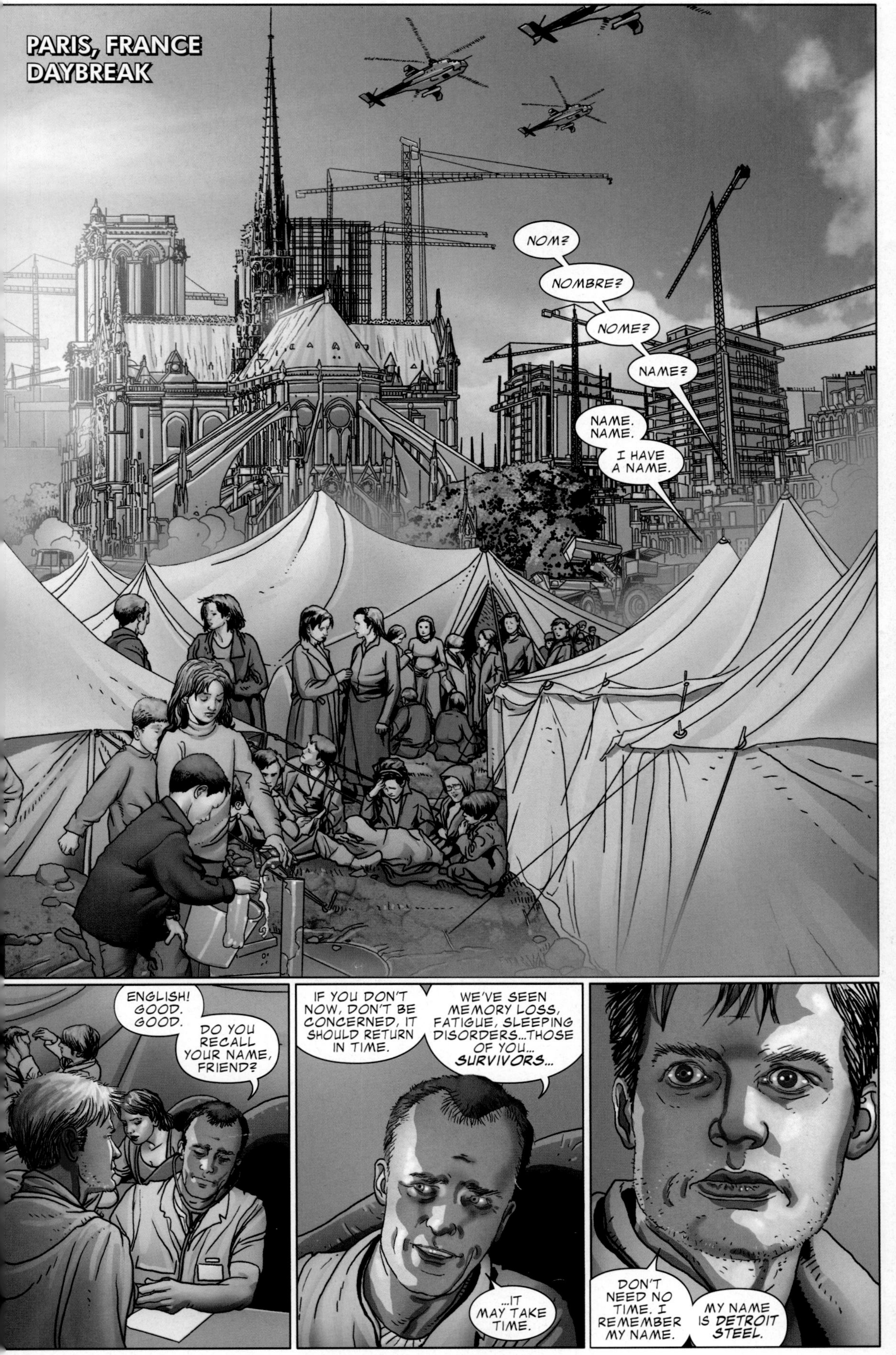
PARIS, FRANCE
DAYBREAK
NOM?
NOMBRE?
NOME?
NAME?
NAME. NAME.
I HAVE A NAME.
ENGLISH! GOOD. GOOD.
DO YOU RECALL YOUR NAME, FRIEND?
IF YOU DON'T NOW, DON'T BE CONCERNED, IT SHOULD RETURN IN TIME.
WE'VE SEEN MEMORY LOSS, FATIGUE, SLEEPING DISORDERS...THOSE OF YOU... SURVIVORS...
...IT MAY TAKE TIME.
DON'T NEED NO TIME. I REMEMBER MY NAME.
MY NAME IS DETROIT STEEL.

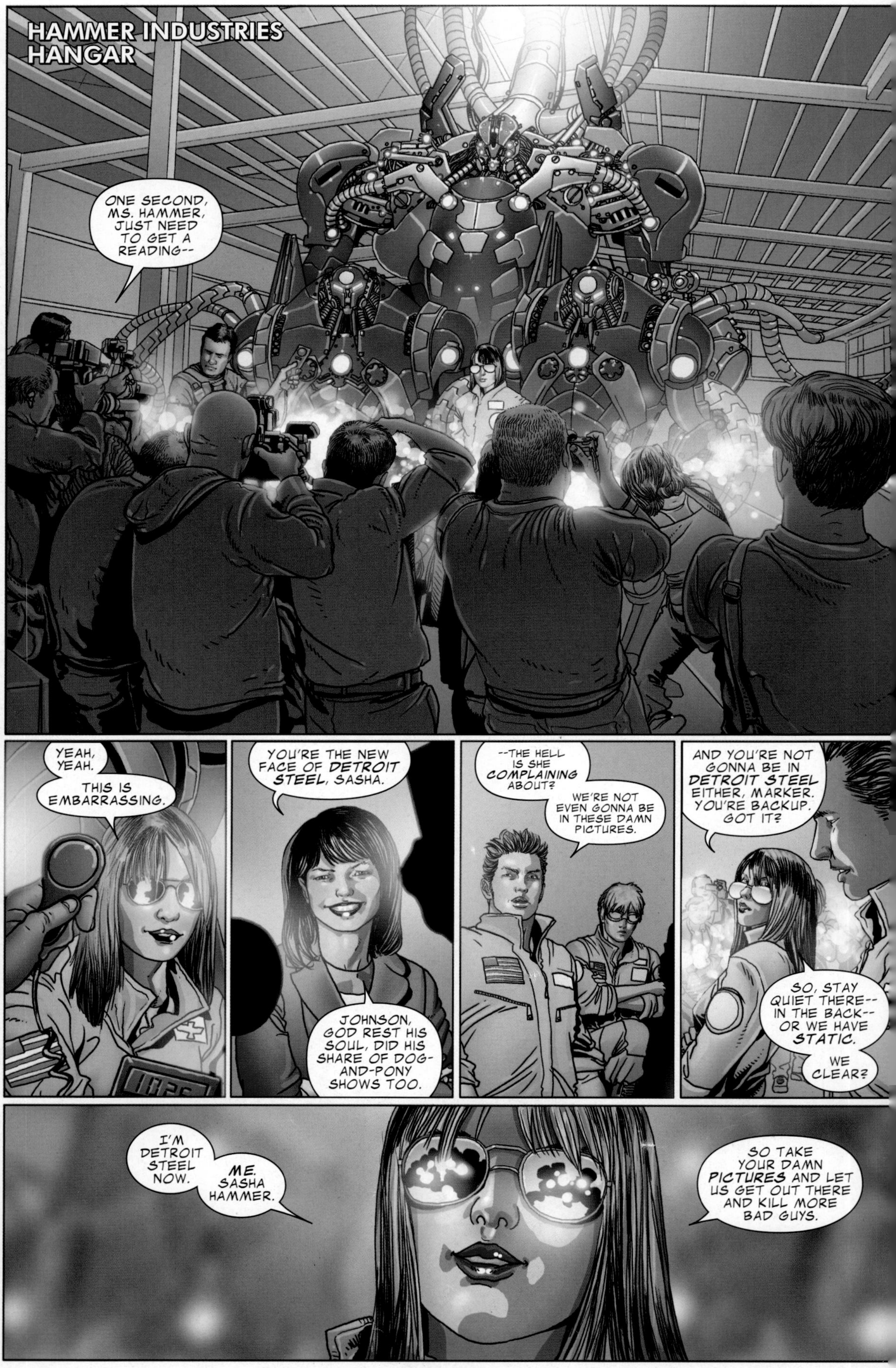
HAMMER INDUSTRIES HANGAR
ONE SECOND, MS. HAMMER, JUST NEED TO GET A READING--
YEAH, YEAH.
THIS IS EMBARRASSING.
YOU'RE THE NEW FACE OF DETROIT STEEL, SASHA.
JOHNSON, GOD REST HIS SOUL, DID HIS SHARE OF DOG-AND-PONY SHOWS TOO.
--THE HELL IS SHE COMPLAINING ABOUT?
WE'RE NOT EVEN GONNA BE IN THESE DAMN PICTURES.
AND YOU'RE NOT GONNA BE IN DETROIT STEEL EITHER, MARKER. YOU'RE BACKUP. GOT IT?
SO, STAY QUIET THERE-- IN THE BACK-- OR WE HAVE STATIC.
WE CLEAR?
I'M DETROIT STEEL NOW.
ME. SASHA HAMMER.
SO TAKE YOUR DAMN PICTURES AND LET US GET OUT THERE AND KILL MORE BAD GUYS.

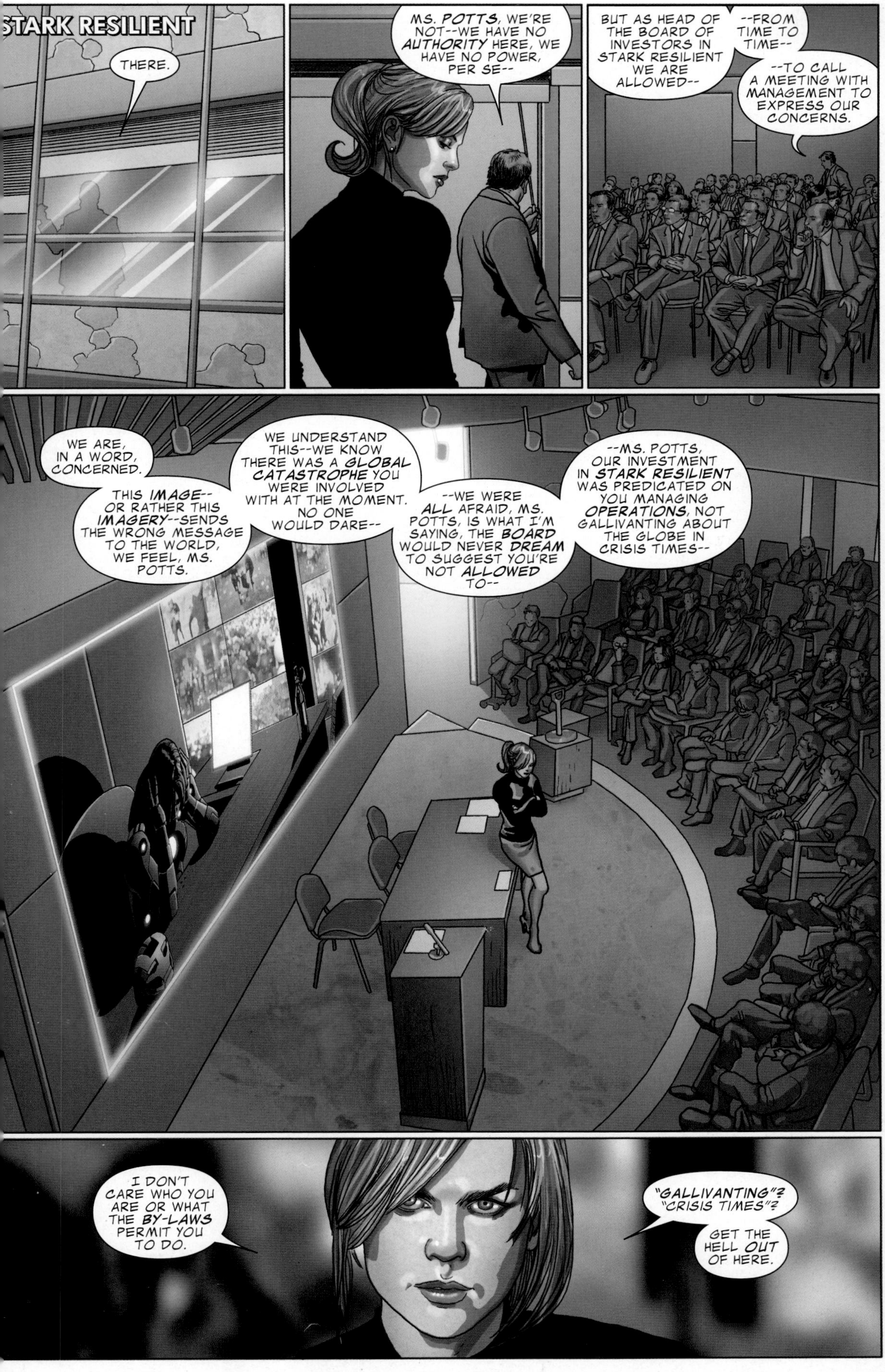
STARK RESILIENT
THERE.
MS. POTTS, WE'RE NOT--WE HAVE NO AUTHORITY HERE, WE HAVE NO POWER, PER SE--
BUT AS HEAD OF THE BOARD OF INVESTORS IN STARK RESILIENT WE ARE ALLOWED--
--FROM TIME TO TIME--
--TO CALL A MEETING WITH MANAGEMENT TO EXPRESS OUR CONCERNS.
WE ARE, IN A WORD, CONCERNED.
THIS IMAGE--OR RATHER THIS IMAGERY--SENDS THE WRONG MESSAGE TO THE WORLD, WE FEEL, MS. POTTS.
WE UNDERSTAND THIS--WE KNOW THERE WAS A GLOBAL CATASTROPHE YOU WERE INVOLVED WITH AT THE MOMENT. NO ONE WOULD DARE--
--WE WERE ALL AFRAID, MS. POTTS, IS WHAT I'M SAYING, THE BOARD WOULD NEVER DREAM TO SUGGEST YOU'RE NOT ALLOWED TO--
--MS. POTTS, OUR INVESTMENT IN STARK RESILIENT WAS PREDICATED ON YOU MANAGING OPERATIONS, NOT GALLIVANTING ABOUT THE GLOBE IN CRISIS TIMES--
I DON'T CARE WHO YOU ARE OR WHAT THE BY-LAWS PERMIT YOU TO DO.
"GALLIVANTING"? "CRISIS TIMES"?
GET THE HELL OUT OF HERE.

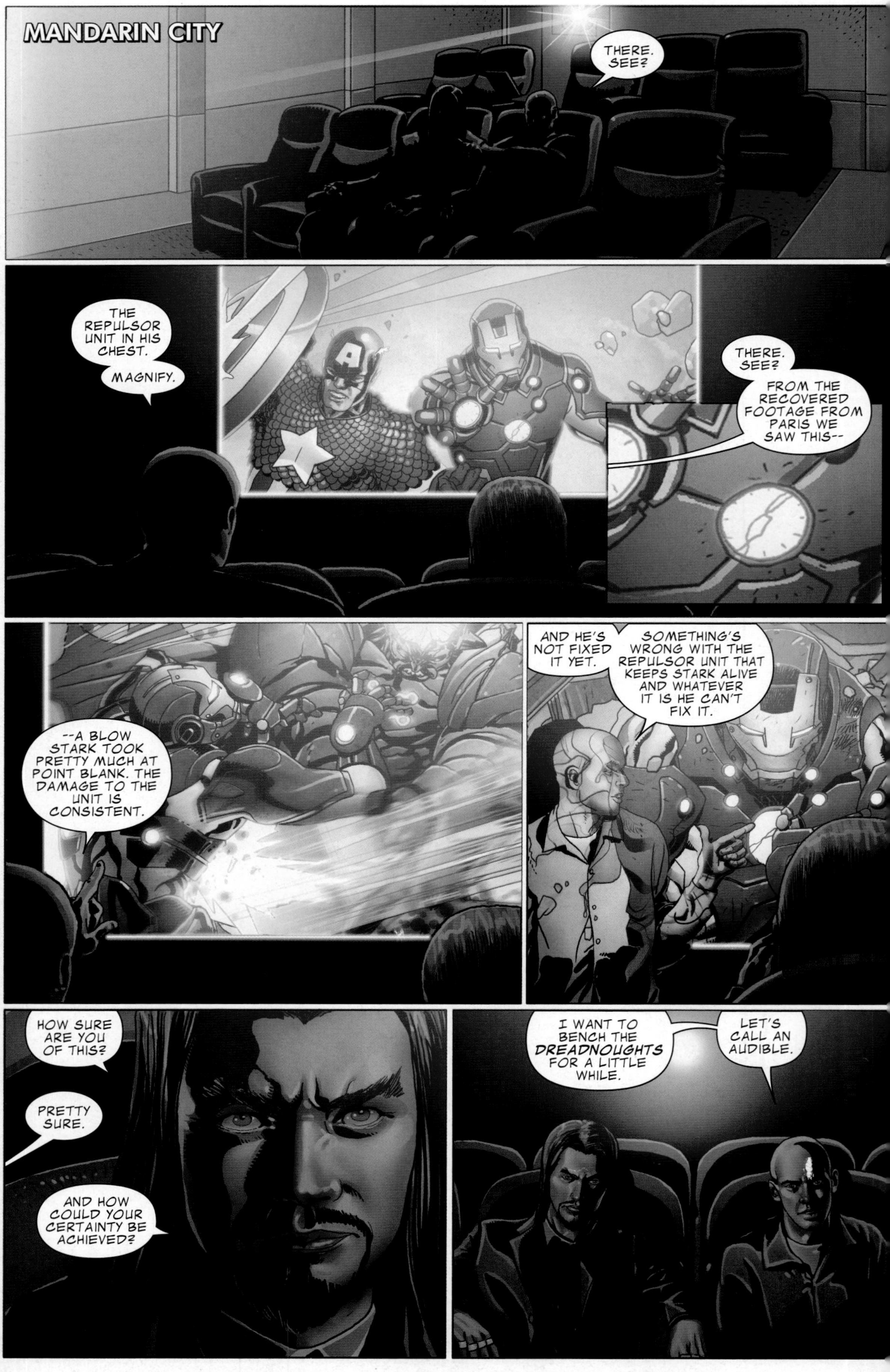
MANDARIN CITY
THERE. SEE?
THE REPULSOR UNIT IN HIS CHEST.
MAGNIFY.
THERE. SEE?
FROM THE RECOVERED FOOTAGE FROM PARIS WE SAW THIS--
--A BLOW STARK TOOK PRETTY MUCH AT POINT BLANK. THE DAMAGE TO THE UNIT IS CONSISTENT.
AND HE'S NOT FIXED IT YET.
SOMETHING'S WRONG WITH THE REPULSOR UNIT THAT KEEPS STARK ALIVE AND WHATEVER IT IS HE CAN'T FIX IT.
HOW SURE ARE YOU OF THIS?
PRETTY SURE.
AND HOW COULD YOUR CERTAINTY BE ACHIEVED?
LET'S CALL AN AUDIBLE.
I WANT TO BENCH THE *DREADNOUGHTS* FOR A LITTLE WHILE.

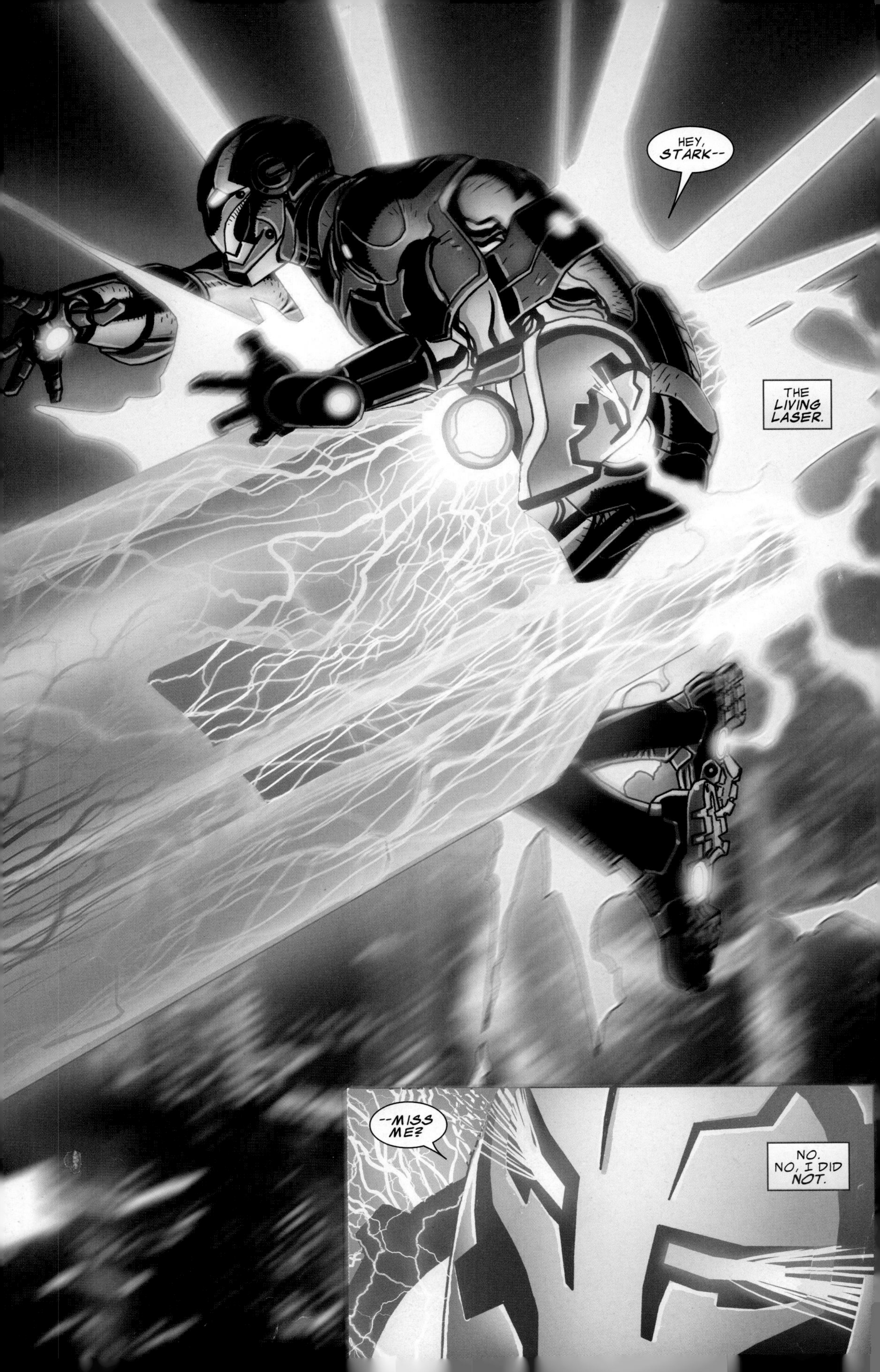
HEY, STARK--
THE LIVING LASER.
--MISS ME?
NO. NO, I DID NOT.

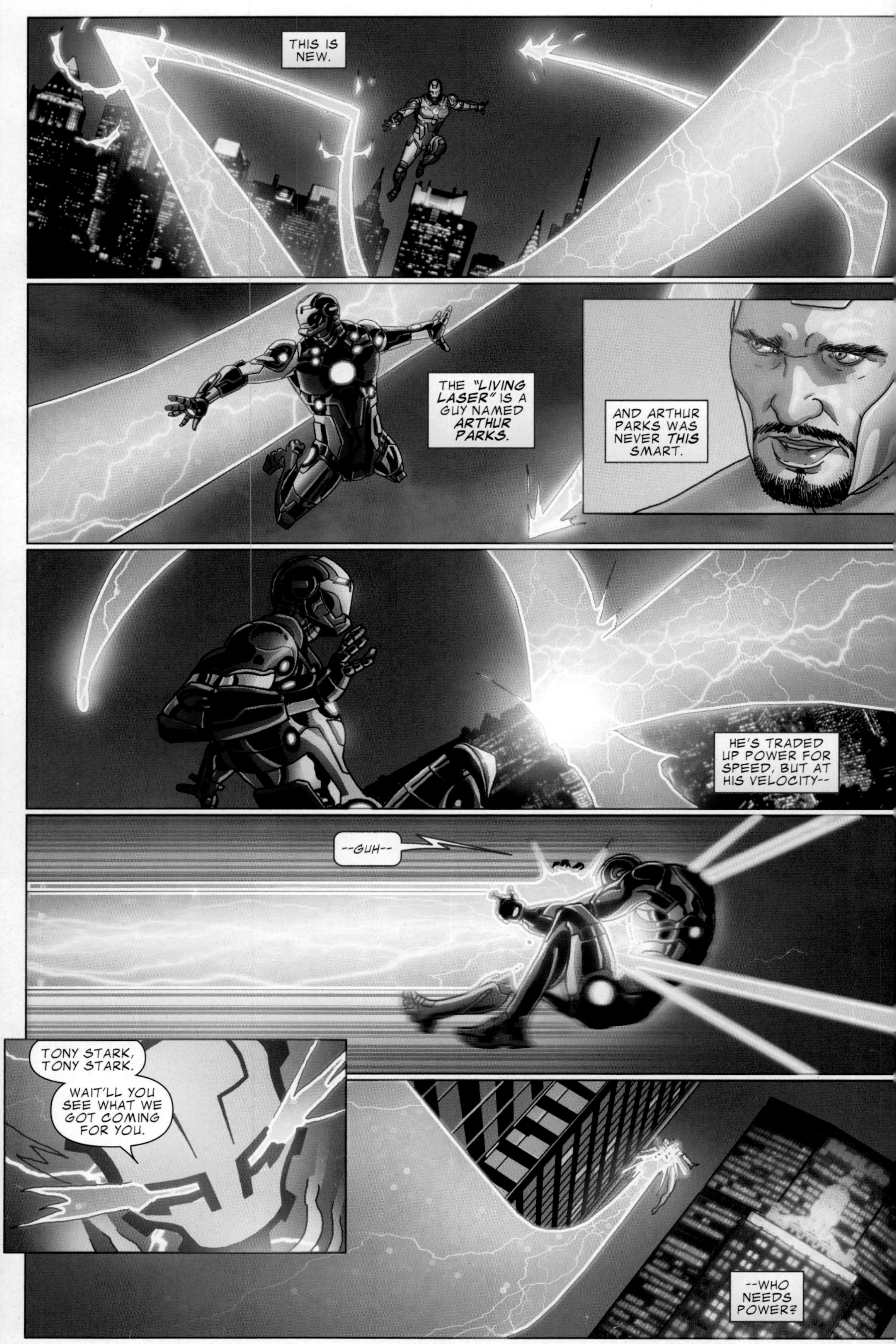
THIS IS NEW.
THE "LIVING LASER" IS A GUY NAMED ARTHUR PARKS.
AND ARTHUR PARKS WAS NEVER THIS SMART.
HE'S TRADED UP POWER FOR SPEED, BUT AT HIS VELOCITY--
--GUH--
TONY STARK, TONY STARK.
WAIT'LL YOU SEE WHAT WE GOT COMING FOR YOU.
--WHO NEEDS POWER?

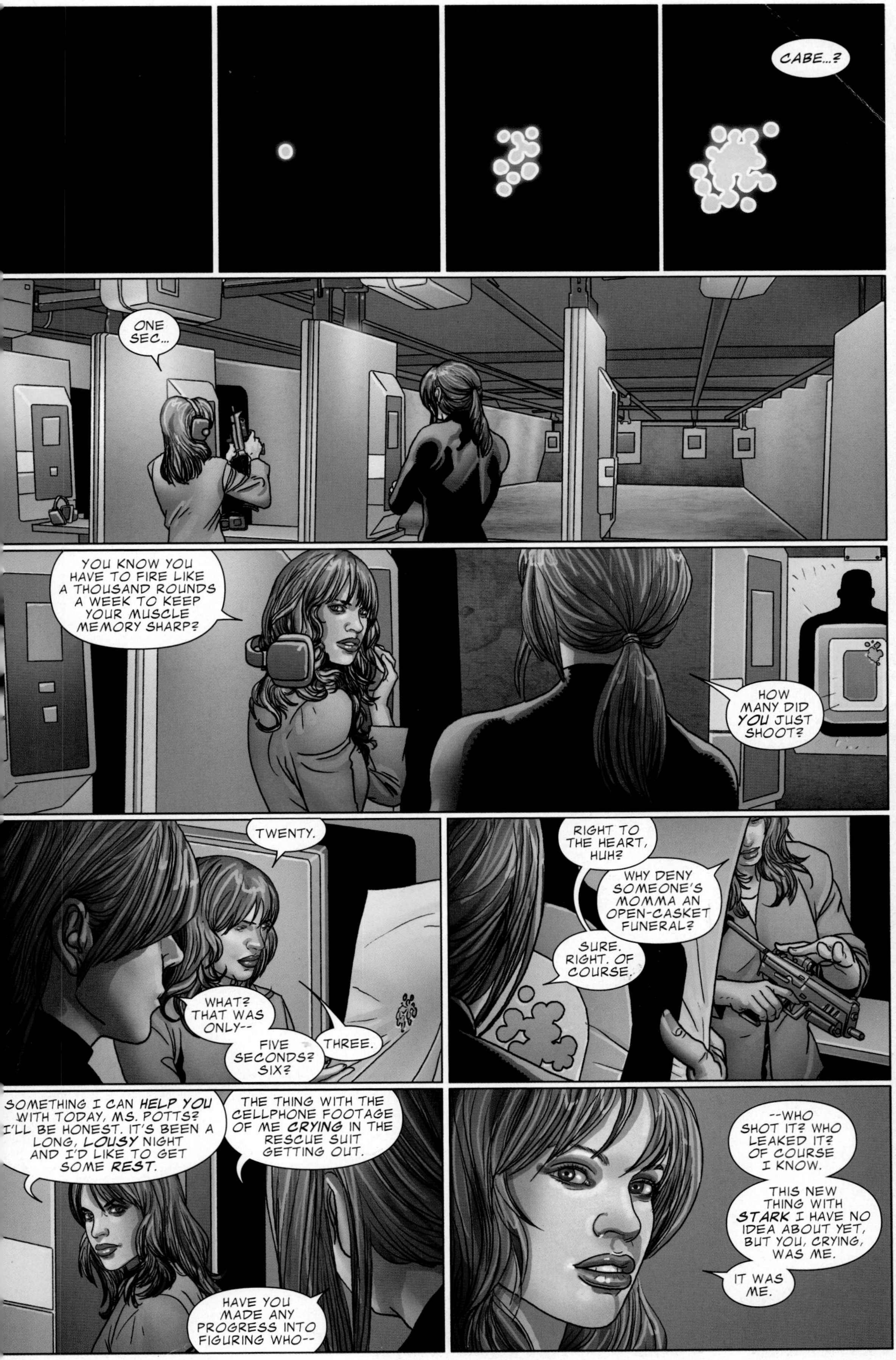
CABE...?
ONE SEC...
YOU KNOW YOU HAVE TO FIRE LIKE A THOUSAND ROUNDS A WEEK TO KEEP YOUR MUSCLE MEMORY SHARP?
HOW MANY DID YOU JUST SHOOT?
TWENTY.
WHAT? THAT WAS ONLY--
FIVE SECONDS? SIX?
THREE.
RIGHT TO THE HEART, HUH?
WHY DENY SOMEONE'S MOMMA AN OPEN-CASKET FUNERAL?
SURE. RIGHT. OF COURSE.
SOMETHING I CAN HELP YOU WITH TODAY, MS. POTTS? I'LL BE HONEST. IT'S BEEN A LONG, LOUSY NIGHT AND I'D LIKE TO GET SOME REST.
THE THING WITH THE CELLPHONE FOOTAGE OF ME CRYING IN THE RESCUE SUIT GETTING OUT.
HAVE YOU MADE ANY PROGRESS INTO FIGURING WHO--
--WHO SHOT IT? WHO LEAKED IT? OF COURSE I KNOW.
THIS NEW THING WITH STARK I HAVE NO IDEA ABOUT YET, BUT YOU, CRYING, WAS ME.
IT WAS ME.

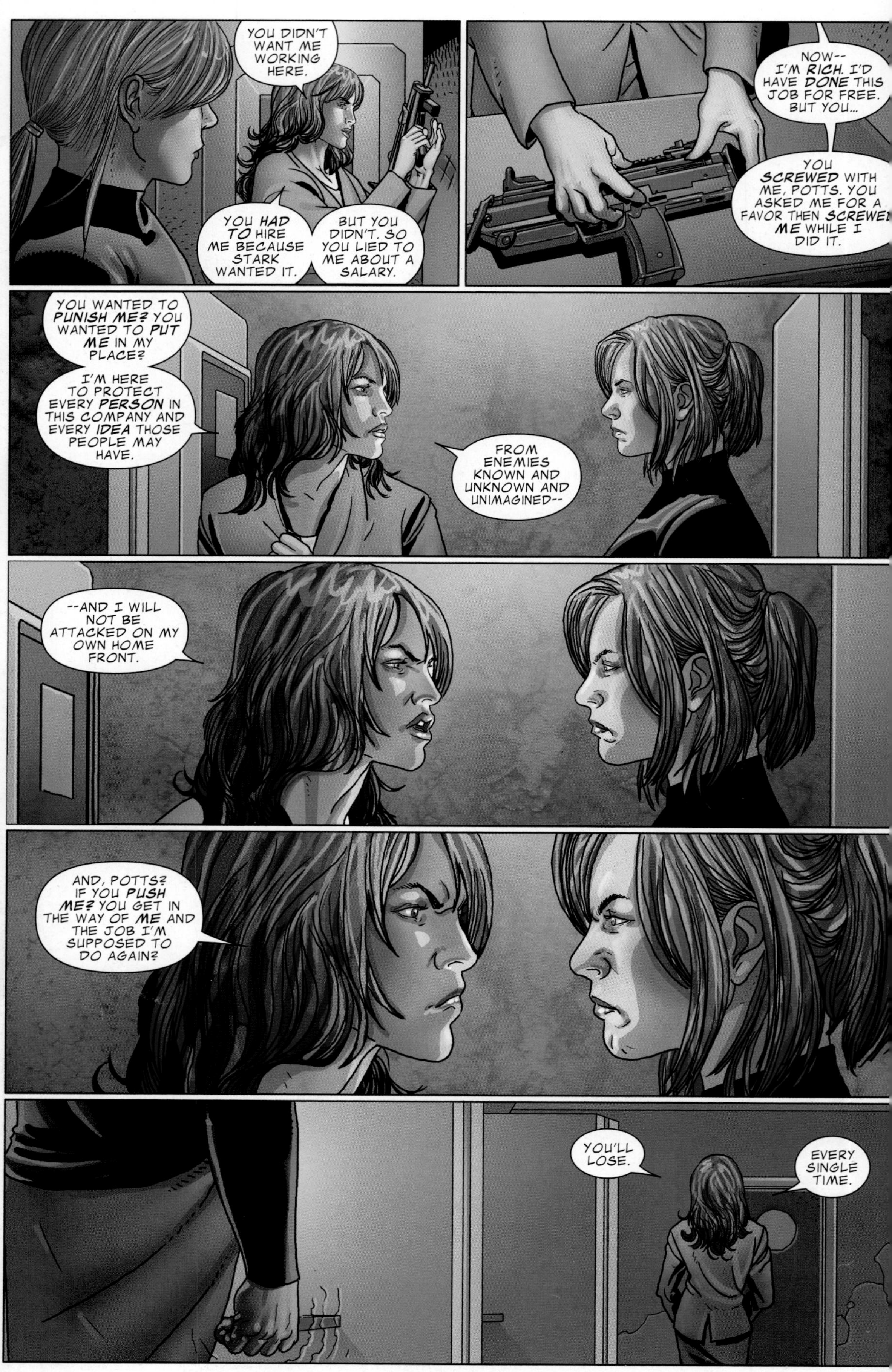
YOU DIDN'T WANT ME WORKING HERE.
YOU HAD TO HIRE ME BECAUSE STARK WANTED IT.
BUT YOU DIDN'T. SO YOU LIED TO ME ABOUT A SALARY.
NOW-- I'M RICH. I'D HAVE DONE THIS JOB FOR FREE. BUT YOU...
YOU SCREWED WITH ME, POTTS. YOU ASKED ME FOR A FAVOR THEN SCREWED ME WHILE I DID IT.
YOU WANTED TO PUNISH ME? YOU WANTED TO PUT ME IN MY PLACE?
I'M HERE TO PROTECT EVERY PERSON IN THIS COMPANY AND EVERY IDEA THOSE PEOPLE MAY HAVE.
FROM ENEMIES KNOWN AND UNKNOWN AND UNIMAGINED--
--AND I WILL NOT BE ATTACKED ON MY OWN HOME FRONT.
AND, POTTS? IF YOU PUSH ME? YOU GET IN THE WAY OF ME AND THE JOB I'M SUPPOSED TO DO AGAIN?
YOU'LL LOSE.
EVERY SINGLE TIME.

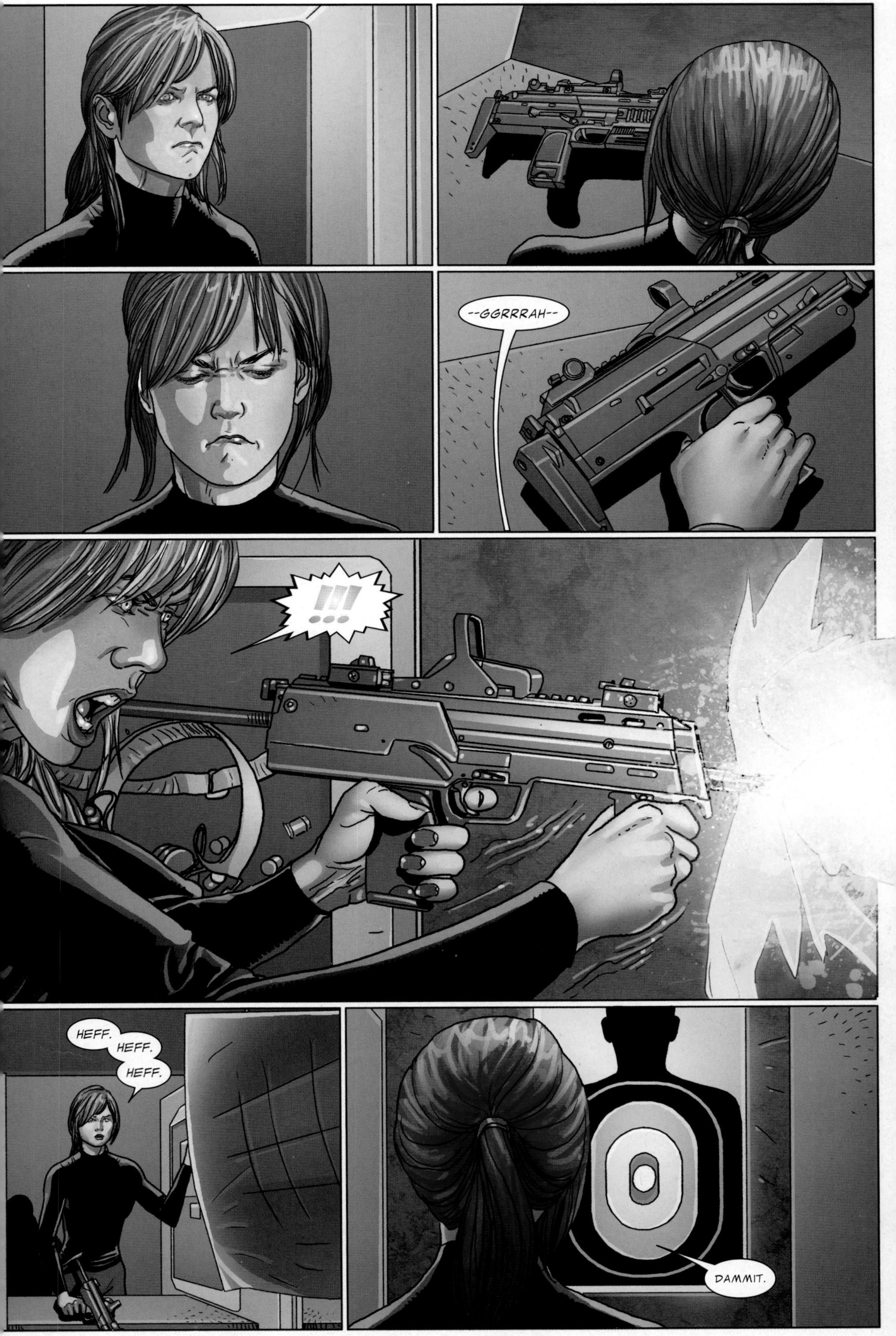
--GGRRRAH--
!!!
...
HEFF.
HEFF.
HEFF.
DAMMIT.

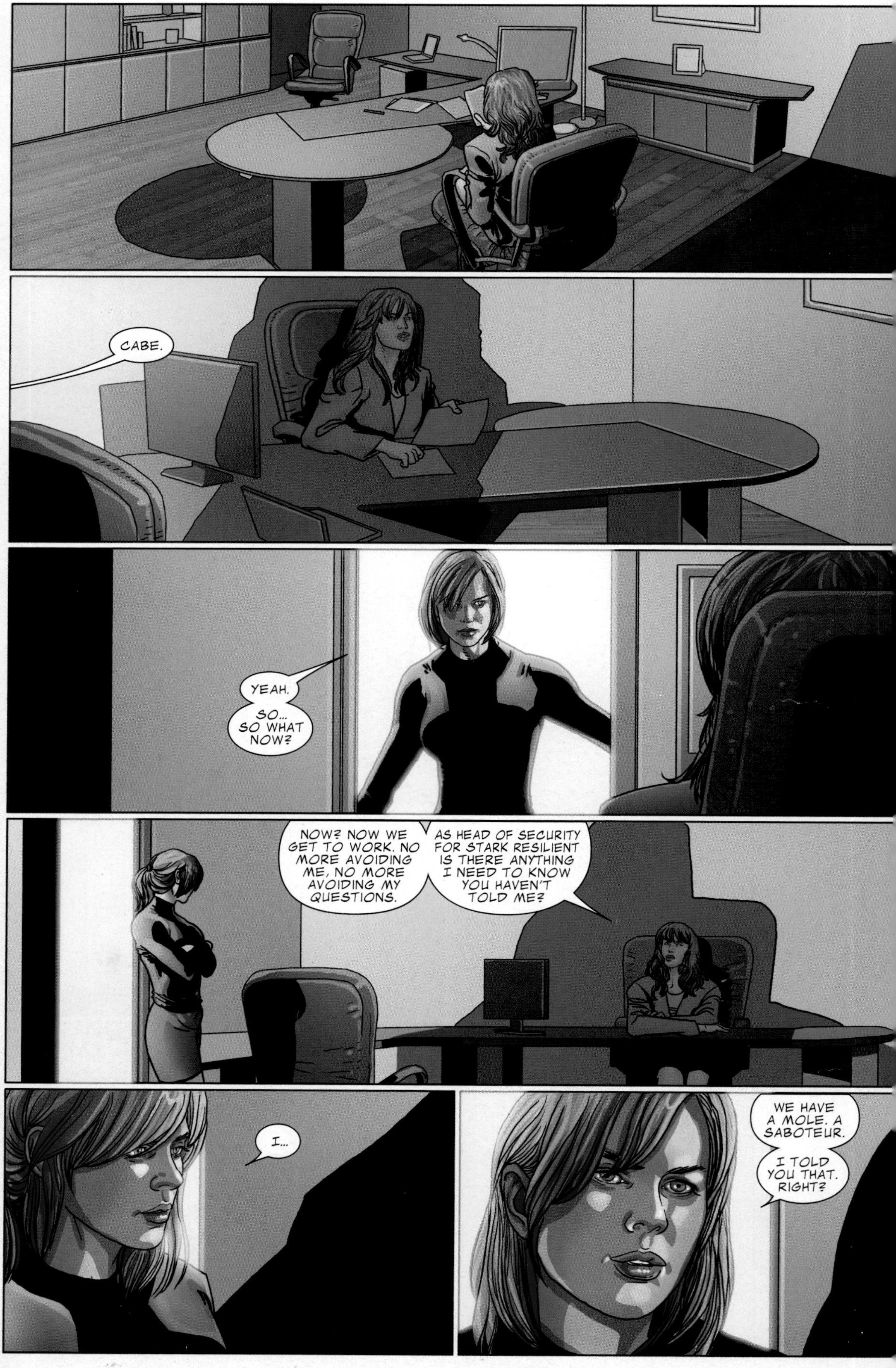
CABE.
YEAH.
SO... SO WHAT NOW?
NOW? NOW WE GET TO WORK. NO MORE AVOIDING ME, NO MORE AVOIDING MY QUESTIONS.
AS HEAD OF SECURITY FOR STARK RESILIENT IS THERE ANYTHING I NEED TO KNOW YOU HAVEN'T TOLD ME?
I...
WE HAVE A MOLE. A SABOTEUR.
I TOLD YOU THAT. RIGHT?

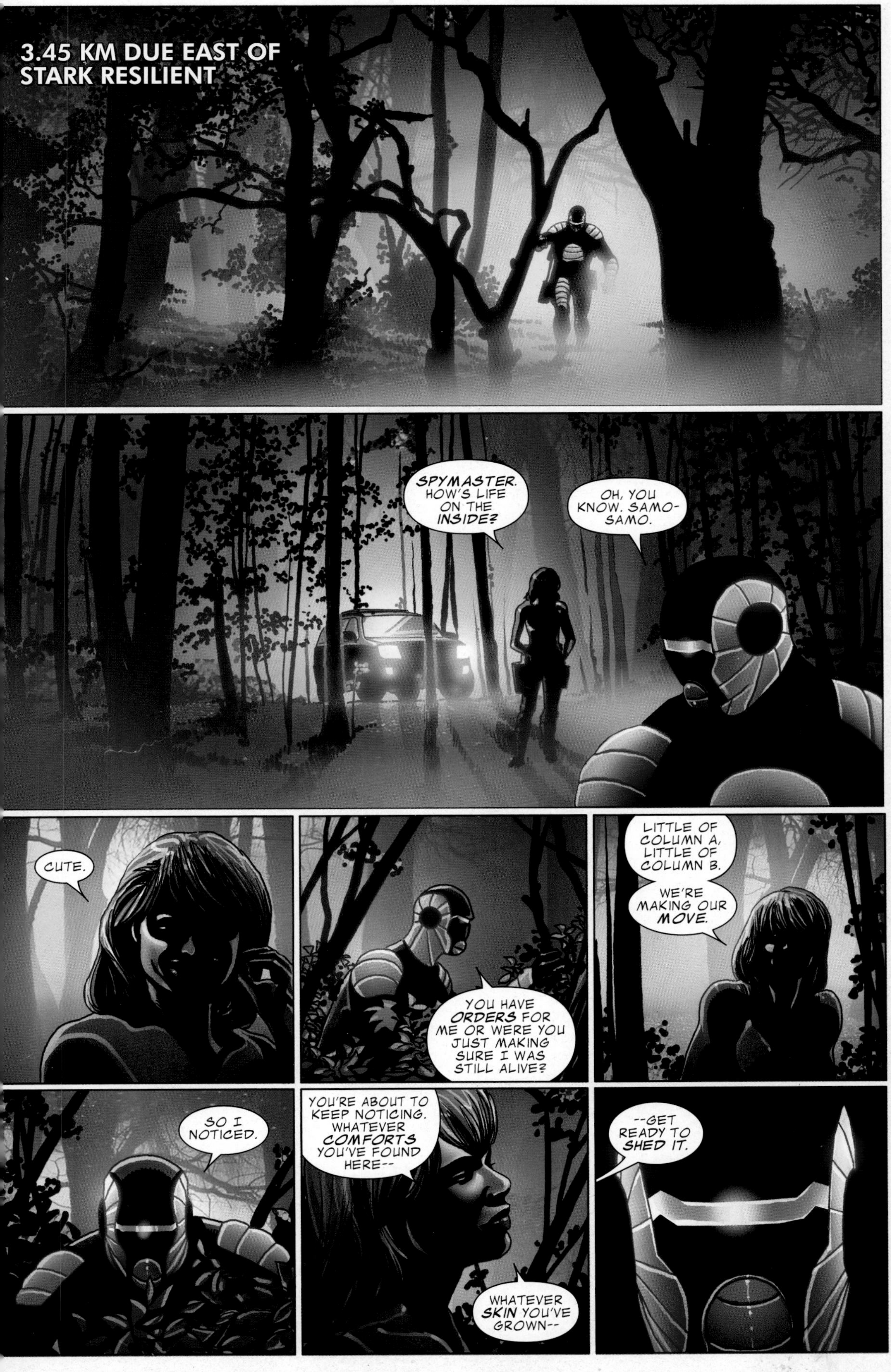
3.45 KM DUE EAST OF STARK RESILIENT
SPYMASTER. HOW'S LIFE ON THE INSIDE?
OH, YOU KNOW. SAMO-SAMO.
CUTE.
YOU HAVE ORDERS FOR ME OR WERE YOU JUST MAKING SURE I WAS STILL ALIVE?
LITTLE OF COLUMN A, LITTLE OF COLUMN B.
WE'RE MAKING OUR MOVE.
SO I NOTICED.
YOU'RE ABOUT TO KEEP NOTICING. WHATEVER COMFORTS YOU'VE FOUND HERE--
WHATEVER SKIN YOU'VE GROWN--
--GET READY TO SHED IT.

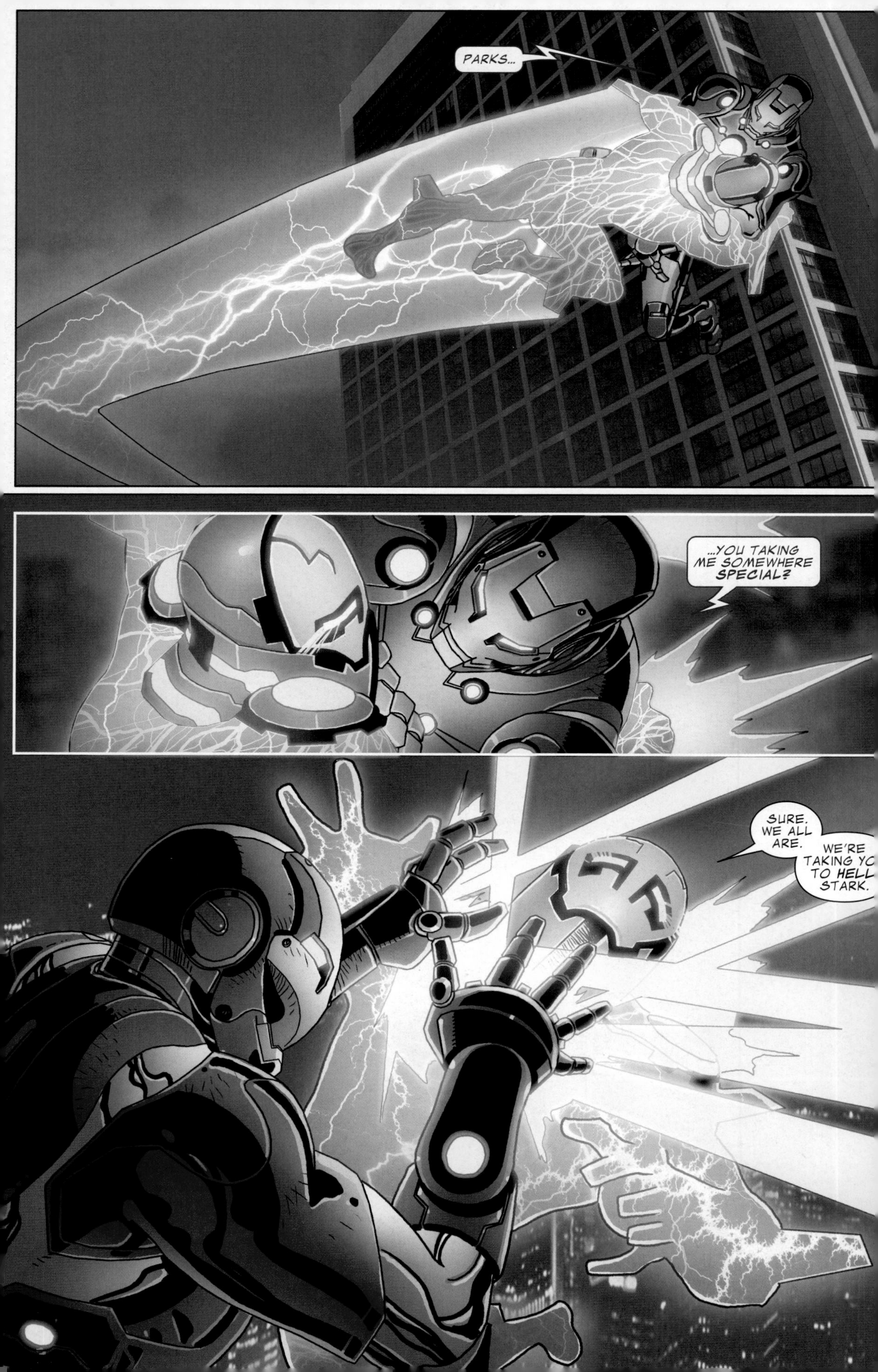
PARKS...
...YOU TAKING ME SOMEWHERE SPECIAL?
SURE. WE ALL ARE.
WE'RE TAKING YO TO HELL STARK.

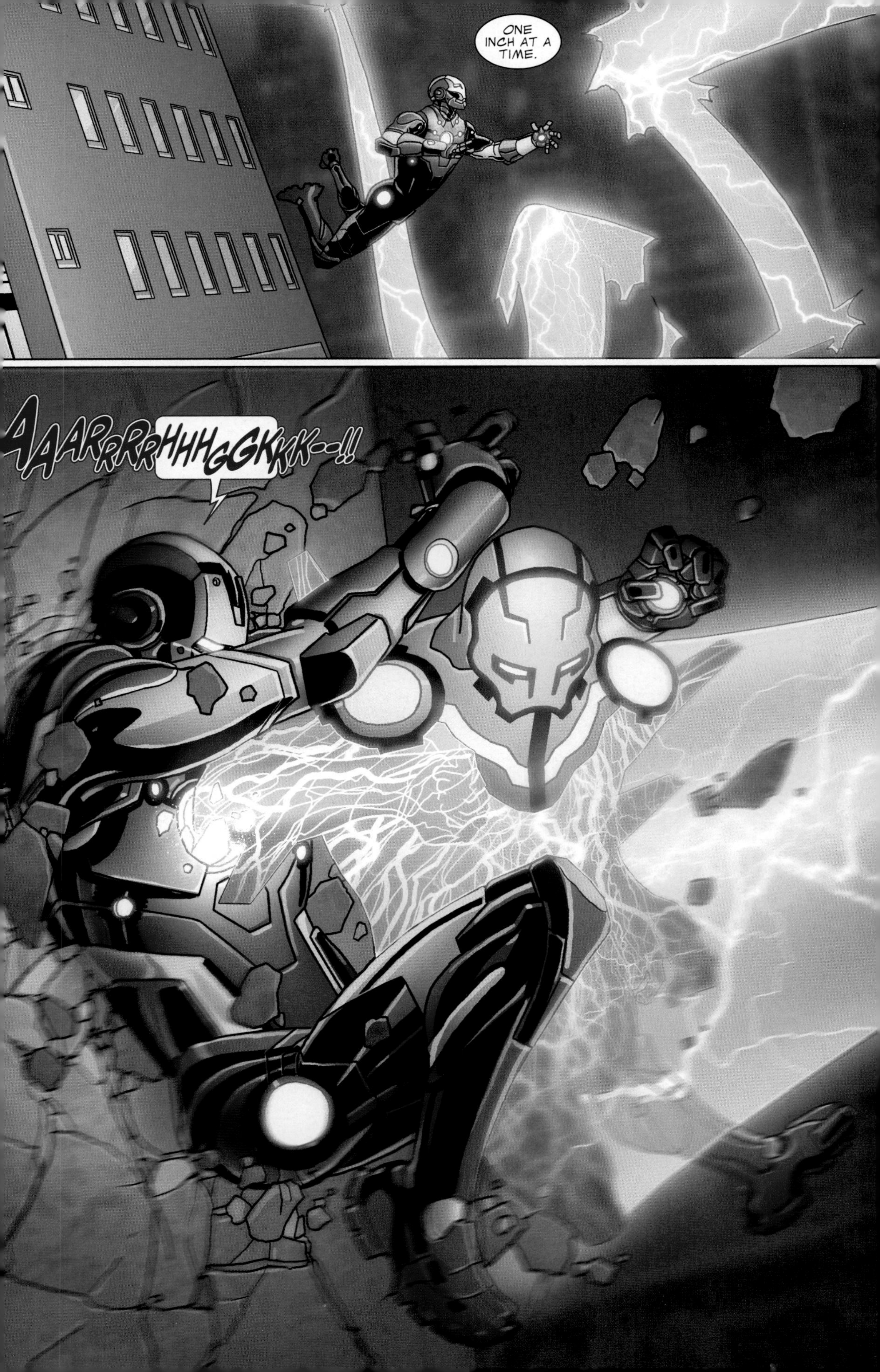
ONE INCH AT A TIME.
AAARRRRHHHGGKKKK--!!

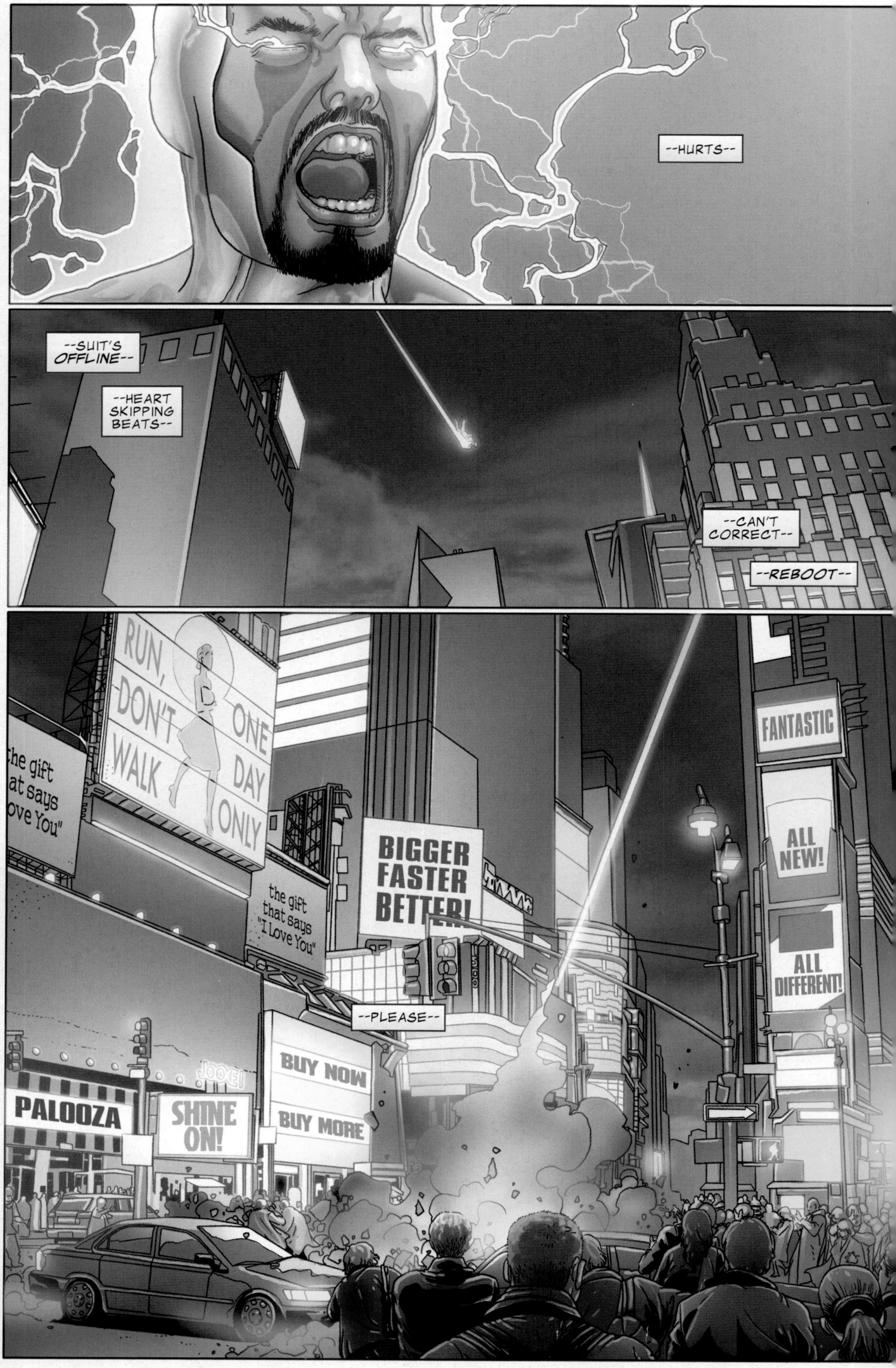
--HURTS--
--SUIT'S OFFLINE--
--HEART SKIPPING BEATS--
--CAN'T CORRECT--
--REBOOT--
RUN, DON'T WALK
ONE DAY ONLY
the gift that says "I Love You"
FANTASTIC
ALL NEW!
ALL DIFFERENT!
BIGGER FASTER BETTER!
the gift that says "I Love You"
--PLEASE--
BUY NOW
BUY MORE
PALOOZA
SHINE ON!

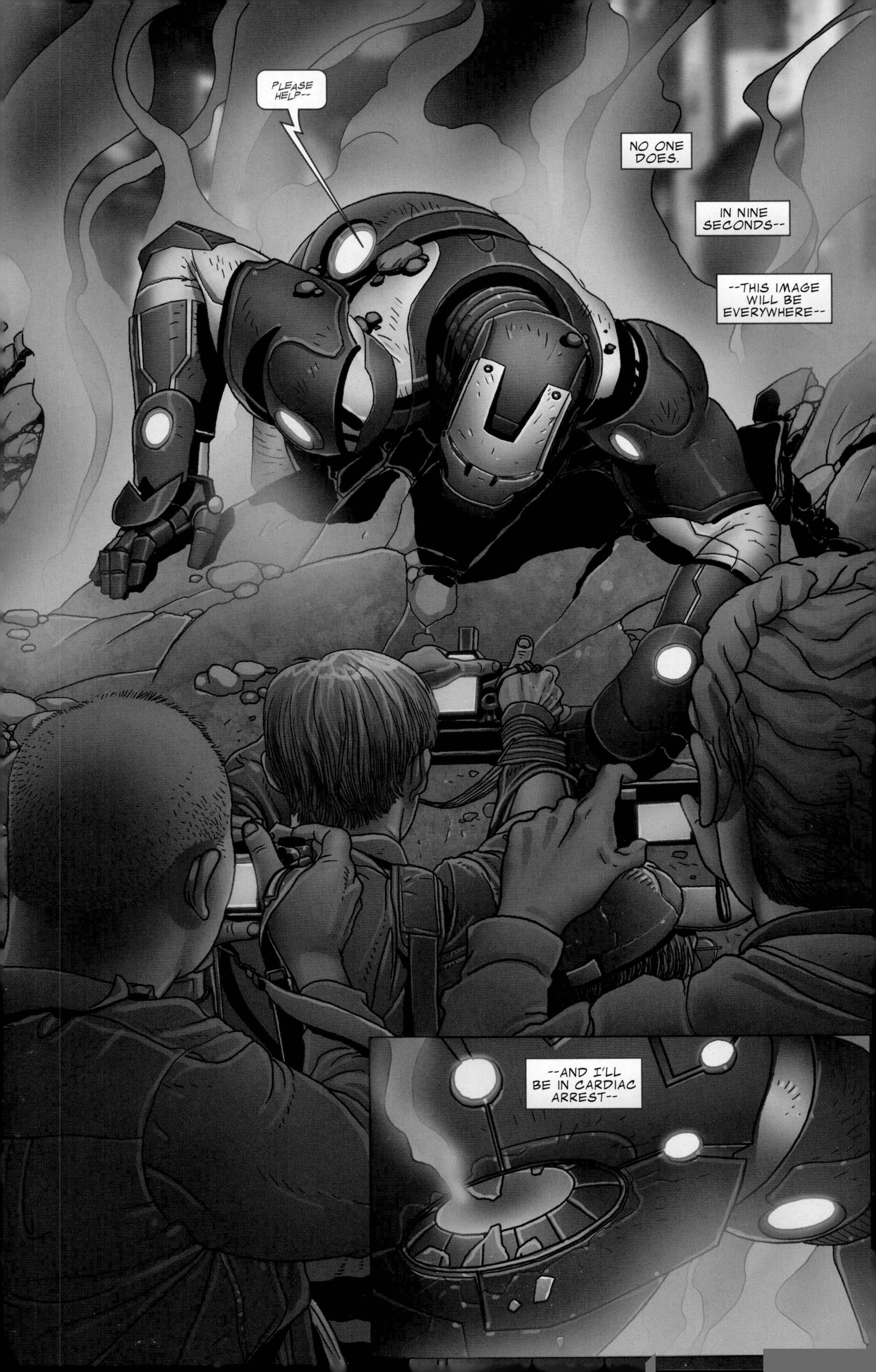
PLEASE HELP--
NO ONE DOES.
IN NINE SECONDS--
--THIS IMAGE WILL BE EVERYWHERE--
--AND I'LL BE IN CARDIAC ARREST--

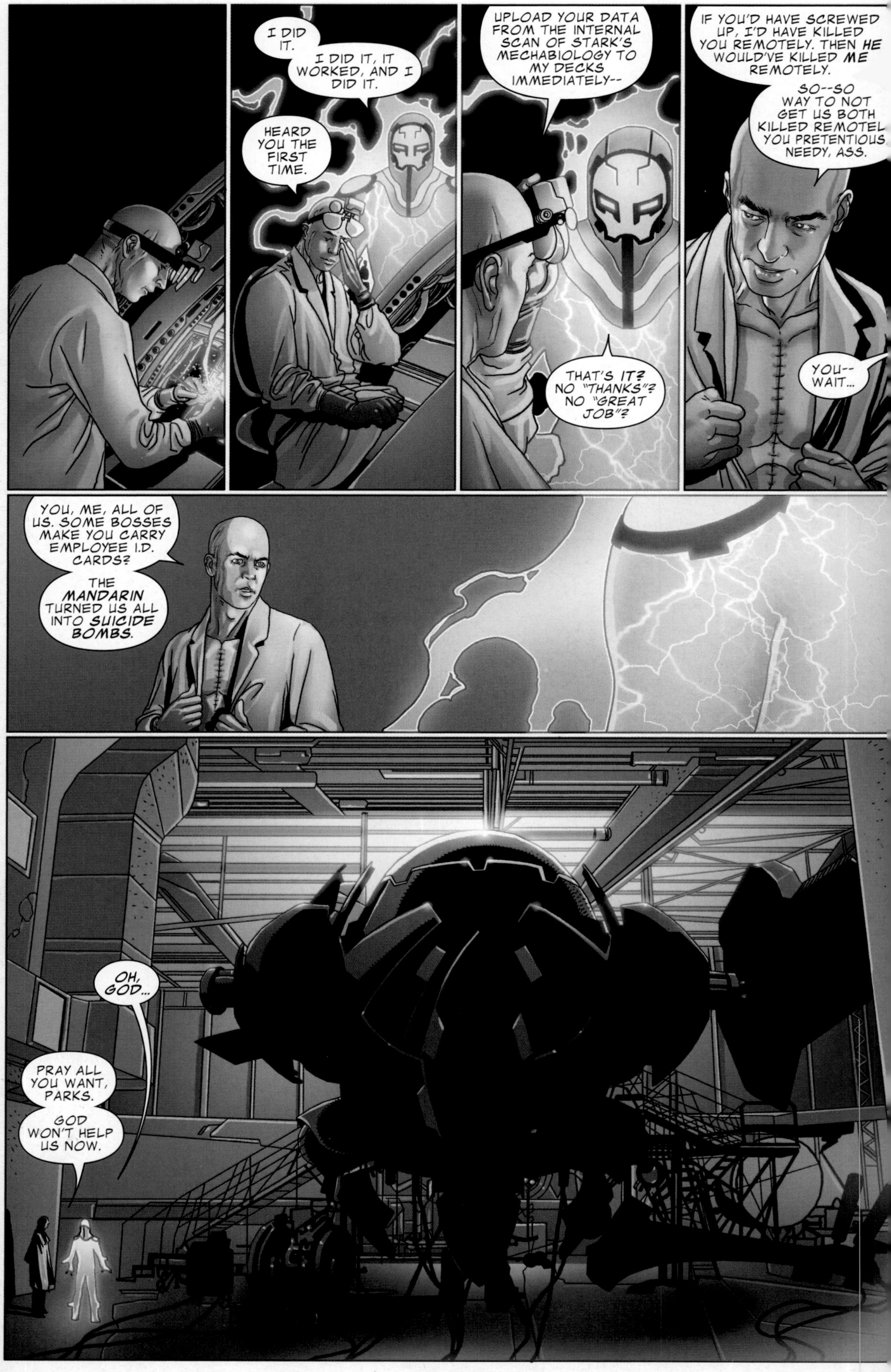
I DID IT.
I DID IT, IT WORKED, AND I DID IT.
HEARD YOU THE FIRST TIME.
UPLOAD YOUR DATA FROM THE INTERNAL SCAN OF STARK'S MECHABIOLOGY TO MY DECKS IMMEDIATELY--
THAT'S IT? NO "THANKS"? NO "GREAT JOB"?
IF YOU'D HAVE SCREWED UP, I'D HAVE KILLED YOU REMOTELY. THEN HE WOULD'VE KILLED ME REMOTELY.
SO--SO WAY TO NOT GET US BOTH KILLED REMOTEL YOU PRETENTIOUS NEEDY, ASS.
YOU-- WAIT...
YOU, ME, ALL OF US. SOME BOSSES MAKE YOU CARRY EMPLOYEE I.D. CARDS?
THE MANDARIN TURNED US ALL INTO SUICIDE BOMBS.
OH, GOD...
PRAY ALL YOU WANT, PARKS.
GOD WON'T HELP US NOW.

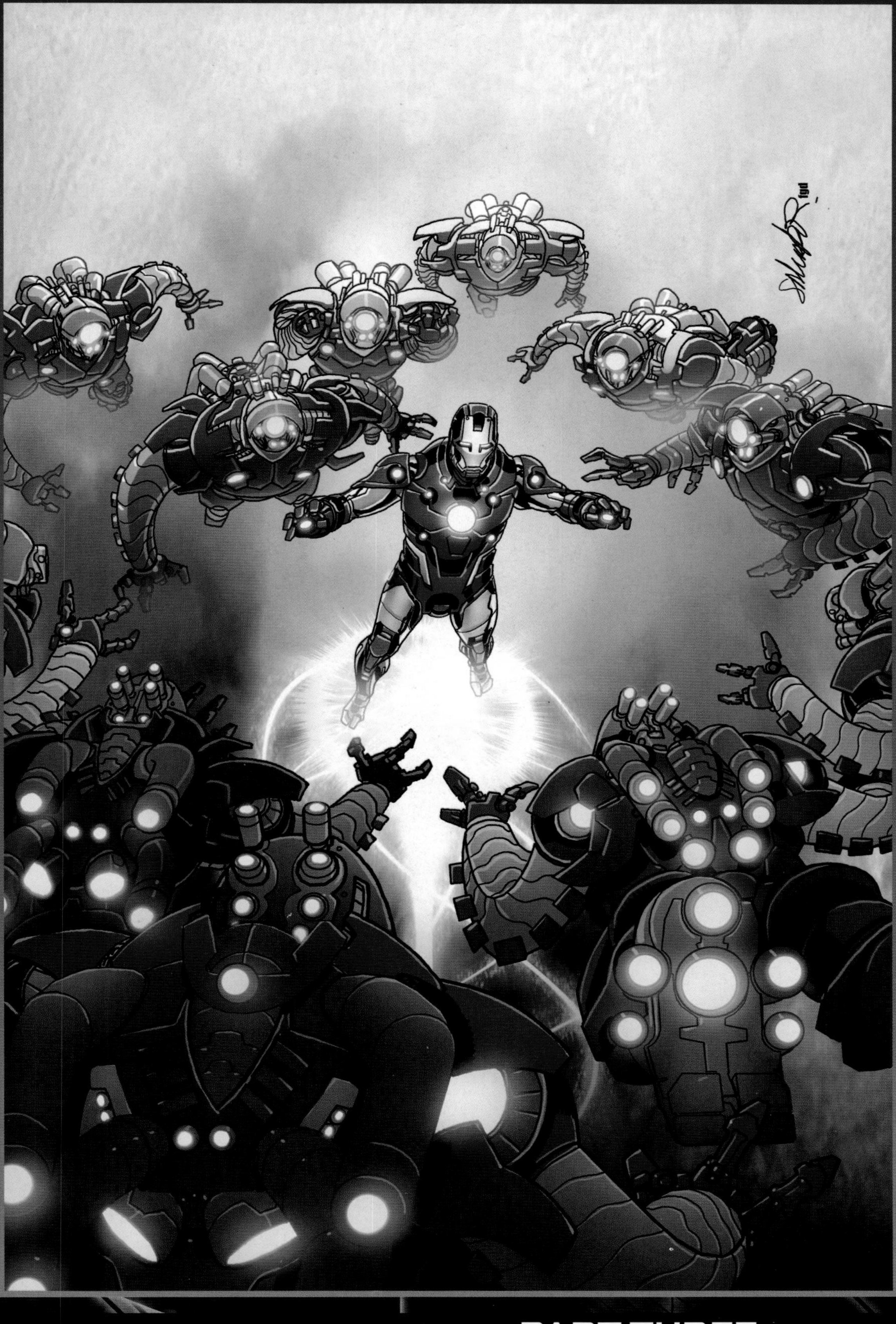

PART THREE: CONTROL 512

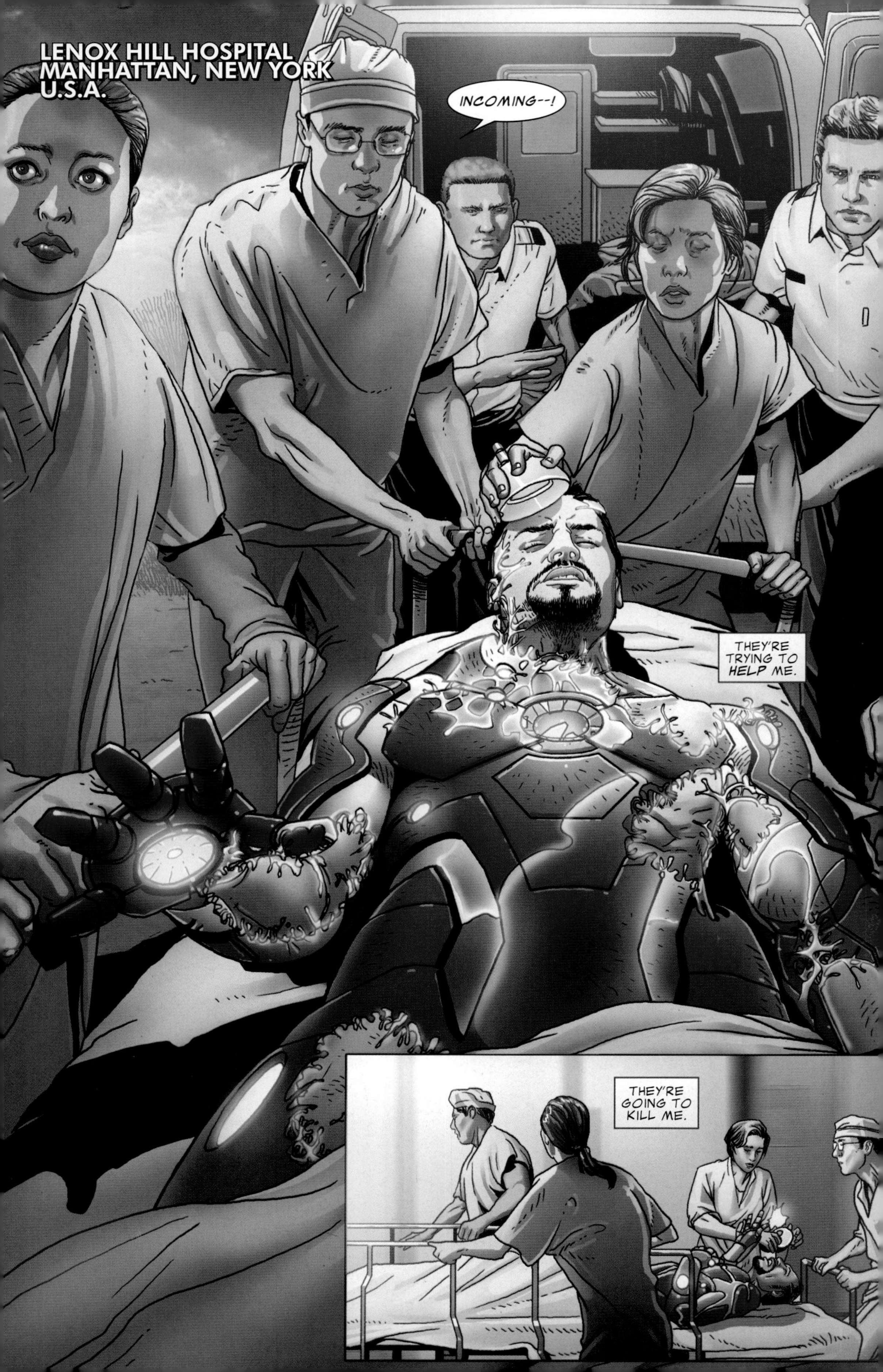
LENOX HILL HOSPITAL
MANHATTAN, NEW YORK
U.S.A.
INCOMING--!
THEY'RE TRYING TO HELP ME.
THEY'RE GOING TO KILL ME.

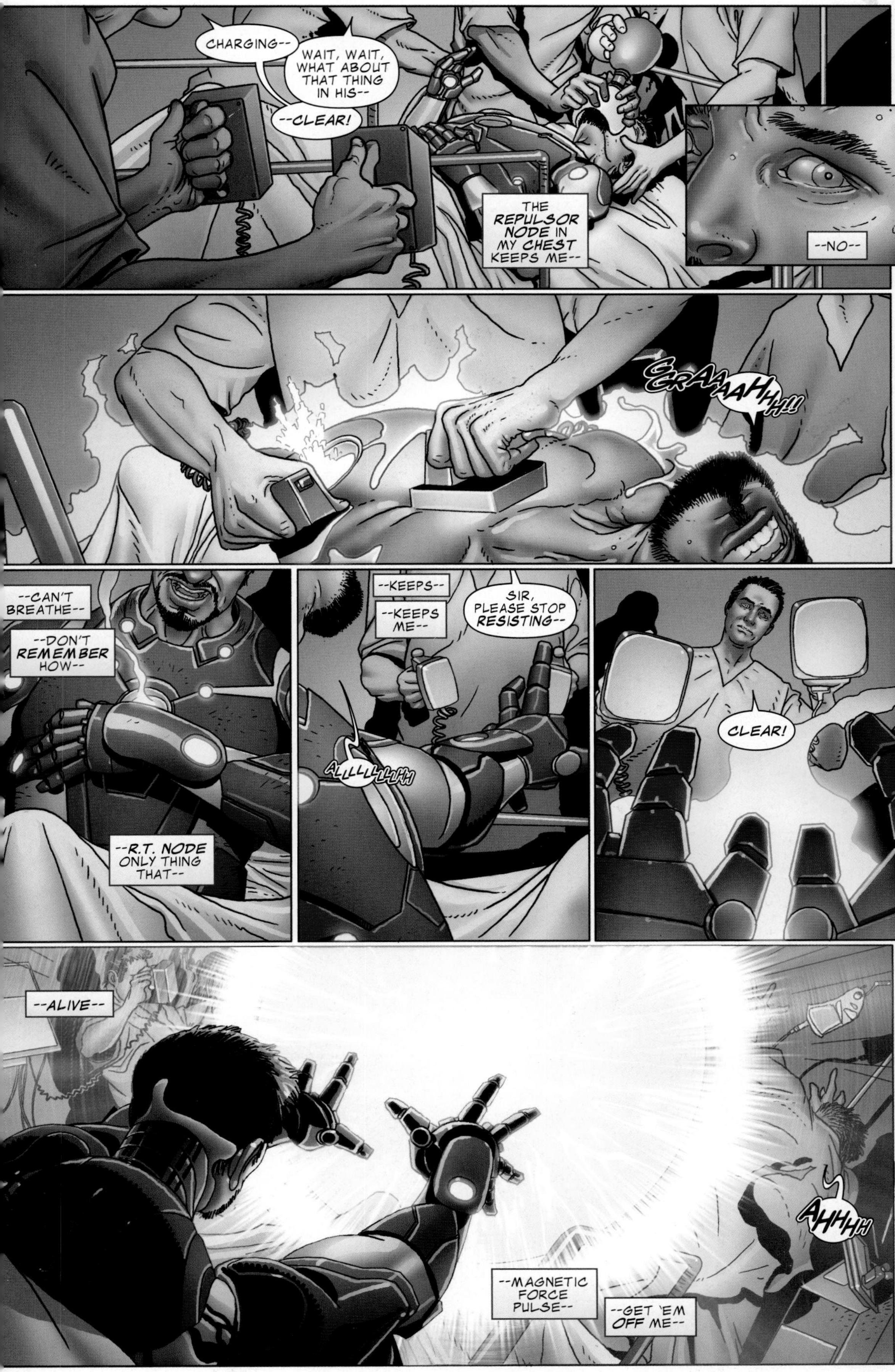
CHARGING--
WAIT, WAIT, WHAT ABOUT THAT THING IN HIS--
--CLEAR!
THE REPULSOR NODE IN MY CHEST KEEPS ME--
--NO--
GGRAAAAHHH!!
--CAN'T BREATHE--
--DON'T REMEMBER HOW--
--R.T. NODE ONLY THING THAT--
--KEEPS--
--KEEPS ME--
SIR, PLEASE STOP RESISTING--
ALLLLLLLLHH
CLEAR!
--ALIVE--
AHHHH
--MAGNETIC FORCE PULSE--
--GET 'EM OFF ME--

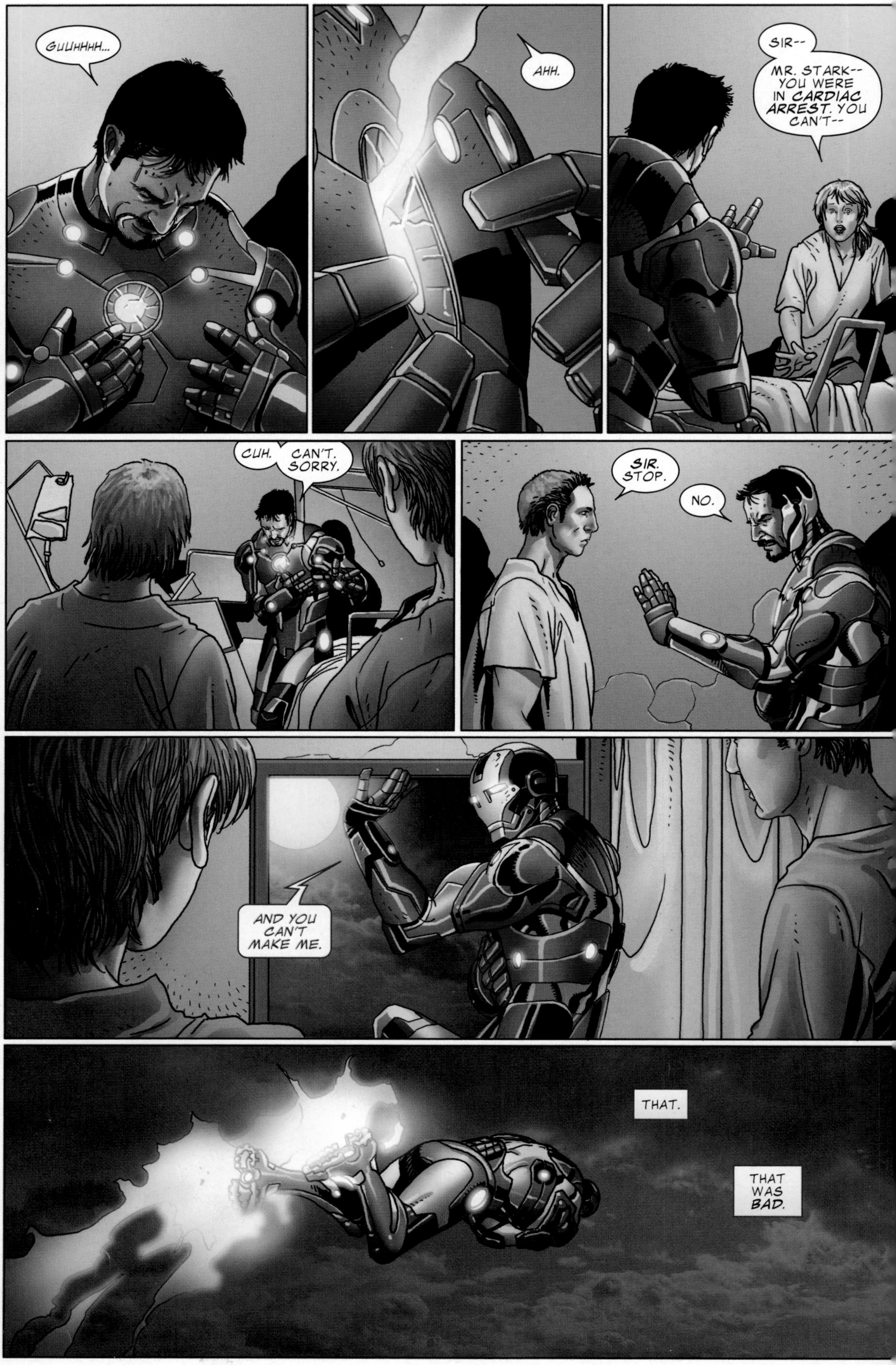
GUUHHHH...
AHH.
SIR--
MR. STARK--YOU WERE IN CARDIAC ARREST. YOU CAN'T--
CUH.
CAN'T. SORRY.
SIR. STOP.
NO.
AND YOU CAN'T MAKE ME.
THAT.
THAT WAS BAD.

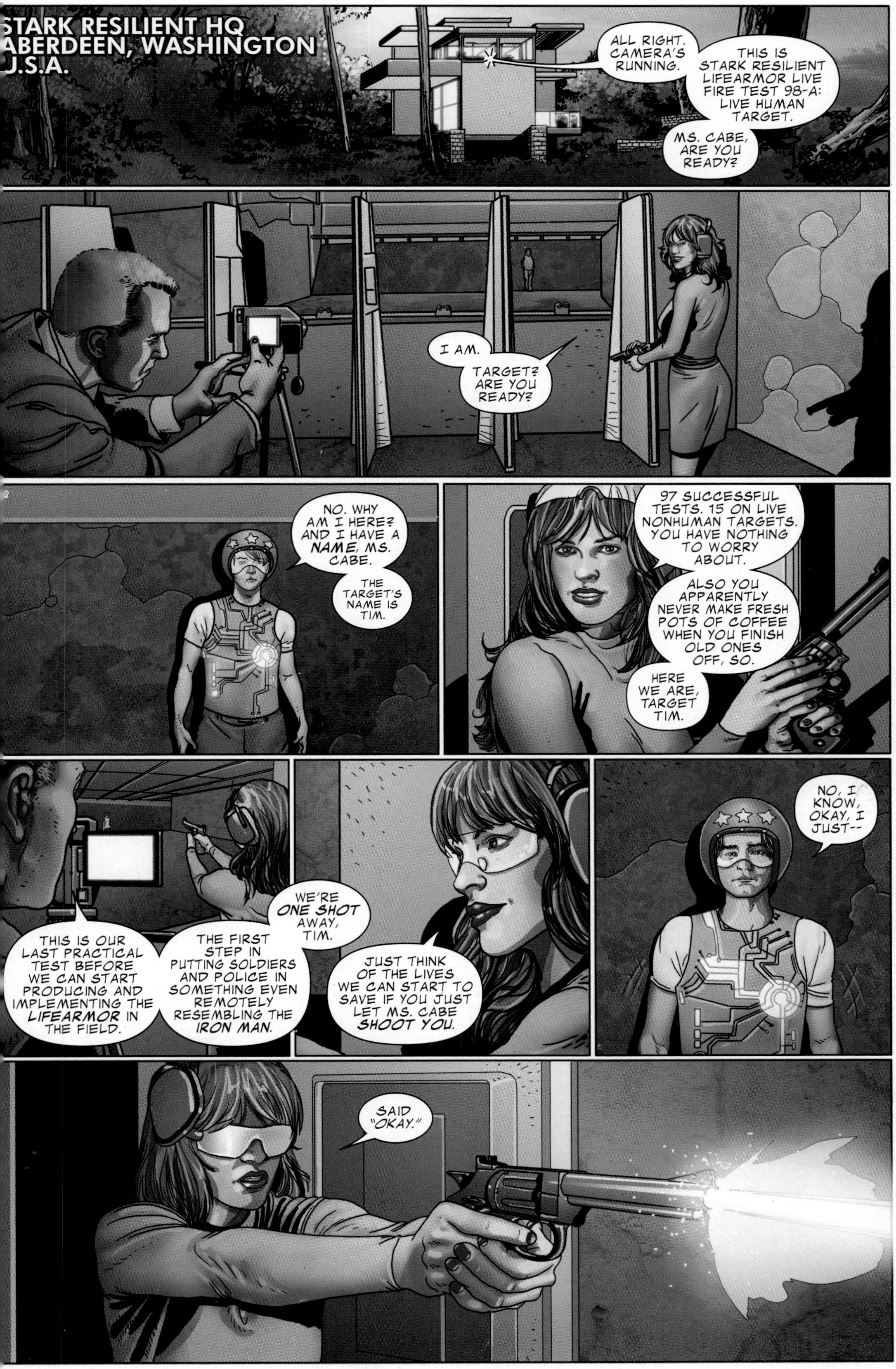
STARK RESILIENT HQ
ABERDEEN, WASHINGTON
U.S.A.
ALL RIGHT. CAMERA'S RUNNING.
THIS IS STARK RESILIENT LIFEARMOR LIVE FIRE TEST 98-A: LIVE HUMAN TARGET.
MS. CABE, ARE YOU READY?
I AM.
TARGET? ARE YOU READY?
NO. WHY AM I HERE? AND I HAVE A NAME, MS. CABE.
THE TARGET'S NAME IS TIM.
97 SUCCESSFUL TESTS. 15 ON LIVE NONHUMAN TARGETS. YOU HAVE NOTHING TO WORRY ABOUT.
ALSO YOU APPARENTLY NEVER MAKE FRESH POTS OF COFFEE WHEN YOU FINISH OLD ONES OFF, SO.
HERE WE ARE, TARGET TIM.
THIS IS OUR LAST PRACTICAL TEST BEFORE WE CAN START PRODUCING AND IMPLEMENTING THE LIFEARMOR IN THE FIELD.
THE FIRST STEP IN PUTTING SOLDIERS AND POLICE IN SOMETHING EVEN REMOTELY RESEMBLING THE IRON MAN.
WE'RE ONE SHOT AWAY, TIM.
JUST THINK OF THE LIVES WE CAN START TO SAVE IF YOU JUST LET MS. CABE SHOOT YOU.
NO, I KNOW, OKAY, I JUST--
SAID "OKAY."

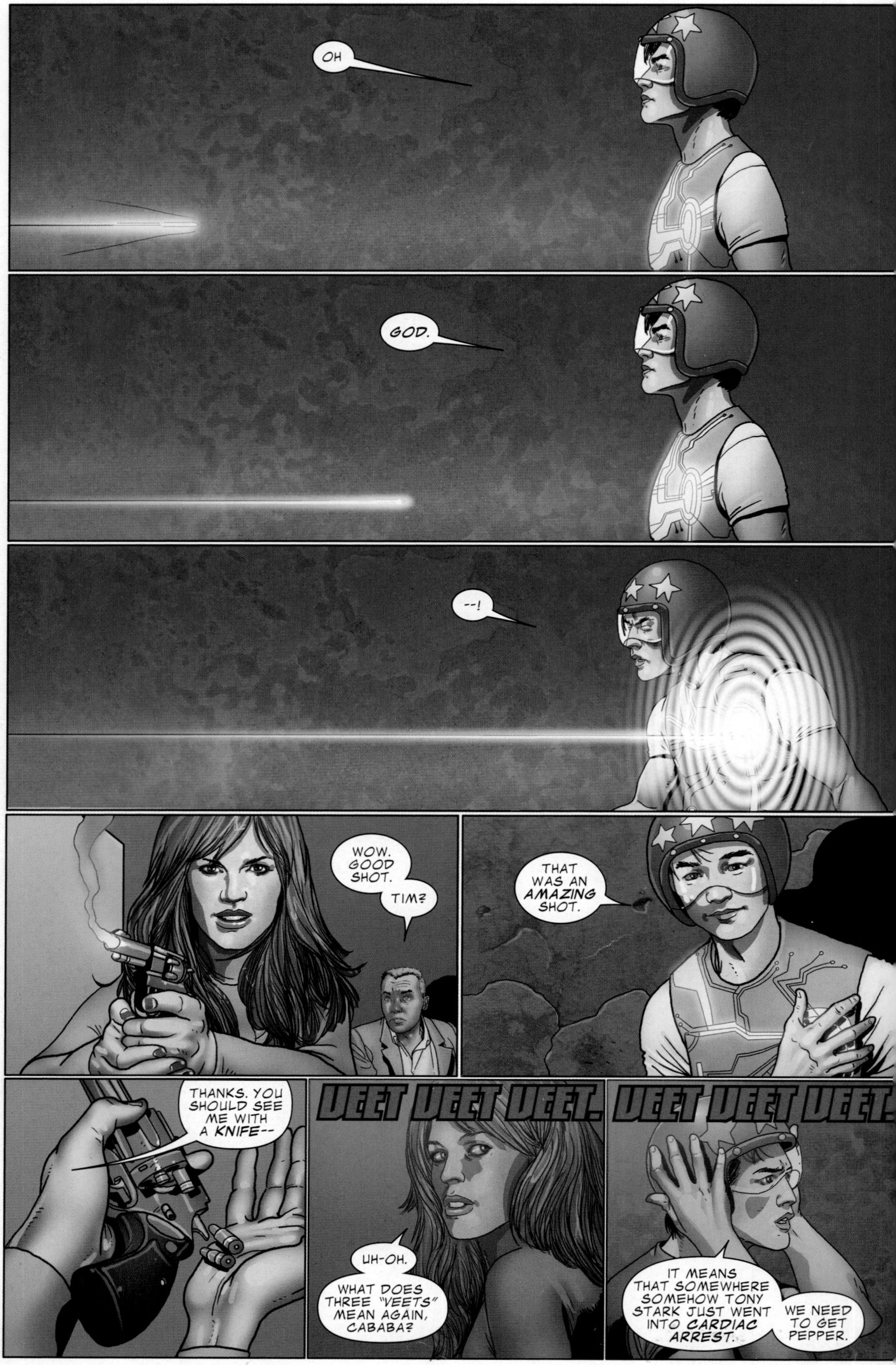
OH
GOD.
--!
WOW. GOOD SHOT.
TIM?
THAT WAS AN AMAZING SHOT.
THANKS. YOU SHOULD SEE ME WITH A KNIFE--
VEET VEET VEET.
UH-OH.
WHAT DOES THREE "VEETS" MEAN AGAIN, CABABA?
VEET VEET VEET.
IT MEANS THAT SOMEWHERE SOMEHOW TONY STARK JUST WENT INTO CARDIAC ARREST.
WE NEED TO GET PEPPER.

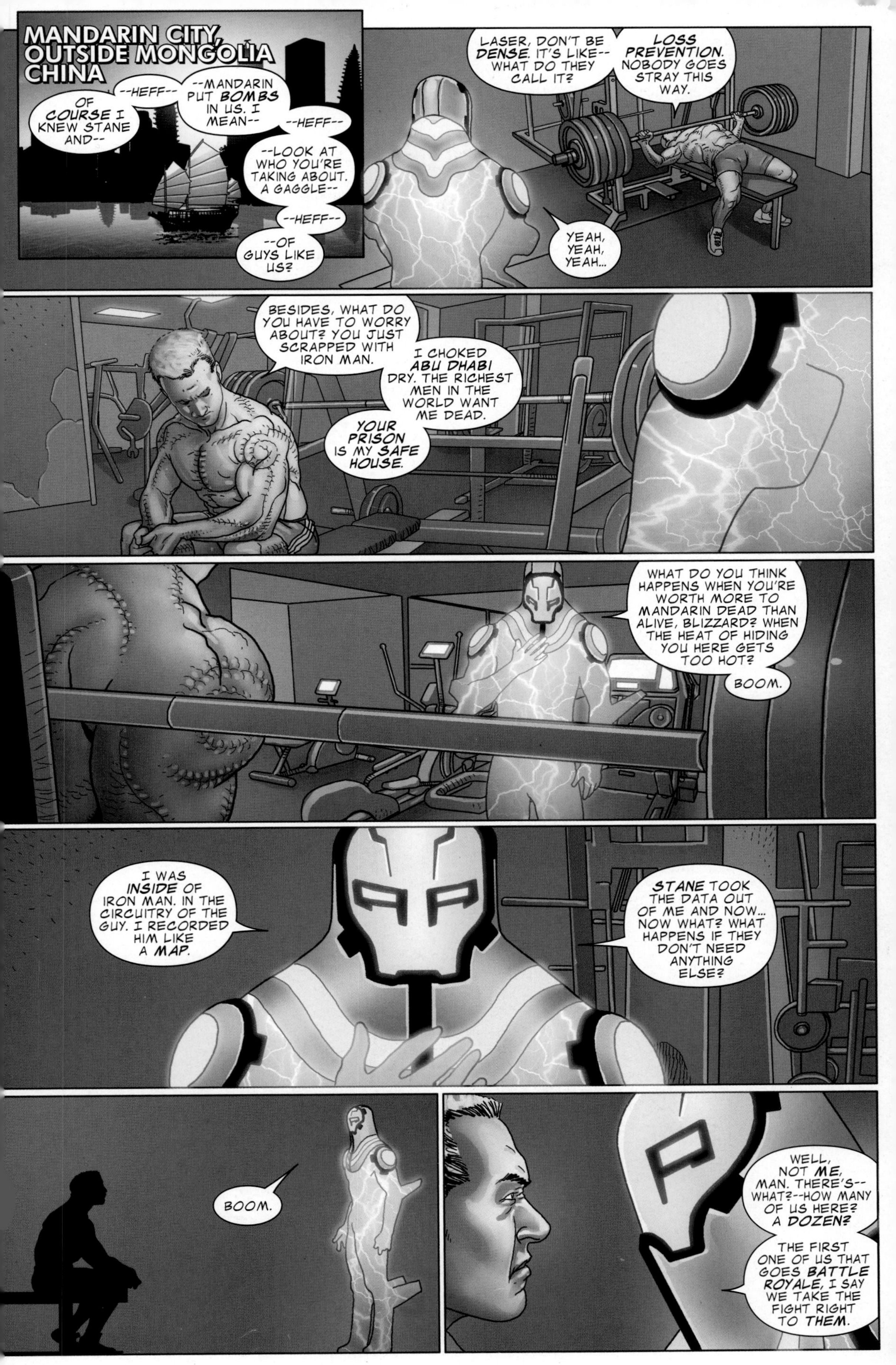
MANDARIN CITY, OUTSIDE MONGOLIA CHINA
OF COURSE I KNEW STANE AND--
--HEFF--
--MANDARIN PUT BOMBS IN US. I MEAN--
--HEFF--
--LOOK AT WHO YOU'RE TAKING ABOUT. A GAGGLE--
--HEFF--
--OF GUYS LIKE US?
LASER, DON'T BE DENSE. IT'S LIKE--WHAT DO THEY CALL IT?
LOSS PREVENTION. NOBODY GOES STRAY THIS WAY.
YEAH, YEAH, YEAH...
BESIDES, WHAT DO YOU HAVE TO WORRY ABOUT? YOU JUST SCRAPPED WITH IRON MAN.
I CHOKED ABU DHABI DRY. THE RICHEST MEN IN THE WORLD WANT ME DEAD.
YOUR PRISON IS MY SAFE HOUSE.
WHAT DO YOU THINK HAPPENS WHEN YOU'RE WORTH MORE TO MANDARIN DEAD THAN ALIVE, BLIZZARD? WHEN THE HEAT OF HIDING YOU HERE GETS TOO HOT?
BOOM.
I WAS INSIDE OF IRON MAN. IN THE CIRCUITRY OF THE GUY. I RECORDED HIM LIKE A MAP.
STANE TOOK THE DATA OUT OF ME AND NOW... NOW WHAT? WHAT HAPPENS IF THEY DON'T NEED ANYTHING ELSE?
BOOM.
WELL, NOT ME, MAN. THERE'S--WHAT?--HOW MANY OF US HERE? A DOZEN?
THE FIRST ONE OF US THAT GOES BATTLE ROYALE, I SAY WE TAKE THE FIGHT RIGHT TO THEM.

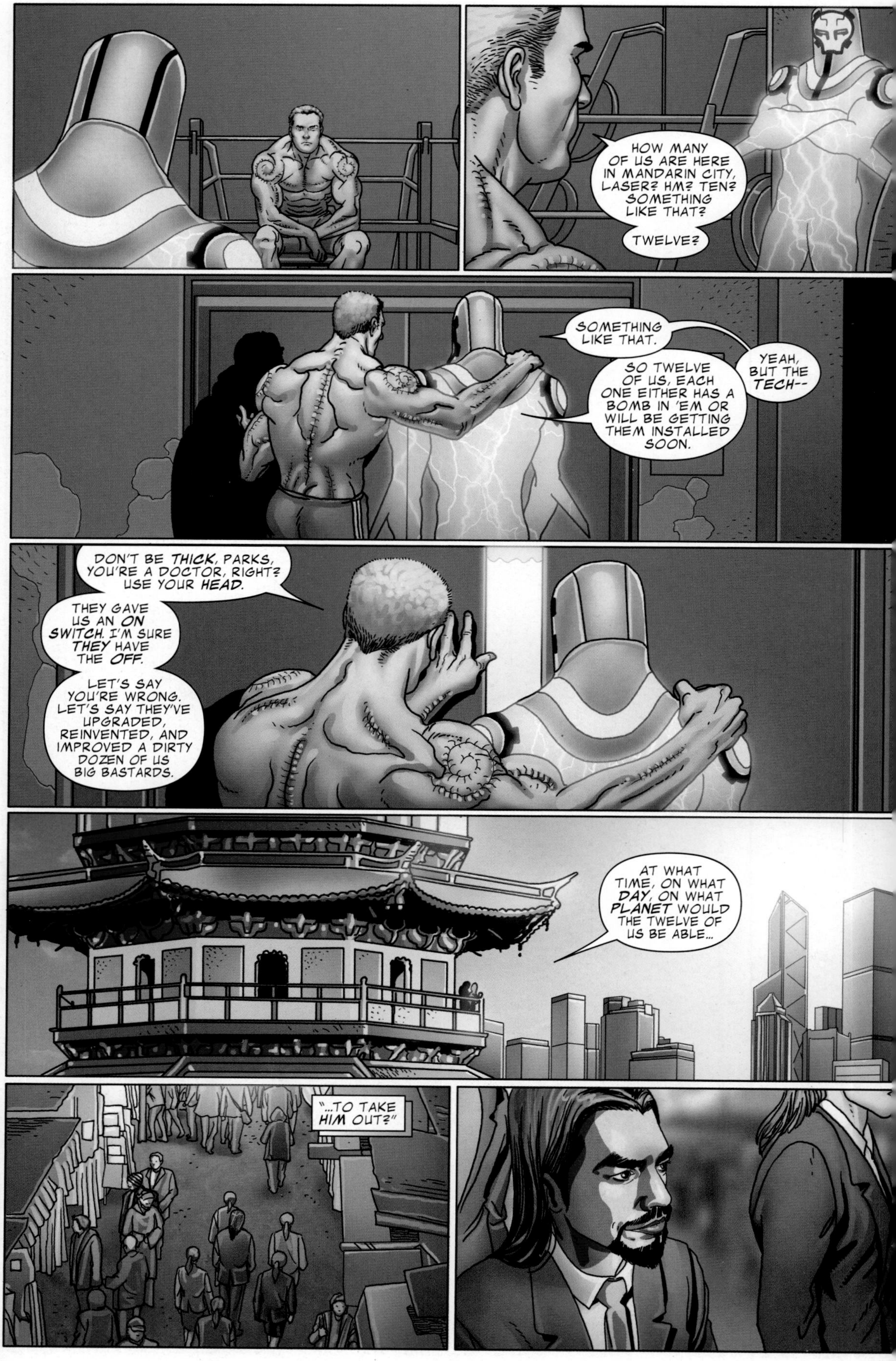
HOW MANY OF US ARE HERE IN MANDARIN CITY, LASER? HM? TEN? SOMETHING LIKE THAT?
TWELVE?
SOMETHING LIKE THAT.
SO TWELVE OF US, EACH ONE EITHER HAS A BOMB IN 'EM OR WILL BE GETTING THEM INSTALLED SOON.
YEAH, BUT THE TECH--
DON'T BE THICK, PARKS, YOU'RE A DOCTOR, RIGHT? USE YOUR HEAD.
THEY GAVE US AN ON SWITCH. I'M SURE THEY HAVE THE OFF.
LET'S SAY YOU'RE WRONG. LET'S SAY THEY'VE UPGRADED, REINVENTED, AND IMPROVED A DIRTY DOZEN OF US BIG BASTARDS.
AT WHAT TIME, ON WHAT DAY, ON WHAT PLANET WOULD THE TWELVE OF US BE ABLE...
"...TO TAKE HIM OUT?"

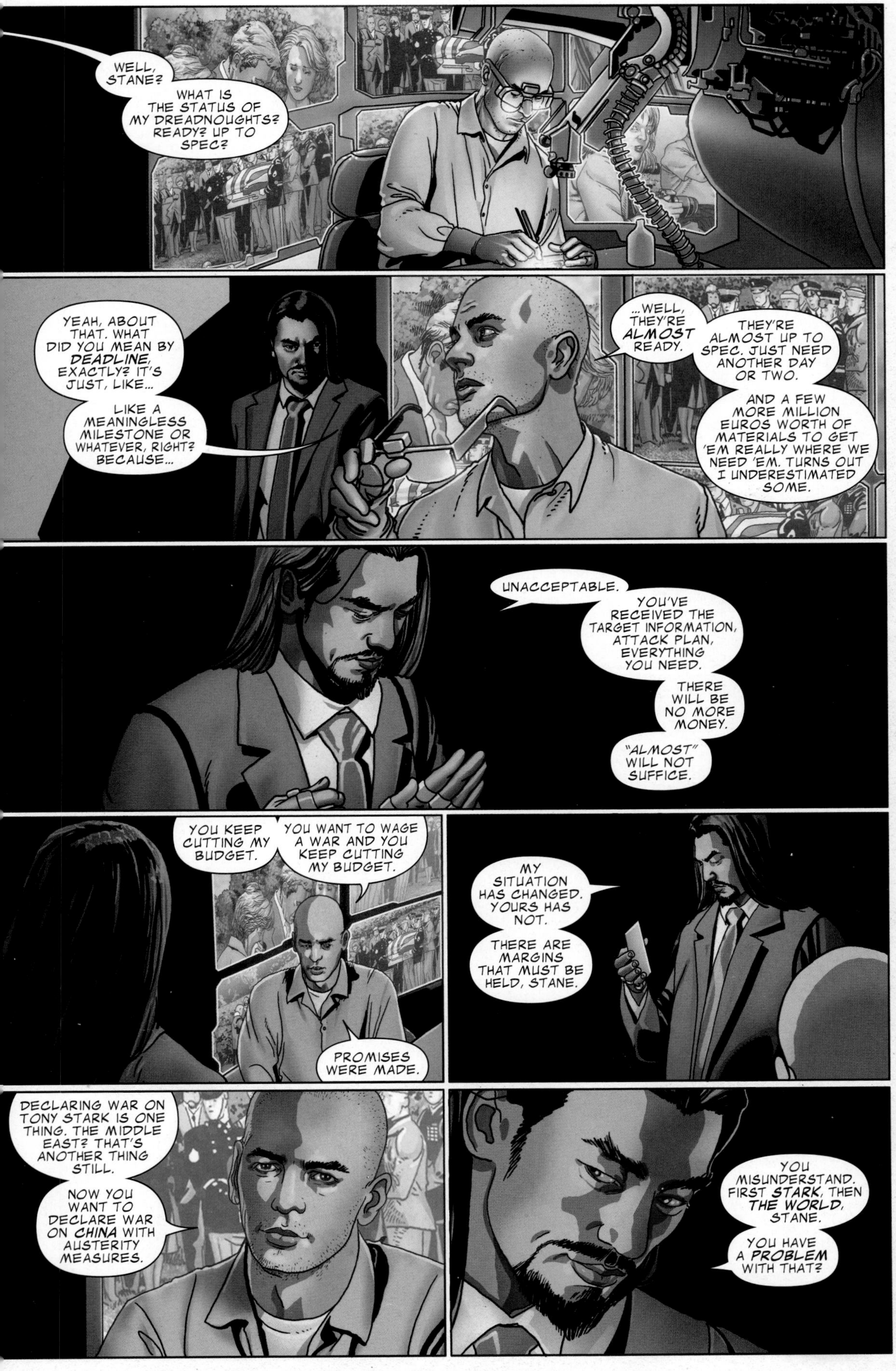
WELL, STANE?
WHAT IS THE STATUS OF MY DREADNOUGHTS? READY? UP TO SPEC?
YEAH, ABOUT THAT. WHAT DID YOU MEAN BY DEADLINE, EXACTLY? IT'S JUST, LIKE...
LIKE A MEANINGLESS MILESTONE OR WHATEVER, RIGHT? BECAUSE...
...WELL, THEY'RE ALMOST READY.
THEY'RE ALMOST UP TO SPEC. JUST NEED ANOTHER DAY OR TWO.
AND A FEW MORE MILLION EUROS WORTH OF MATERIALS TO GET 'EM REALLY WHERE WE NEED 'EM. TURNS OUT I UNDERESTIMATED SOME.
UNACCEPTABLE.
YOU'VE RECEIVED THE TARGET INFORMATION, ATTACK PLAN, EVERYTHING YOU NEED.
THERE WILL BE NO MORE MONEY.
"ALMOST" WILL NOT SUFFICE.
YOU KEEP CUTTING MY BUDGET.
YOU WANT TO WAGE A WAR AND YOU KEEP CUTTING MY BUDGET.
PROMISES WERE MADE.
MY SITUATION HAS CHANGED. YOURS HAS NOT.
THERE ARE MARGINS THAT MUST BE HELD, STANE.
DECLARING WAR ON TONY STARK IS ONE THING. THE MIDDLE EAST? THAT'S ANOTHER THING STILL.
NOW YOU WANT TO DECLARE WAR ON CHINA WITH AUSTERITY MEASURES.
YOU MISUNDERSTAND. FIRST STARK, THEN THE WORLD, STANE.
YOU HAVE A PROBLEM WITH THAT?

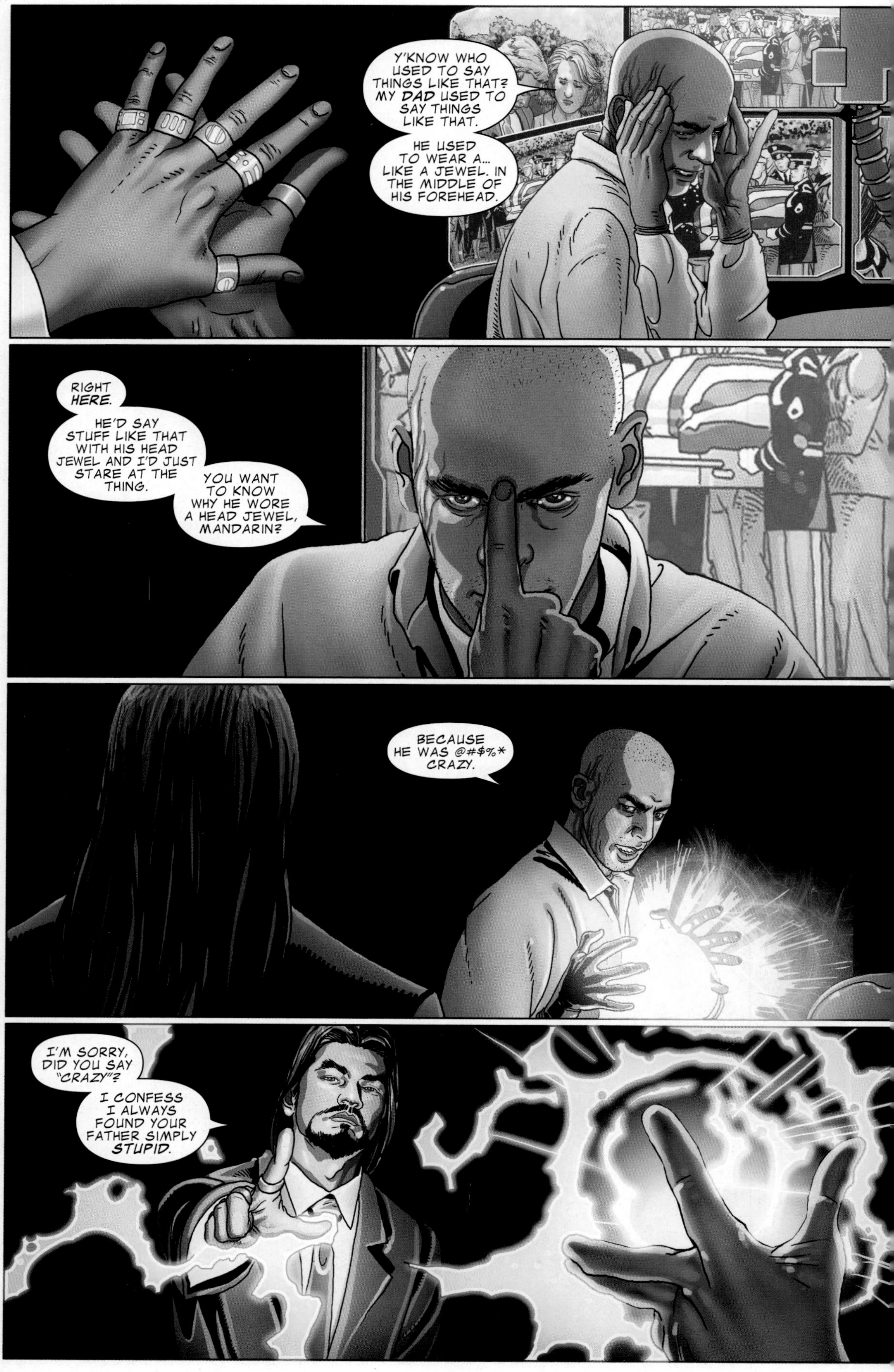
Y'KNOW WHO USED TO SAY THINGS LIKE THAT? MY DAD USED TO SAY THINGS LIKE THAT.
HE USED TO WEAR A... LIKE A JEWEL. IN THE MIDDLE OF HIS FOREHEAD.
RIGHT HERE.
HE'D SAY STUFF LIKE THAT WITH HIS HEAD JEWEL AND I'D JUST STARE AT THE THING.
YOU WANT TO KNOW WHY HE WORE A HEAD JEWEL, MANDARIN?
BECAUSE HE WAS @#$%* CRAZY.
I'M SORRY, DID YOU SAY "CRAZY"?
I CONFESS I ALWAYS FOUND YOUR FATHER SIMPLY STUPID.

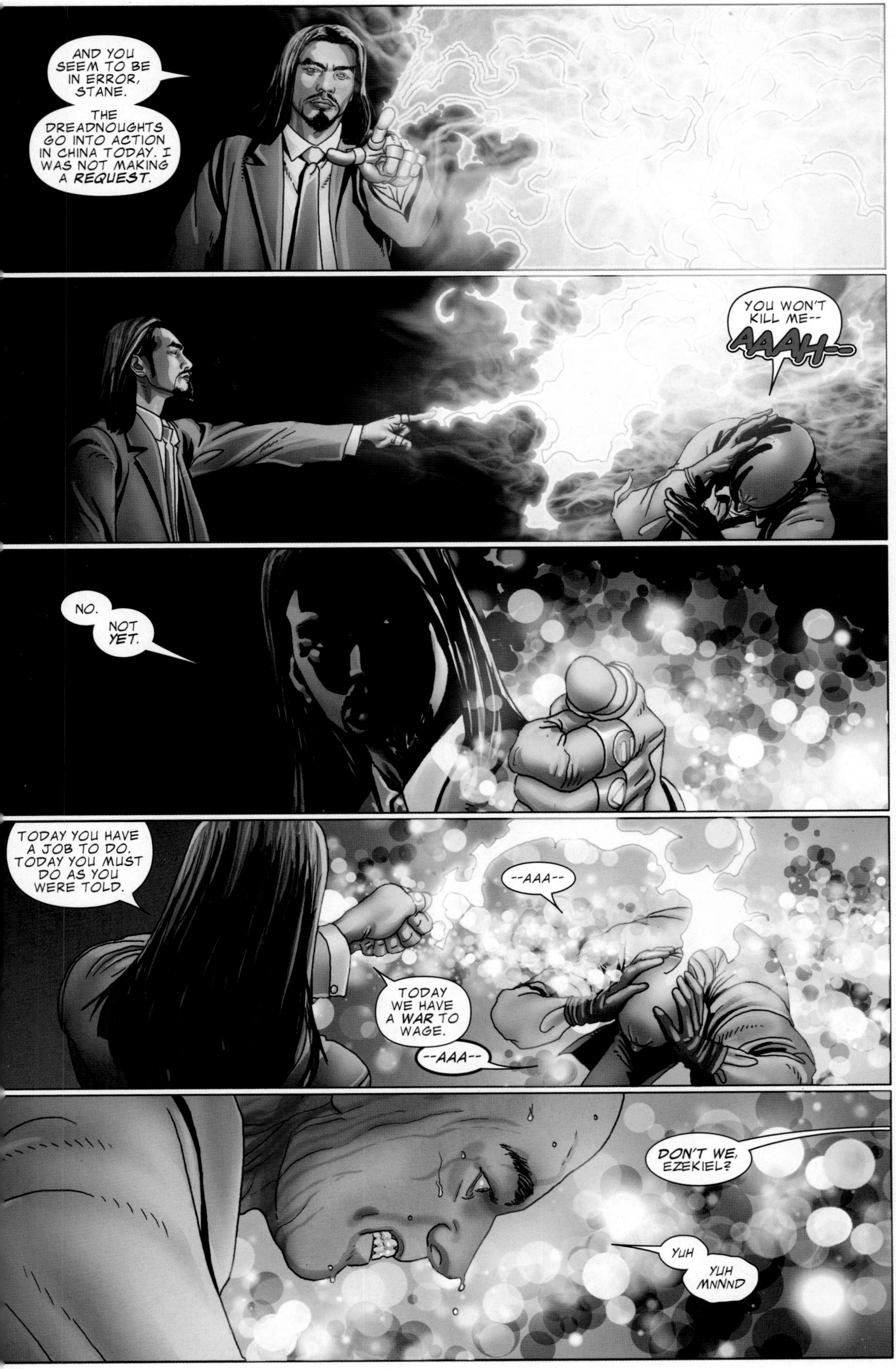
AND YOU SEEM TO BE IN ERROR, STANE.
THE DREADNOUGHTS GO INTO ACTION IN CHINA TODAY. I WAS NOT MAKING A REQUEST.
YOU WON'T KILL ME--
AAAH--
NO.
NOT YET.
TODAY YOU HAVE A JOB TO DO. TODAY YOU MUST DO AS YOU WERE TOLD.
--AAA--
TODAY WE HAVE A WAR TO WAGE.
--AAA--
DON'T WE, EZEKIEL?
YUH
YUH MNNND

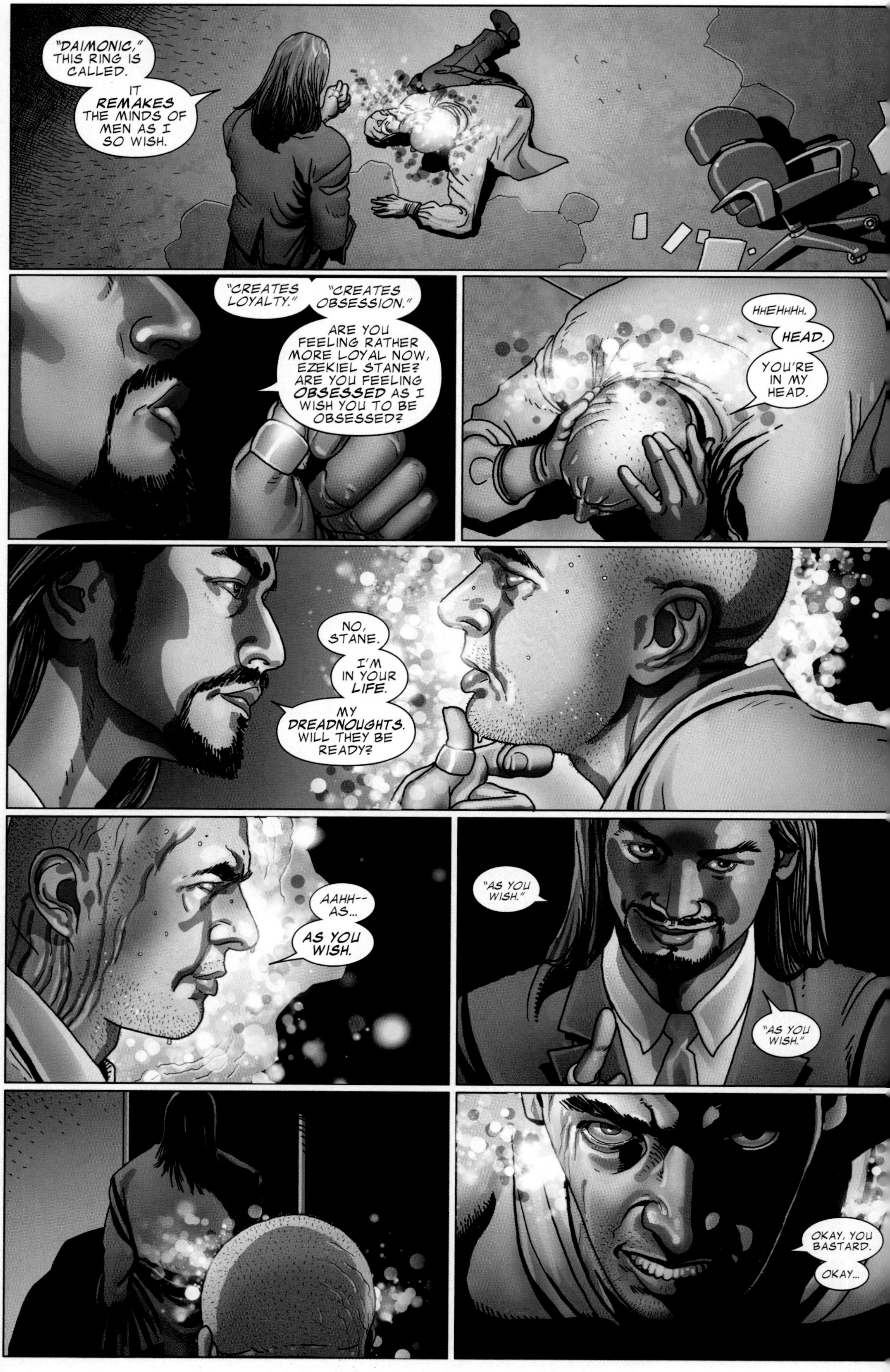
"DAIMONIC," THIS RING IS CALLED.
IT REMAKES THE MINDS OF MEN AS I SO WISH.
"CREATES LOYALTY."
"CREATES OBSESSION."
ARE YOU FEELING RATHER MORE LOYAL NOW, EZEKIEL STANE? ARE YOU FEELING OBSESSED AS I WISH YOU TO BE OBSESSED?
HHEHHHH.
HEAD.
YOU'RE IN MY HEAD.
NO, STANE.
I'M IN YOUR LIFE.
MY DREADNOUGHTS. WILL THEY BE READY?
AAHH-- AS...
AS YOU WISH.
"AS YOU WISH."
"AS YOU WISH."
OKAY, YOU BASTARD.
OKAY...

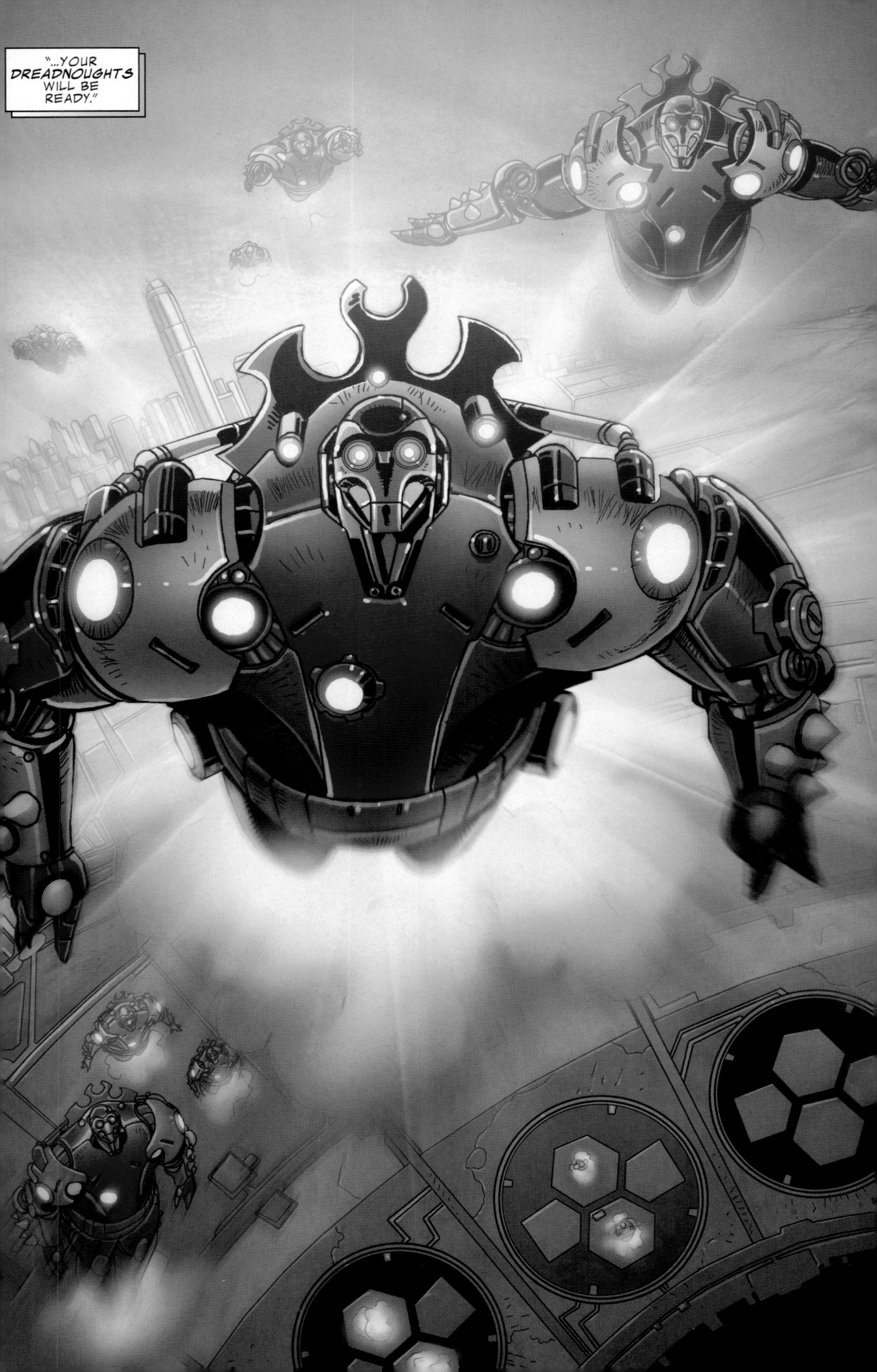
"...YOUR DREADNOUGHTS WILL BE READY."

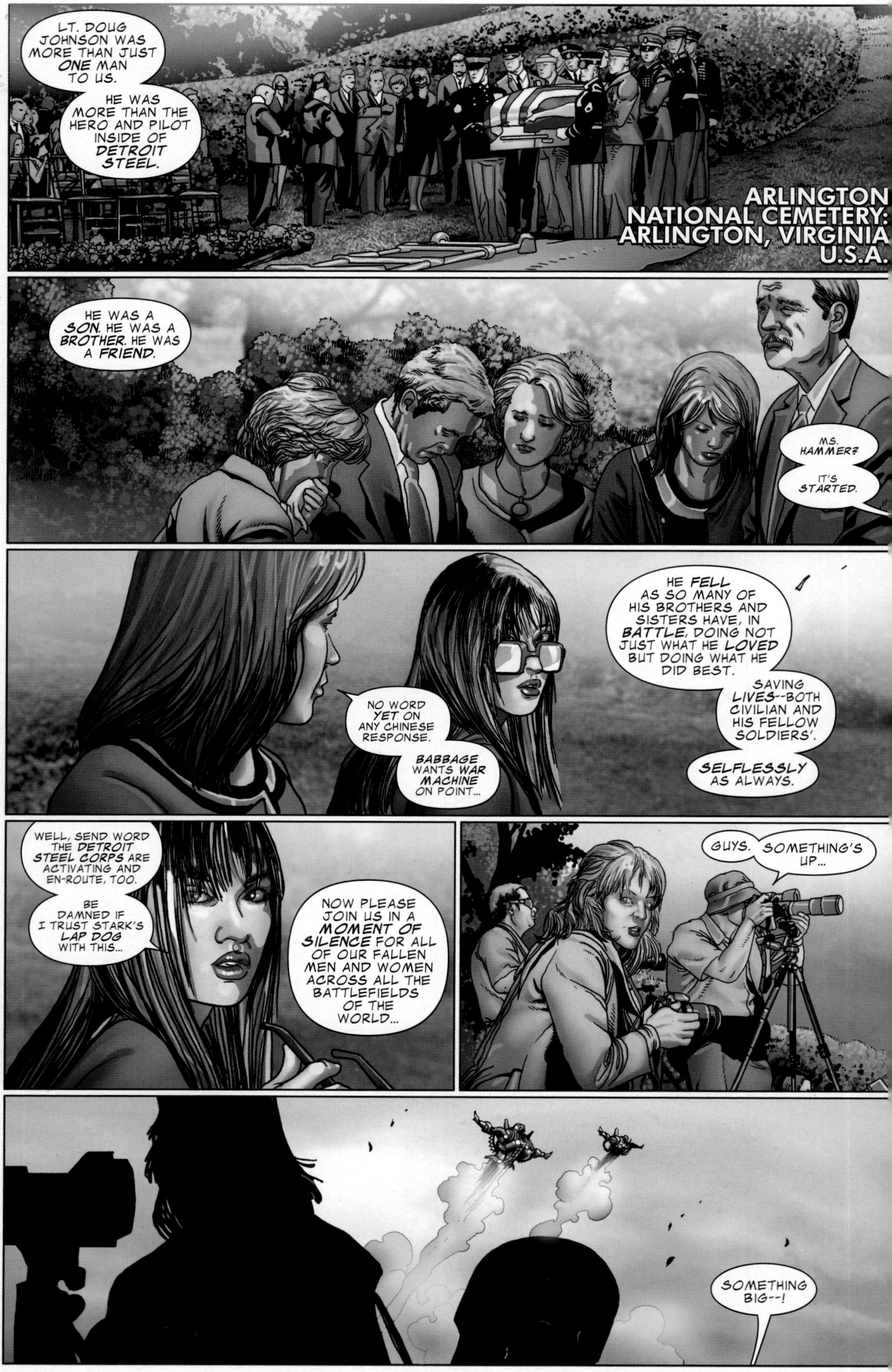
LT. DOUG JOHNSON WAS MORE THAN JUST ONE MAN TO US.
HE WAS MORE THAN THE HERO AND PILOT INSIDE OF DETROIT STEEL.
ARLINGTON NATIONAL CEMETERY: ARLINGTON, VIRGINIA U.S.A.
HE WAS A SON. HE WAS A BROTHER. HE WAS A FRIEND.
MS. HAMMER?
IT'S STARTED.
NO WORD YET ON ANY CHINESE RESPONSE.
BABBAGE WANTS WAR MACHINE ON POINT...
HE FELL AS SO MANY OF HIS BROTHERS AND SISTERS HAVE, IN BATTLE, DOING NOT JUST WHAT HE LOVED BUT DOING WHAT HE DID BEST.
SAVING LIVES--BOTH CIVILIAN AND HIS FELLOW SOLDIERS'.
SELFLESSLY AS ALWAYS.
WELL, SEND WORD THE DETROIT STEEL CORPS ARE ACTIVATING AND EN-ROUTE, TOO.
BE DAMNED IF I TRUST STARK'S LAP DOG WITH THIS...
NOW PLEASE JOIN US IN A MOMENT OF SILENCE FOR ALL OF OUR FALLEN MEN AND WOMEN ACROSS ALL THE BATTLEFIELDS OF THE WORLD...
GUYS.
SOMETHING'S UP...
SOMETHING BIG--!

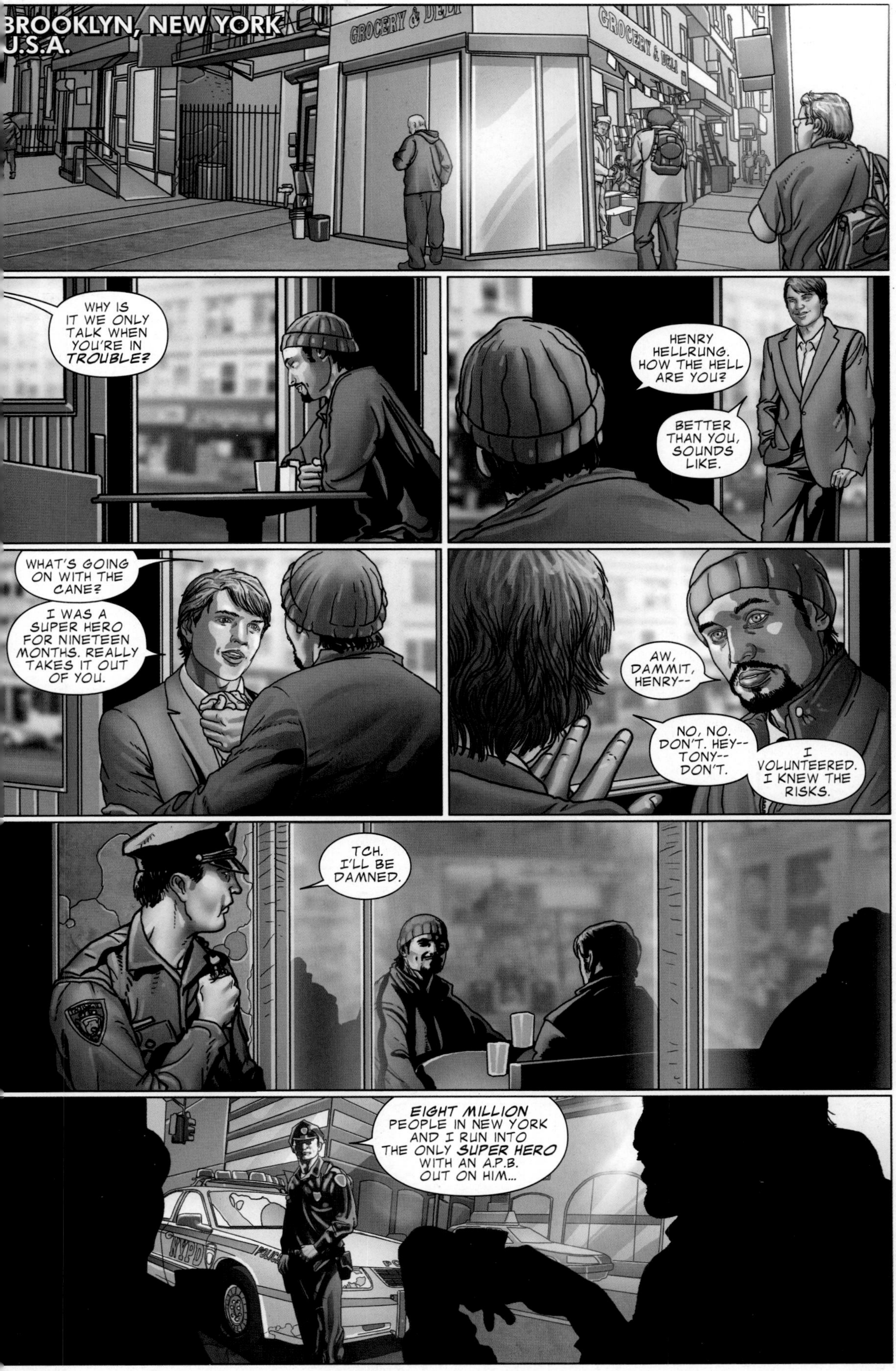
BROOKLYN, NEW YORK U.S.A.
GROCERY & DELI
GROCERY & DELI
WHY IS IT WE ONLY TALK WHEN YOU'RE IN *TROUBLE?*
HENRY HELLRUNG. HOW THE HELL ARE YOU?
BETTER THAN YOU, SOUNDS LIKE.
WHAT'S GOING ON WITH THE CANE?
I WAS A SUPER HERO FOR NINETEEN MONTHS. REALLY TAKES IT OUT OF YOU.
AW, DAMMIT, HENRY--
NO, NO. DON'T. HEY-- TONY-- DON'T.
I VOLUNTEERED. I KNEW THE RISKS.
TCH. I'LL BE DAMNED.
EIGHT MILLION PEOPLE IN NEW YORK AND I RUN INTO THE ONLY *SUPER HERO* WITH AN A.P.B. OUT ON HIM...
NYPD

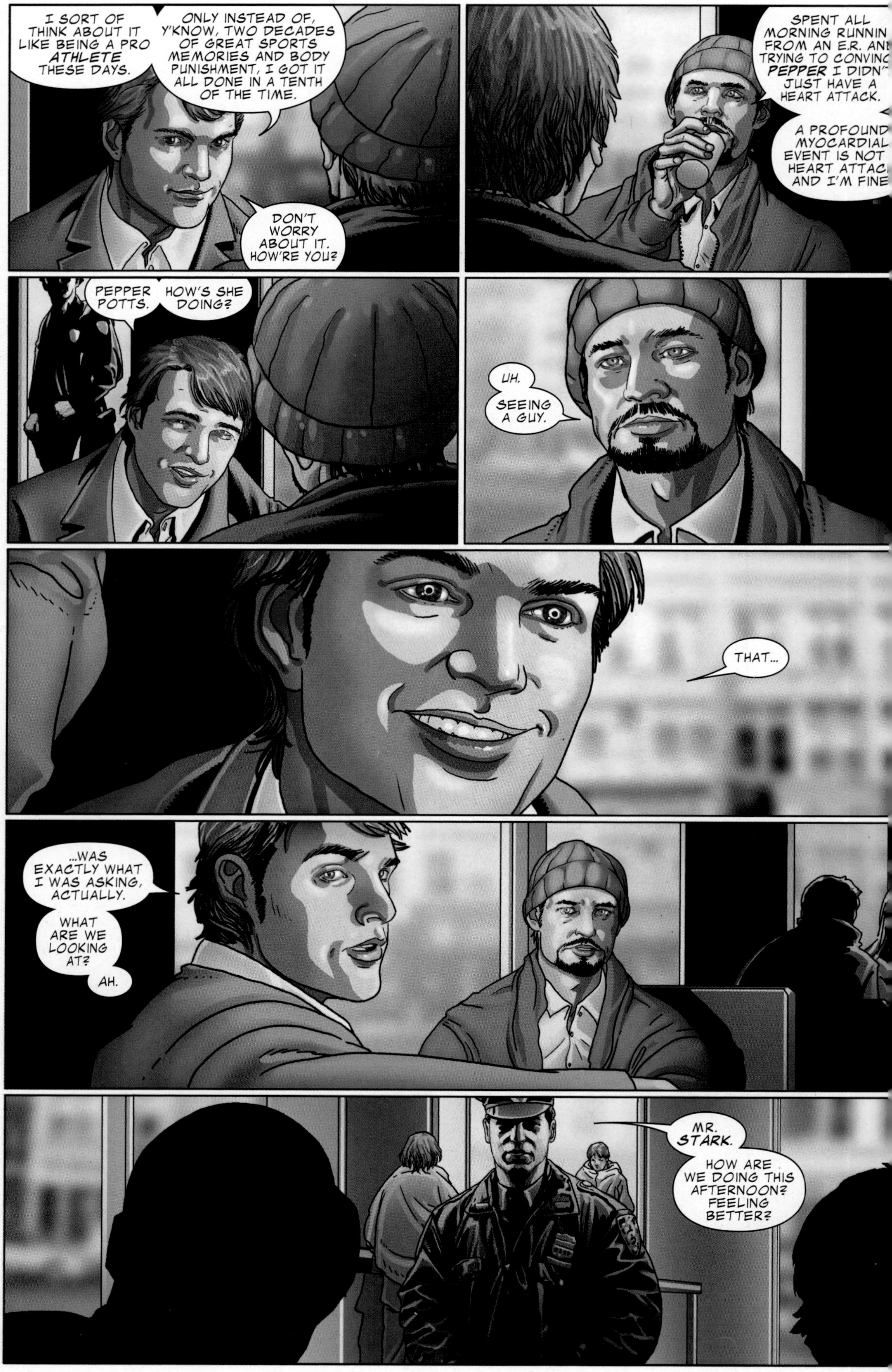
I SORT OF THINK ABOUT IT LIKE BEING A PRO ATHLETE THESE DAYS.
ONLY INSTEAD OF, Y'KNOW, TWO DECADES OF GREAT SPORTS MEMORIES AND BODY PUNISHMENT, I GOT IT ALL DONE IN A TENTH OF THE TIME.
DON'T WORRY ABOUT IT. HOW'RE YOU?
SPENT ALL MORNING RUNNIN FROM AN E.R. AN TRYING TO CONVINC PEPPER I DIDN' JUST HAVE A HEART ATTACK.
A PROFOUND MYOCARDIAL EVENT IS NOT HEART ATTAC AND I'M FINE
PEPPER POTTS.
HOW'S SHE DOING?
UH.
SEEING A GUY.
THAT...
...WAS EXACTLY WHAT I WAS ASKING, ACTUALLY.
WHAT ARE WE LOOKING AT?
AH.
MR. STARK.
HOW ARE WE DOING THIS AFTERNOON? FEELING BETTER?

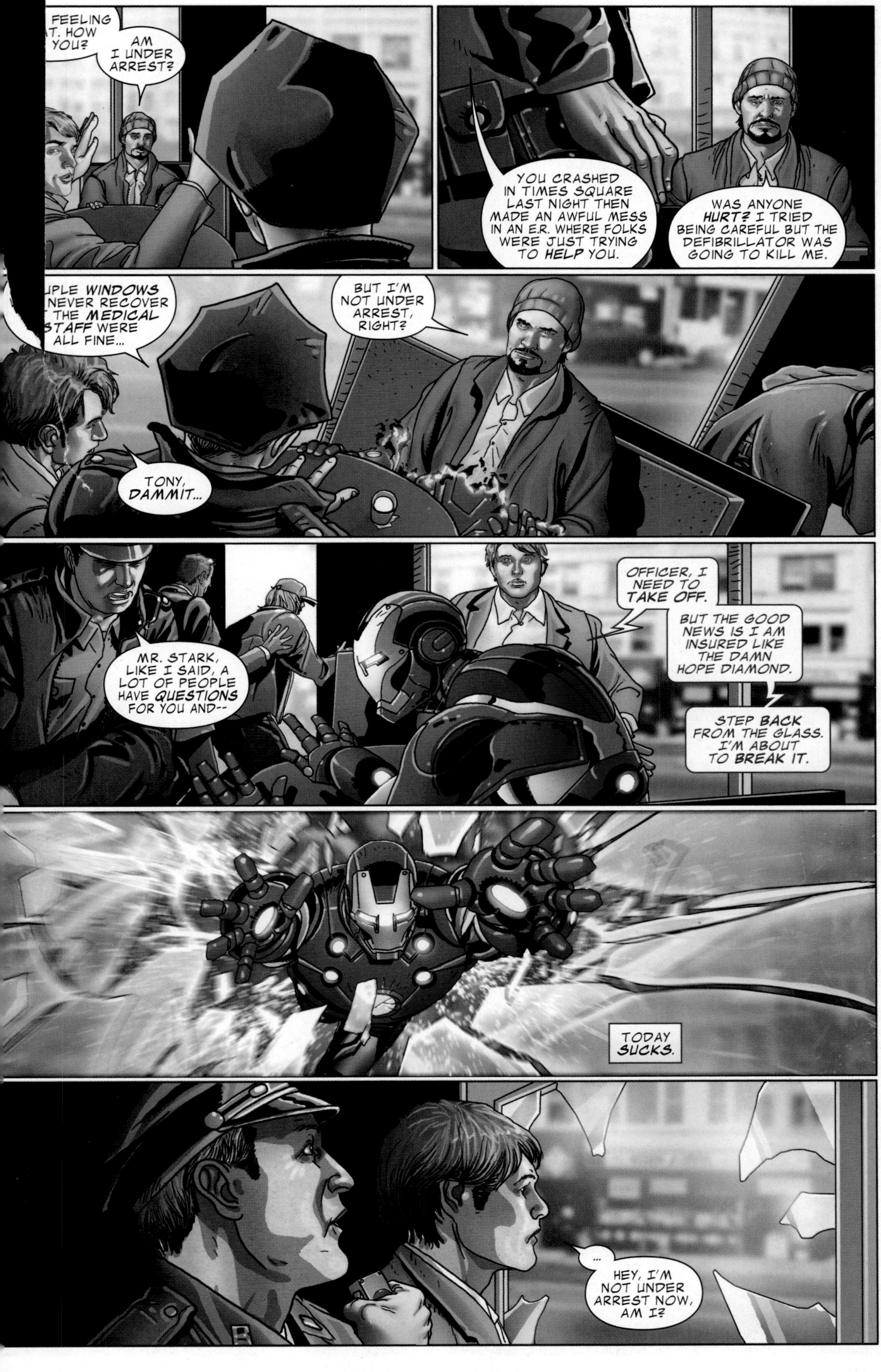
FEELING
AT. HOW
YOU?
AM I UNDER ARREST?
YOU CRASHED IN TIMES SQUARE LAST NIGHT THEN MADE AN AWFUL MESS IN AN E.R. WHERE FOLKS WERE JUST TRYING TO HELP YOU.
WAS ANYONE HURT? I TRIED BEING CAREFUL BUT THE DEFIBRILLATOR WAS GOING TO KILL ME.
UPLE WINDOWS
NEVER RECOVER
T THE MEDICAL
STAFF WERE ALL FINE...
BUT I'M NOT UNDER ARREST, RIGHT?
TONY, DAMMIT...
MR. STARK, LIKE I SAID, A LOT OF PEOPLE HAVE QUESTIONS FOR YOU AND--
OFFICER, I NEED TO TAKE OFF.
BUT THE GOOD NEWS IS I AM INSURED LIKE THE DAMN HOPE DIAMOND.
STEP BACK FROM THE GLASS. I'M ABOUT TO BREAK IT.
TODAY SUCKS.
... HEY, I'M NOT UNDER ARREST NOW, AM I?

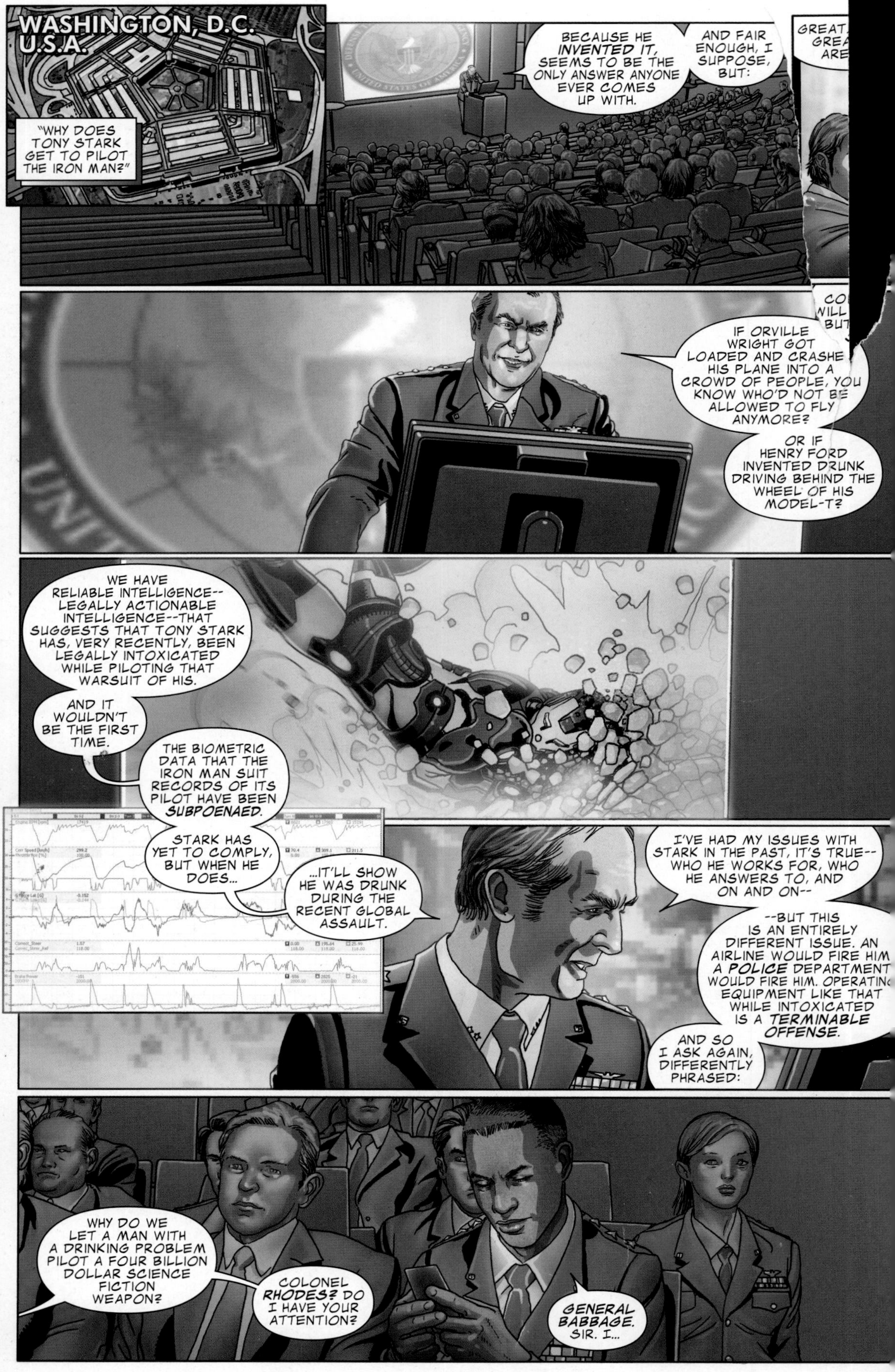
WASHINGTON, D.C. U.S.A.
"WHY DOES TONY STARK GET TO PILOT THE IRON MAN?"
BECAUSE HE INVENTED IT, SEEMS TO BE THE ONLY ANSWER ANYONE EVER COMES UP WITH.
AND FAIR ENOUGH, I SUPPOSE, BUT:
IF ORVILLE WRIGHT GOT LOADED AND CRASHE HIS PLANE INTO A CROWD OF PEOPLE, YOU KNOW WHO'D NOT BE ALLOWED TO FLY ANYMORE?
OR IF HENRY FORD INVENTED DRUNK DRIVING BEHIND THE WHEEL OF HIS MODEL-T?
WE HAVE RELIABLE INTELLIGENCE--LEGALLY ACTIONABLE INTELLIGENCE--THAT SUGGESTS THAT TONY STARK HAS, VERY RECENTLY, BEEN LEGALLY INTOXICATED WHILE PILOTING THAT WARSUIT OF HIS.
AND IT WOULDN'T BE THE FIRST TIME.
THE BIOMETRIC DATA THAT THE IRON MAN SUIT RECORDS OF ITS PILOT HAVE BEEN SUBPOENAED.
STARK HAS YET TO COMPLY, BUT WHEN HE DOES...
...IT'LL SHOW HE WAS DRUNK DURING THE RECENT GLOBAL ASSAULT.
I'VE HAD MY ISSUES WITH STARK IN THE PAST, IT'S TRUE--WHO HE WORKS FOR, WHO HE ANSWERS TO, AND ON AND ON--
--BUT THIS IS AN ENTIRELY DIFFERENT ISSUE. AN AIRLINE WOULD FIRE HIM A POLICE DEPARTMENT WOULD FIRE HIM. OPERATIN EQUIPMENT LIKE THAT WHILE INTOXICATED IS A TERMINABLE OFFENSE.
AND SO I ASK AGAIN, DIFFERENTLY PHRASED:
WHY DO WE LET A MAN WITH A DRINKING PROBLEM PILOT A FOUR BILLION DOLLAR SCIENCE FICTION WEAPON?
COLONEL RHODES? DO I HAVE YOUR ATTENTION?
GENERAL BABBAGE. SIR. I...

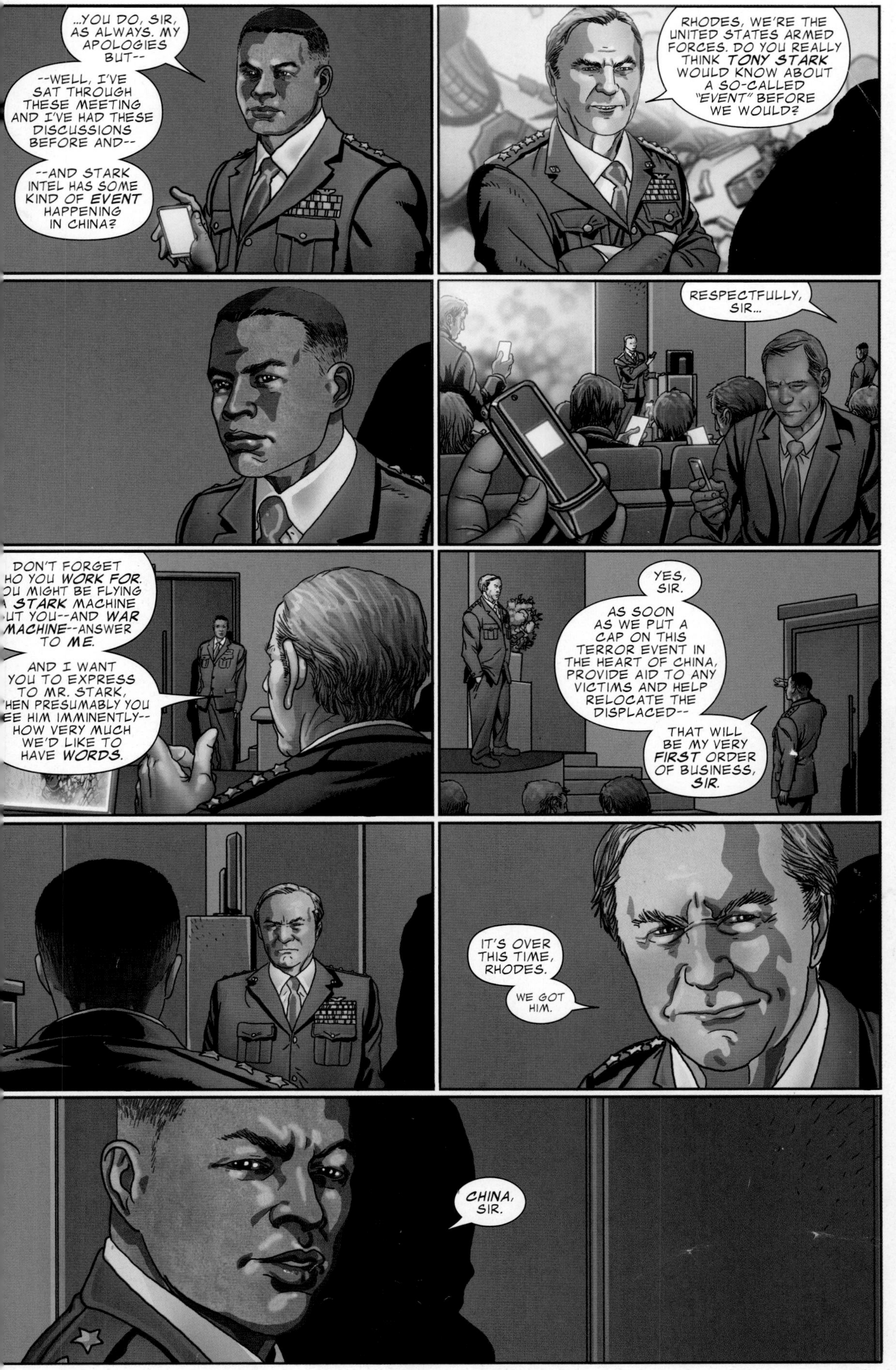
...YOU DO, SIR, AS ALWAYS. MY APOLOGIES BUT--
--WELL, I'VE SAT THROUGH THESE MEETING AND I'VE HAD THESE DISCUSSIONS BEFORE AND--
--AND STARK INTEL HAS SOME KIND OF EVENT HAPPENING IN CHINA?
RHODES, WE'RE THE UNITED STATES ARMED FORCES. DO YOU REALLY THINK TONY STARK WOULD KNOW ABOUT A SO-CALLED "EVENT" BEFORE WE WOULD?
RESPECTFULLY, SIR...
DON'T FORGET HO YOU WORK FOR. OU MIGHT BE FLYING STARK MACHINE UT YOU--AND WAR MACHINE--ANSWER TO ME.
AND I WANT YOU TO EXPRESS TO MR. STARK, HEN PRESUMABLY YOU EE HIM IMMINENTLY--HOW VERY MUCH WE'D LIKE TO HAVE WORDS.
YES, SIR.
AS SOON AS WE PUT A CAP ON THIS TERROR EVENT IN THE HEART OF CHINA, PROVIDE AID TO ANY VICTIMS AND HELP RELOCATE THE DISPLACED--
THAT WILL BE MY VERY FIRST ORDER OF BUSINESS, SIR.
IT'S OVER THIS TIME, RHODES.
WE GOT HIM.
CHINA, SIR.

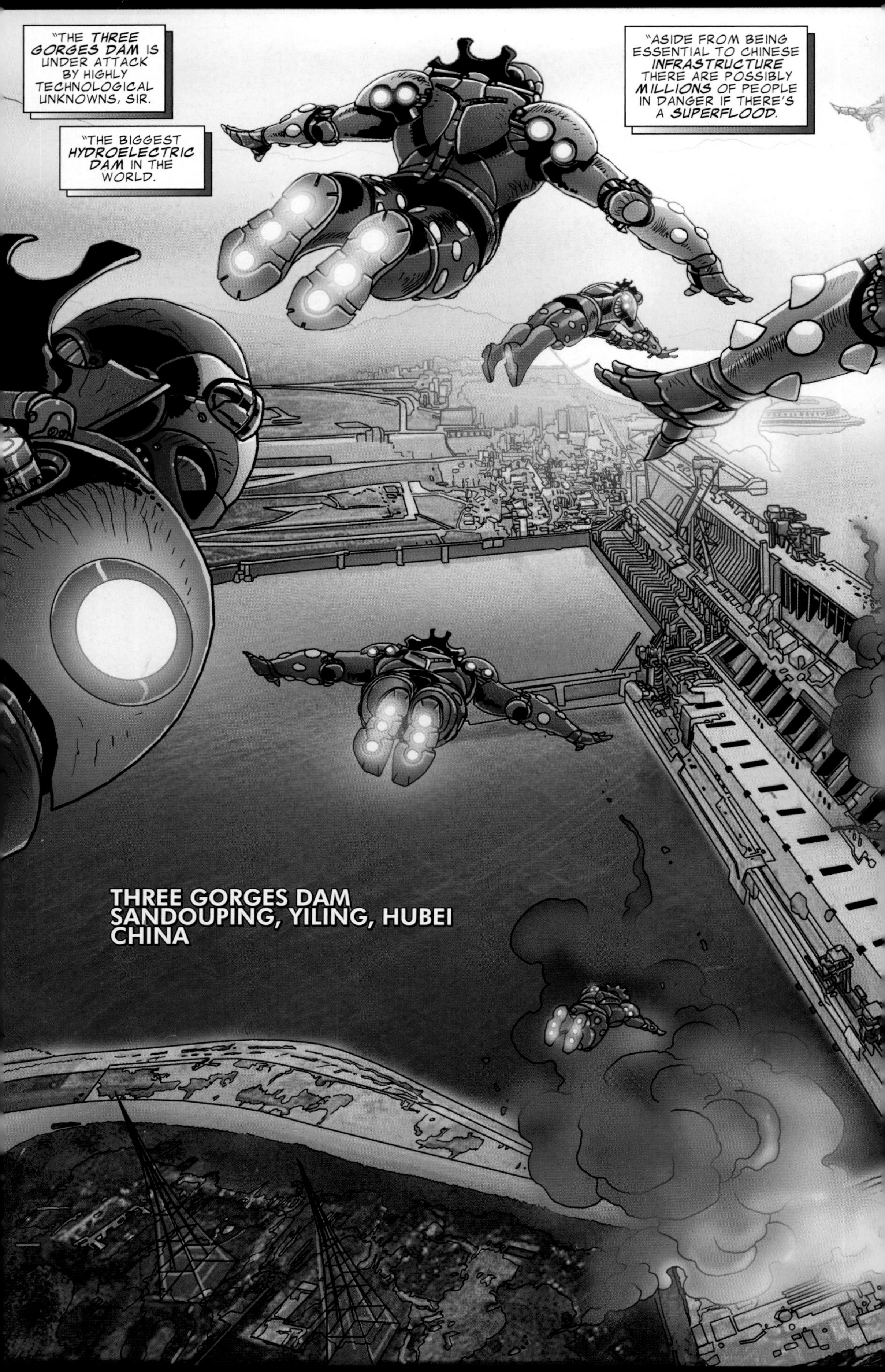
"THE THREE GORGES DAM IS UNDER ATTACK BY HIGHLY TECHNOLOGICAL UNKNOWNS, SIR.
"THE BIGGEST HYDROELECTRIC DAM IN THE WORLD.
"ASIDE FROM BEING ESSENTIAL TO CHINESE INFRASTRUCTURE THERE ARE POSSIBLY MILLIONS OF PEOPLE IN DANGER IF THERE'S A SUPERFLOOD.
THREE GORGES DAM
SANDOUPING, YILING, HUBEI
CHINA

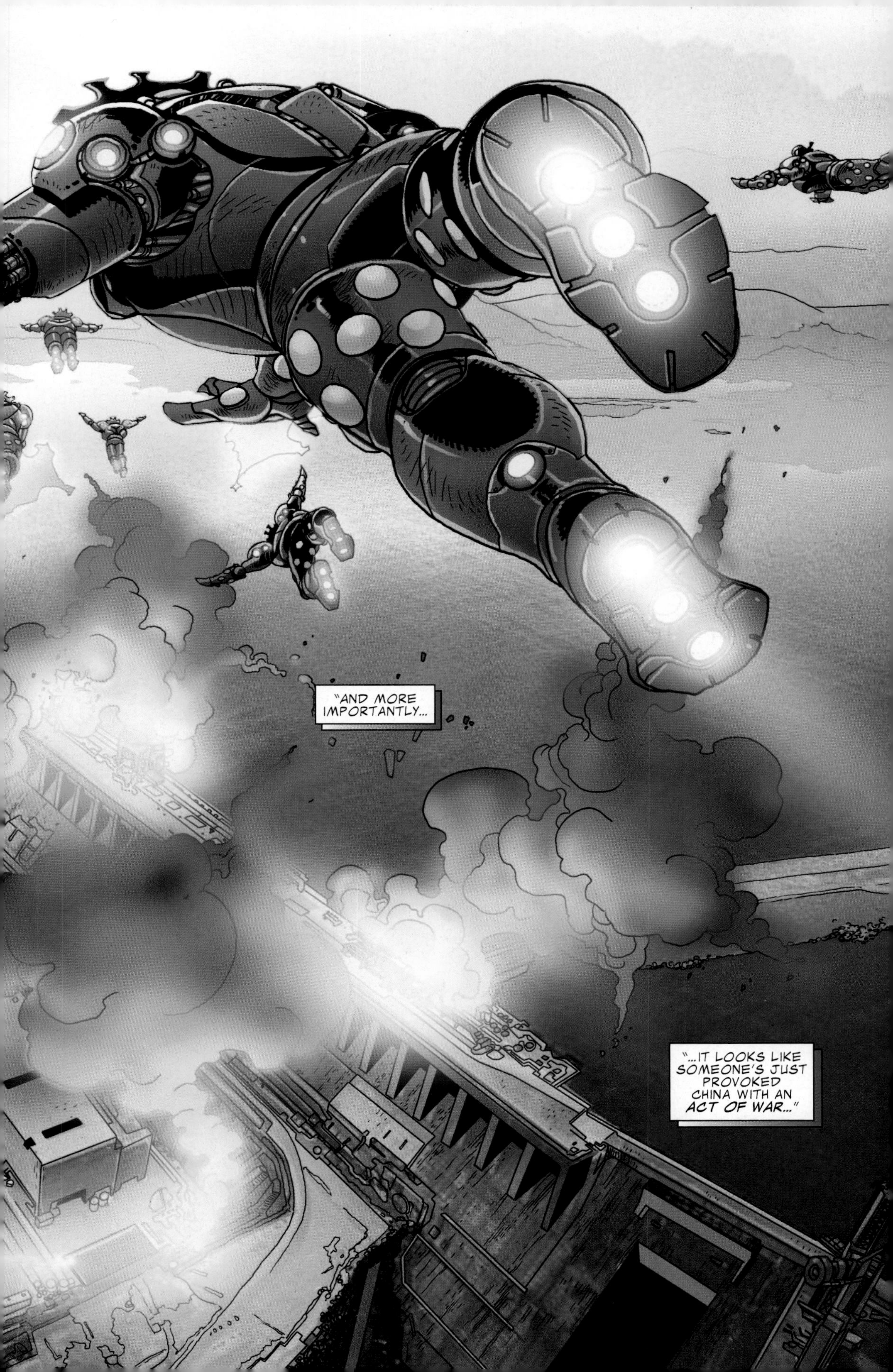
"AND MORE IMPORTANTLY...
"...IT LOOKS LIKE SOMEONE'S JUST PROVOKED CHINA WITH AN ACT OF WAR..."

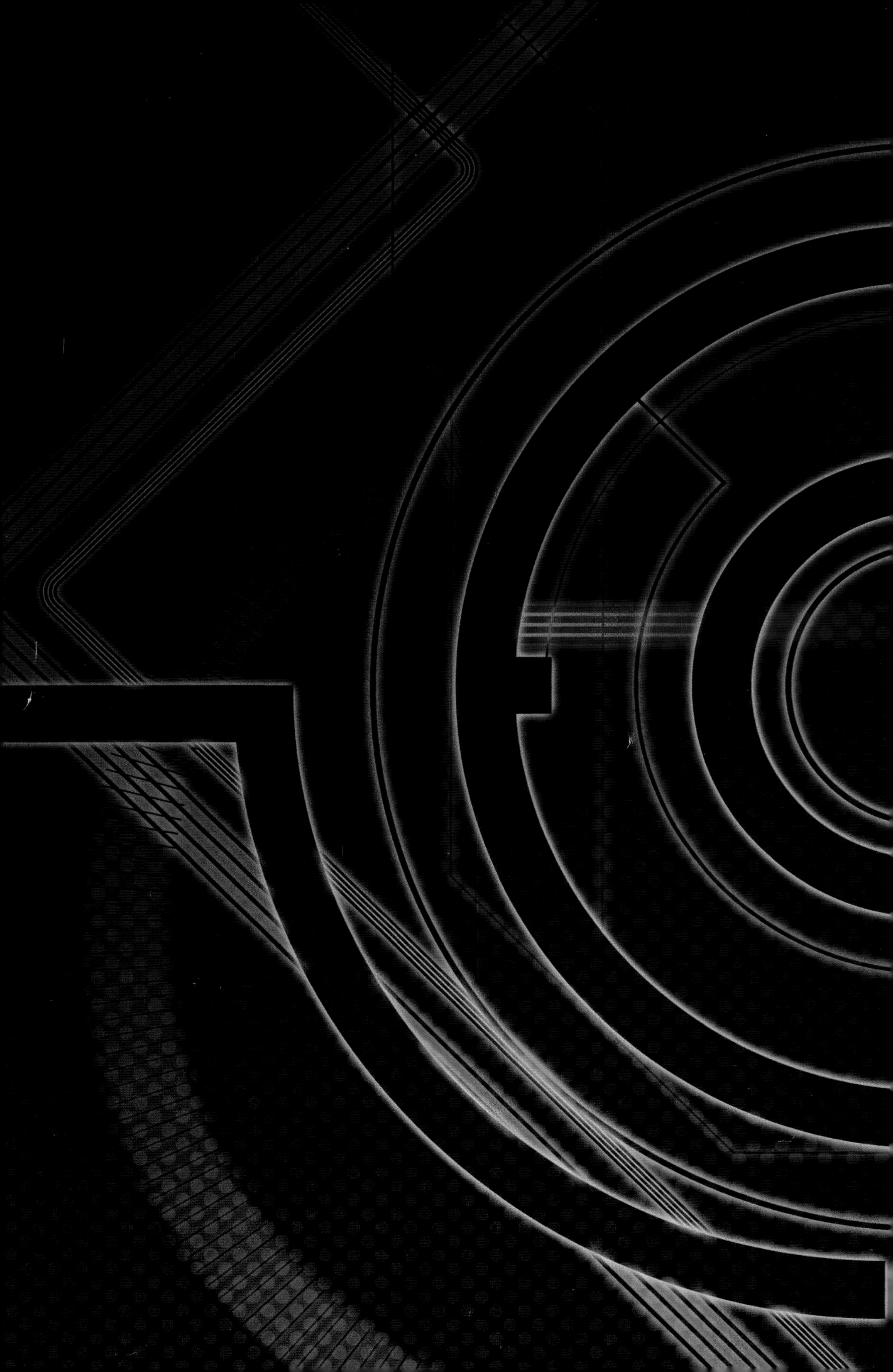

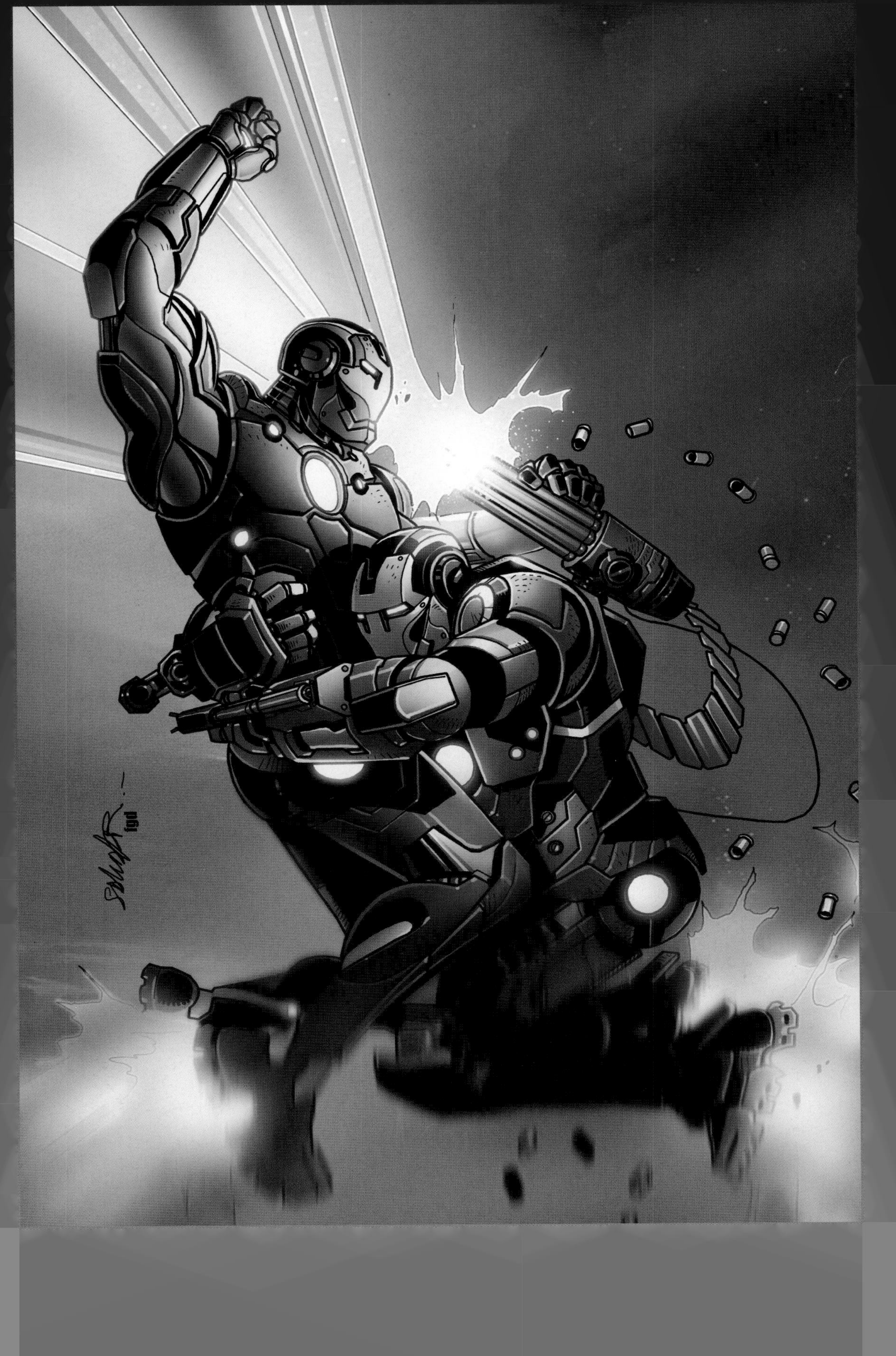

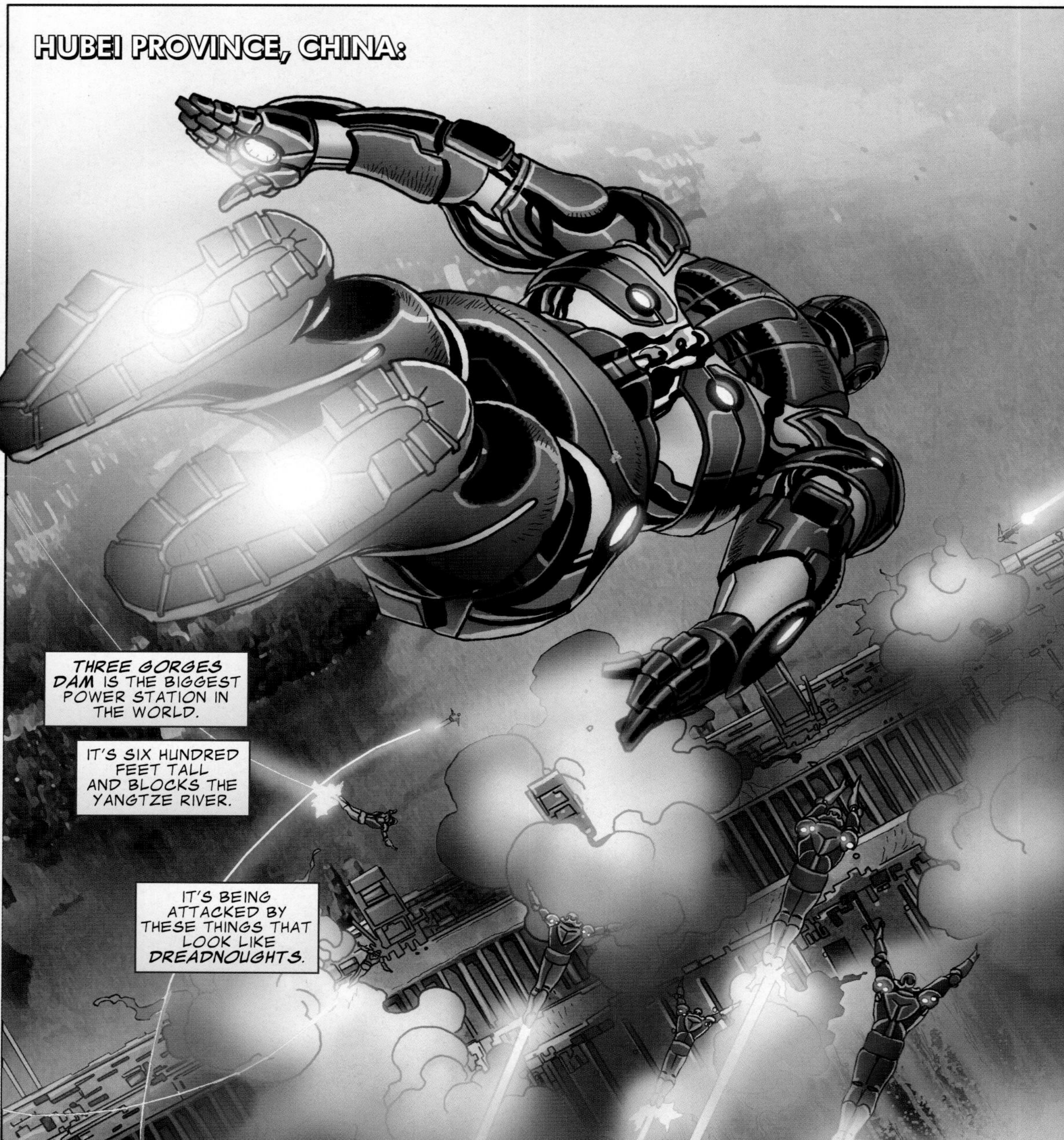
HUBEI PROVINCE, CHINA:
THREE GORGES DAM IS THE BIGGEST POWER STATION IN THE WORLD.
IT'S SIX HUNDRED FEET TALL AND BLOCKS THE YANGTZE RIVER.
IT'S BEING ATTACKED BY THESE THINGS THAT LOOK LIKE DREADNOUGHTS.
LIKE UPDATED, UPGRADED DREADNOUGHTS.

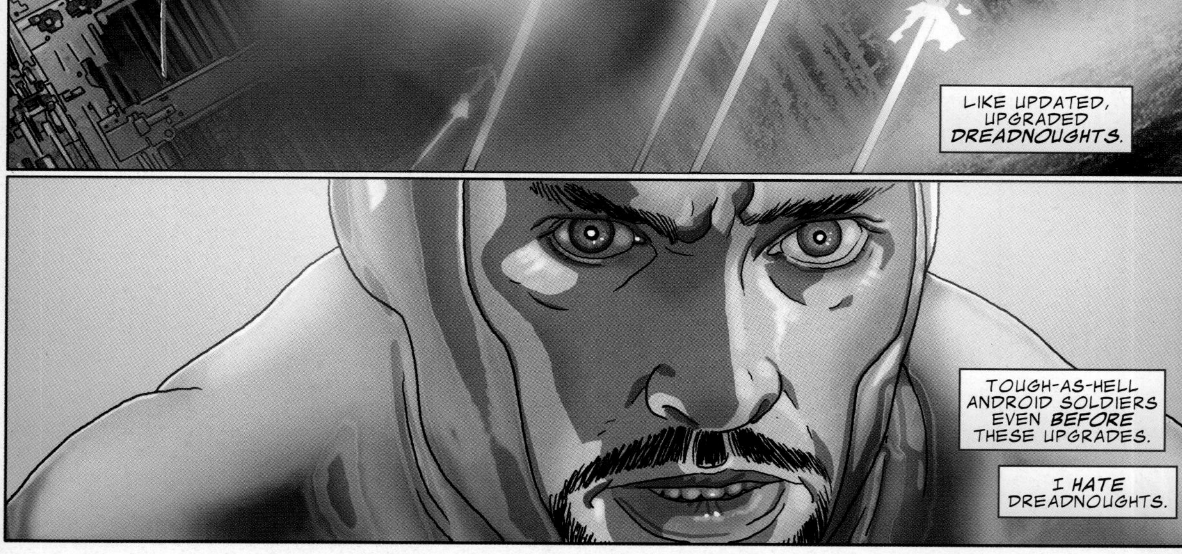
TOUGH-AS-HELL ANDROID SOLDIERS EVEN BEFORE THESE UPGRADES.
I HATE DREADNOUGHTS.

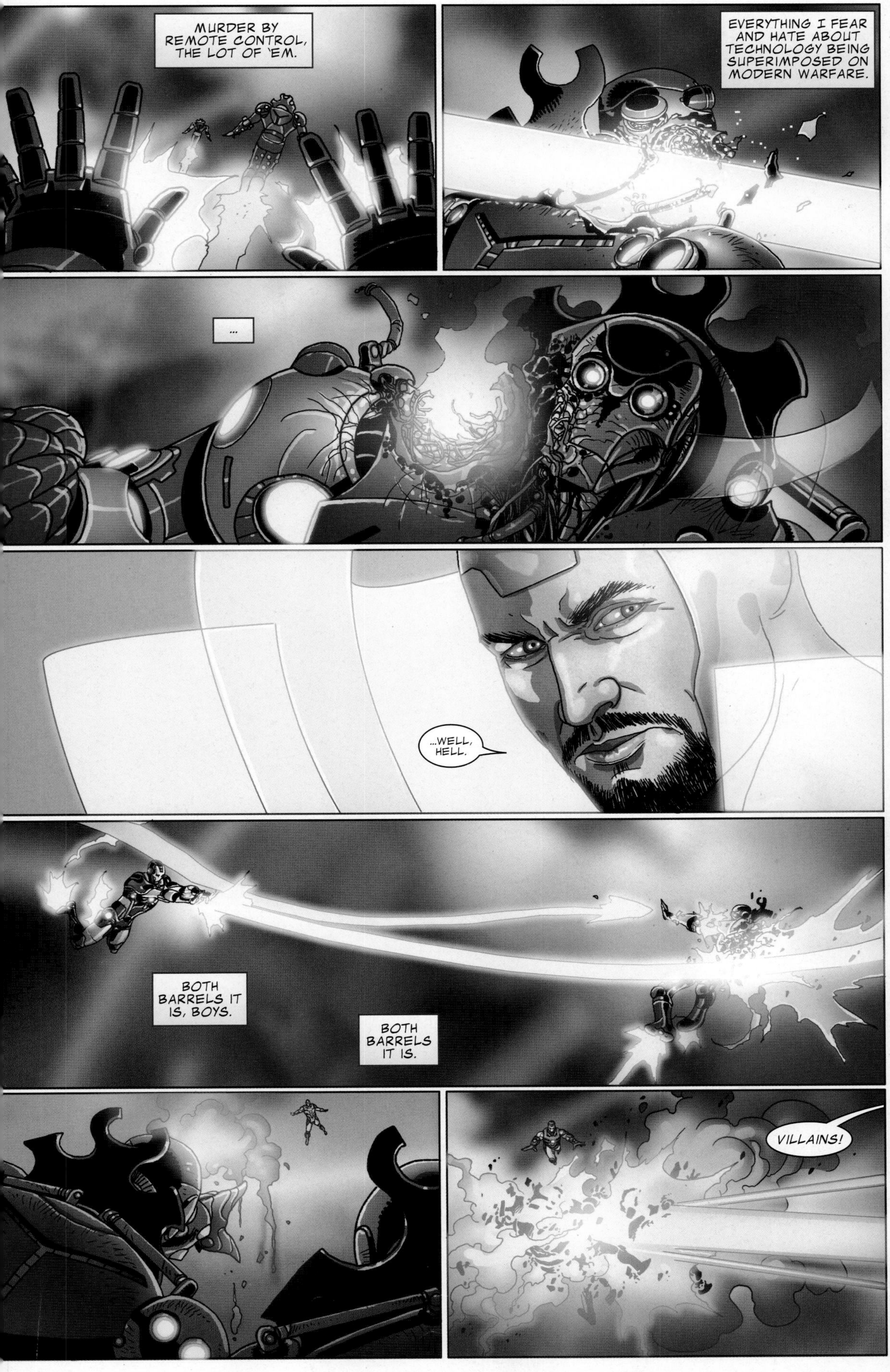
MURDER BY REMOTE CONTROL, THE LOT OF 'EM.
EVERYTHING I FEAR AND HATE ABOUT TECHNOLOGY BEING SUPERIMPOSED ON MODERN WARFARE.
...
...WELL, HELL.
BOTH BARRELS IT IS, BOYS.
BOTH BARRELS IT IS.
VILLAINS!

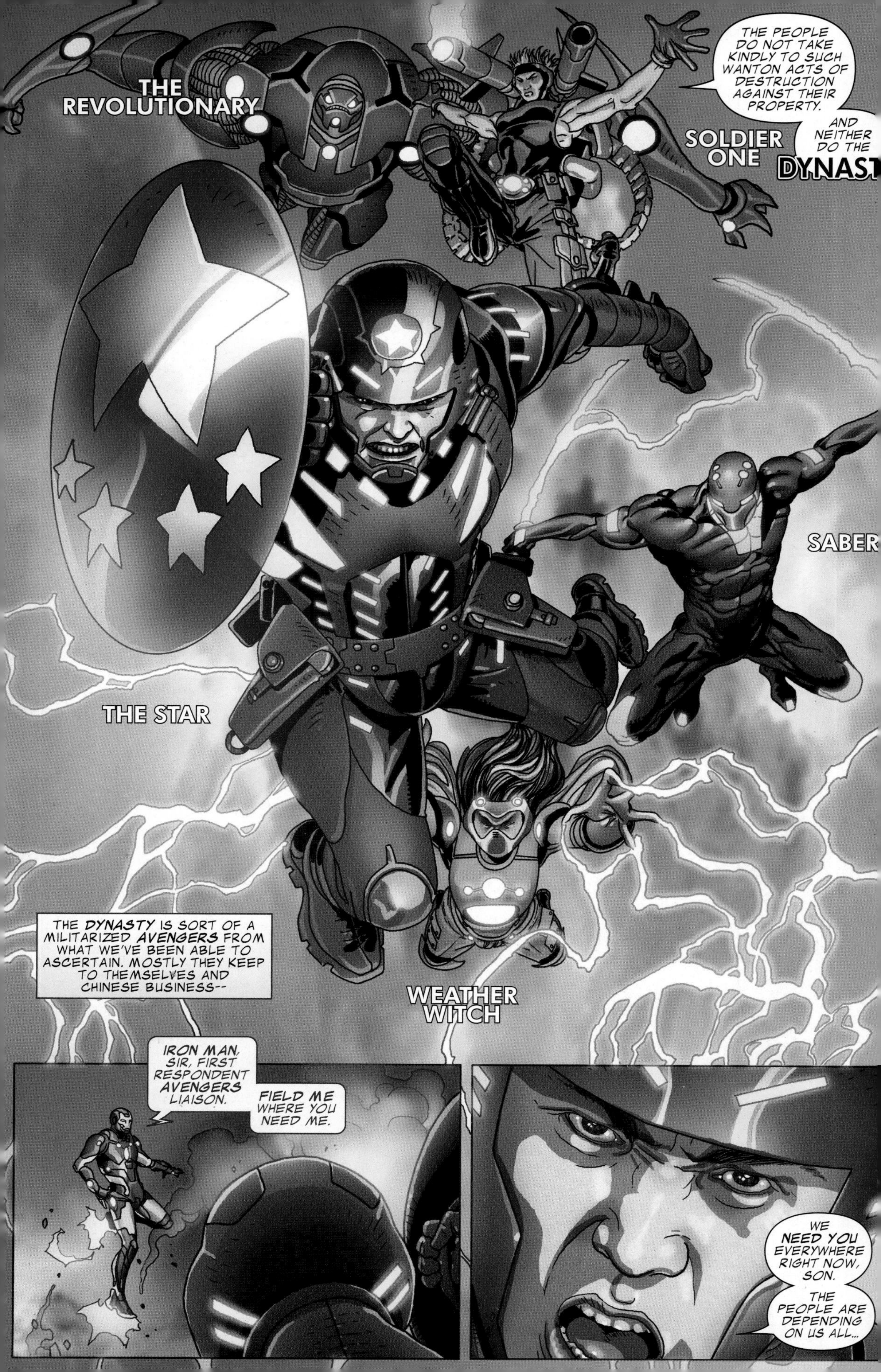
THE REVOLUTIONARY
THE PEOPLE DO NOT TAKE KINDLY TO SUCH WANTON ACTS OF DESTRUCTION AGAINST THEIR PROPERTY.
AND NEITHER DO THE DYNAST
SOLDIER ONE
SABER
THE STAR
THE DYNASTY IS SORT OF A MILITARIZED AVENGERS FROM WHAT WE'VE BEEN ABLE TO ASCERTAIN. MOSTLY THEY KEEP TO THEMSELVES AND CHINESE BUSINESS--
WEATHER WITCH
IRON MAN, SIR, FIRST RESPONDENT AVENGERS LIAISON.
FIELD ME WHERE YOU NEED ME.
WE NEED YOU EVERYWHERE RIGHT NOW, SON.
THE PEOPLE ARE DEPENDING ON US ALL...

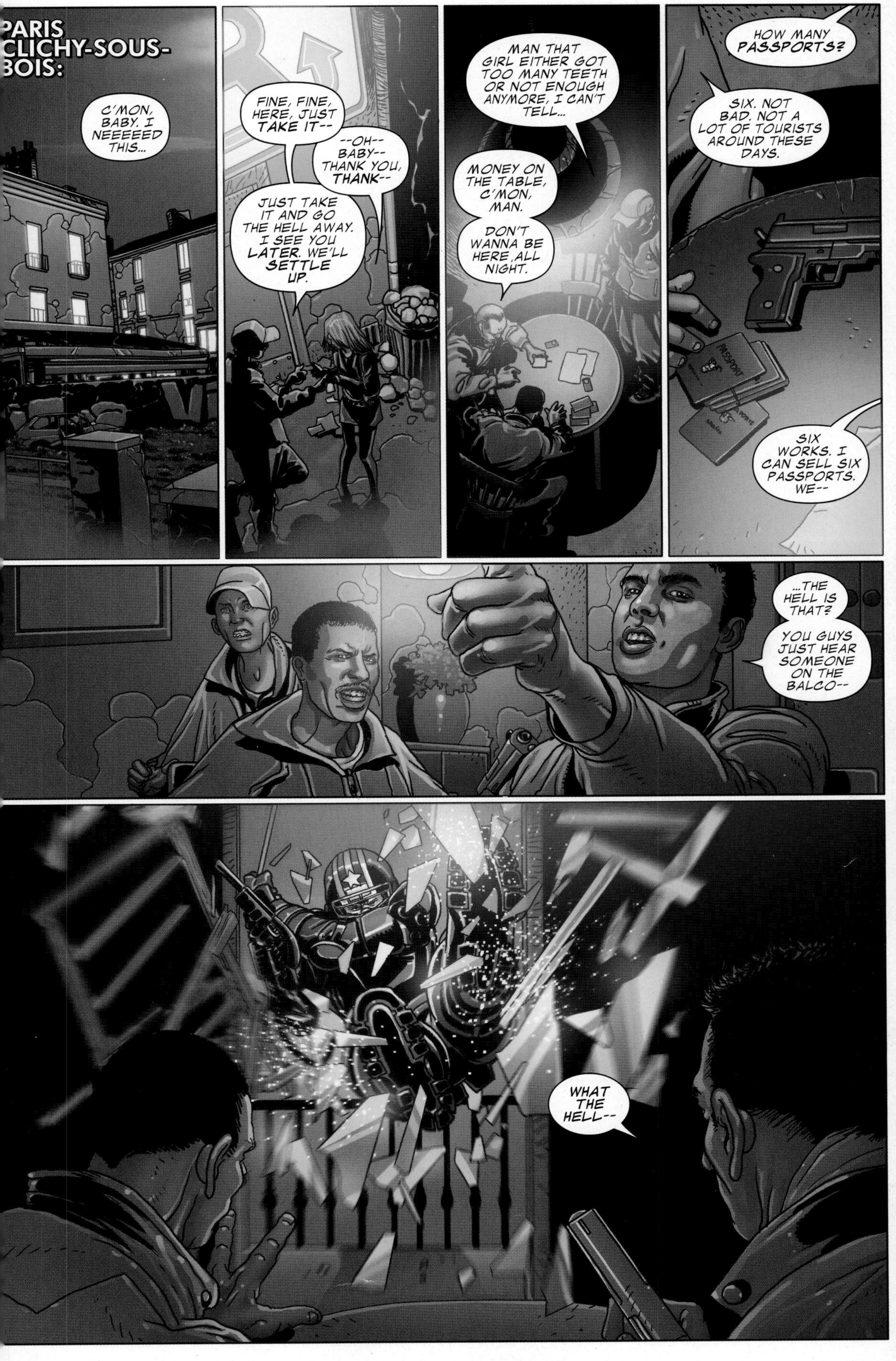
PARIS
CLICHY-SOUS-BOIS:
C'MON, BABY. I NEEEEED THIS...
FINE, FINE, HERE, JUST TAKE IT--
--OH-- BABY-- THANK YOU, THANK--
JUST TAKE IT AND GO THE HELL AWAY. I SEE YOU LATER. WE'LL SETTLE UP.
MAN THAT GIRL EITHER GOT TOO MANY TEETH OR NOT ENOUGH ANYMORE, I CAN'T TELL...
MONEY ON THE TABLE, C'MON, MAN.
DON'T WANNA BE HERE ALL NIGHT.
HOW MANY PASSPORTS?
SIX. NOT BAD. NOT A LOT OF TOURISTS AROUND THESE DAYS.
PASSPORT
SIX WORKS. I CAN SELL SIX PASSPORTS. WE--
...THE HELL IS THAT?
YOU GUYS JUST HEAR SOMEONE ON THE BALCO--
WHAT THE HELL--

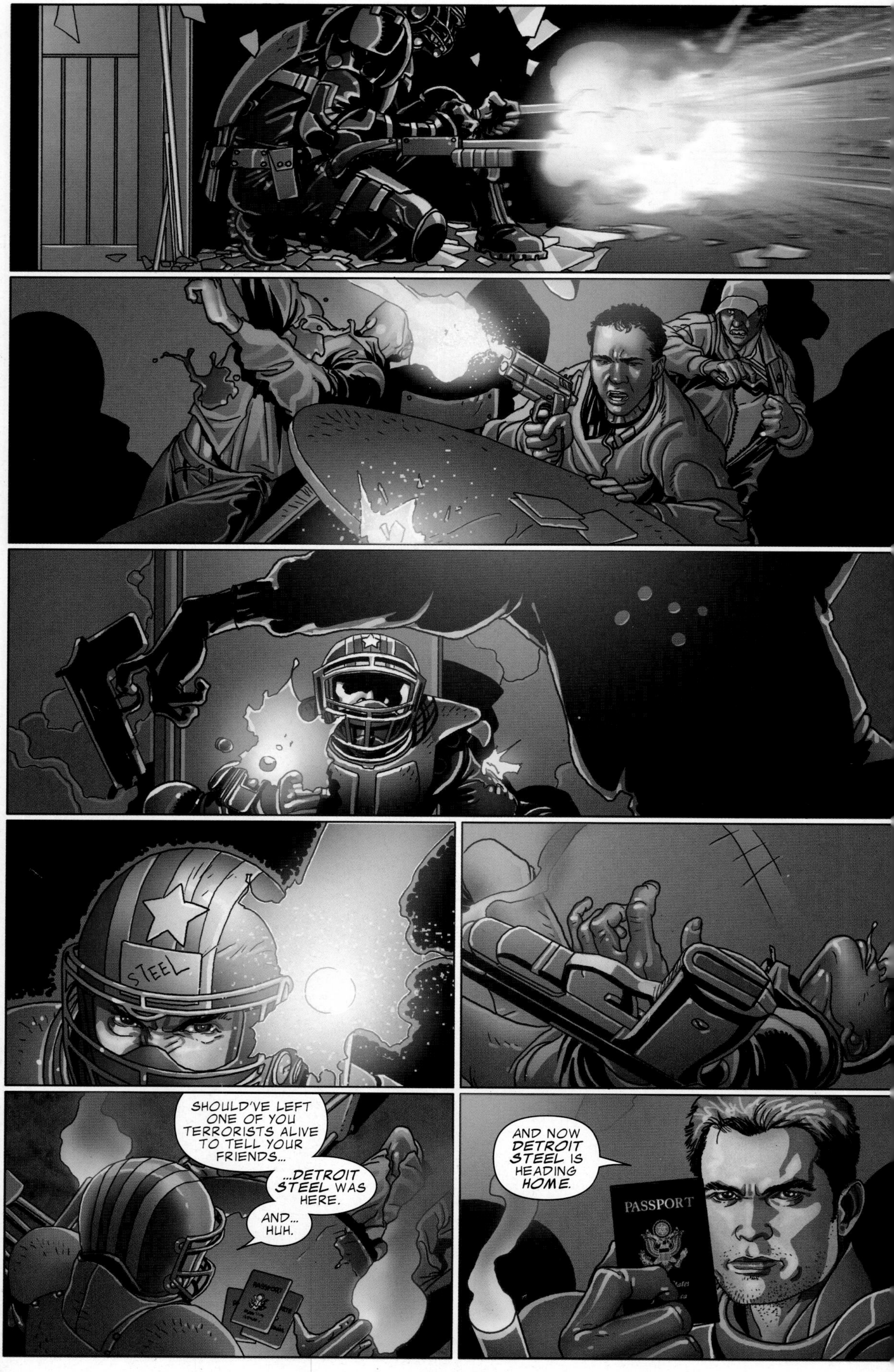
SHOULD'VE LEFT ONE OF YOU TERRORISTS ALIVE TO TELL YOUR FRIENDS...
...DETROIT STEEL WAS HERE.
AND... HUH.
AND NOW DETROIT STEEL IS HEADING HOME.
PASSPORT
STEEL

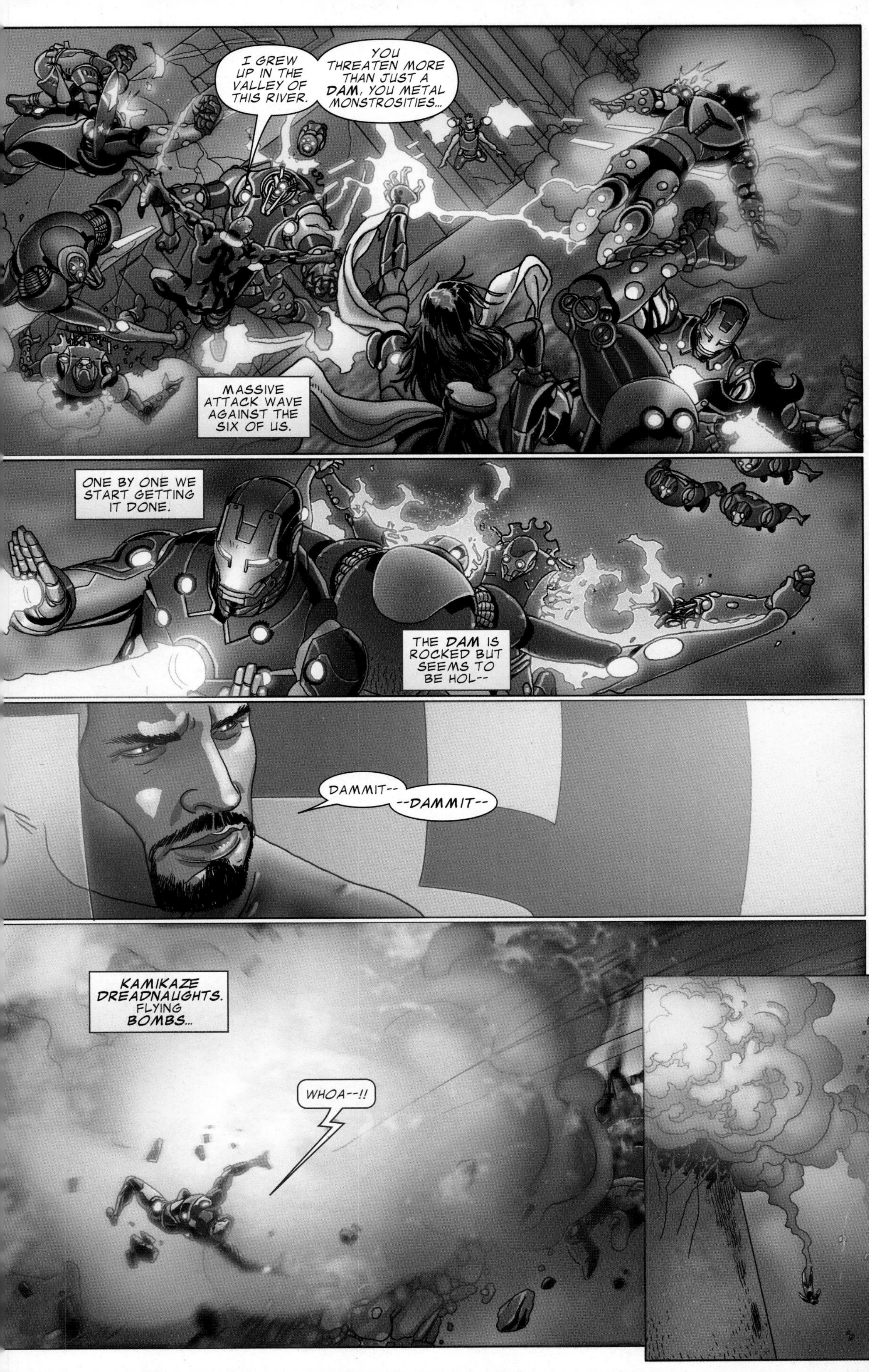
I GREW UP IN THE VALLEY OF THIS RIVER.
YOU THREATEN MORE THAN JUST A DAM, YOU METAL MONSTROSITIES...
MASSIVE ATTACK WAVE AGAINST THE SIX OF US.
ONE BY ONE WE START GETTING IT DONE.
THE DAM IS ROCKED BUT SEEMS TO BE HOL--
DAMMIT--
--DAMMIT--
KAMIKAZE DREADNAUGHTS. FLYING BOMBS...
WHOA--!!

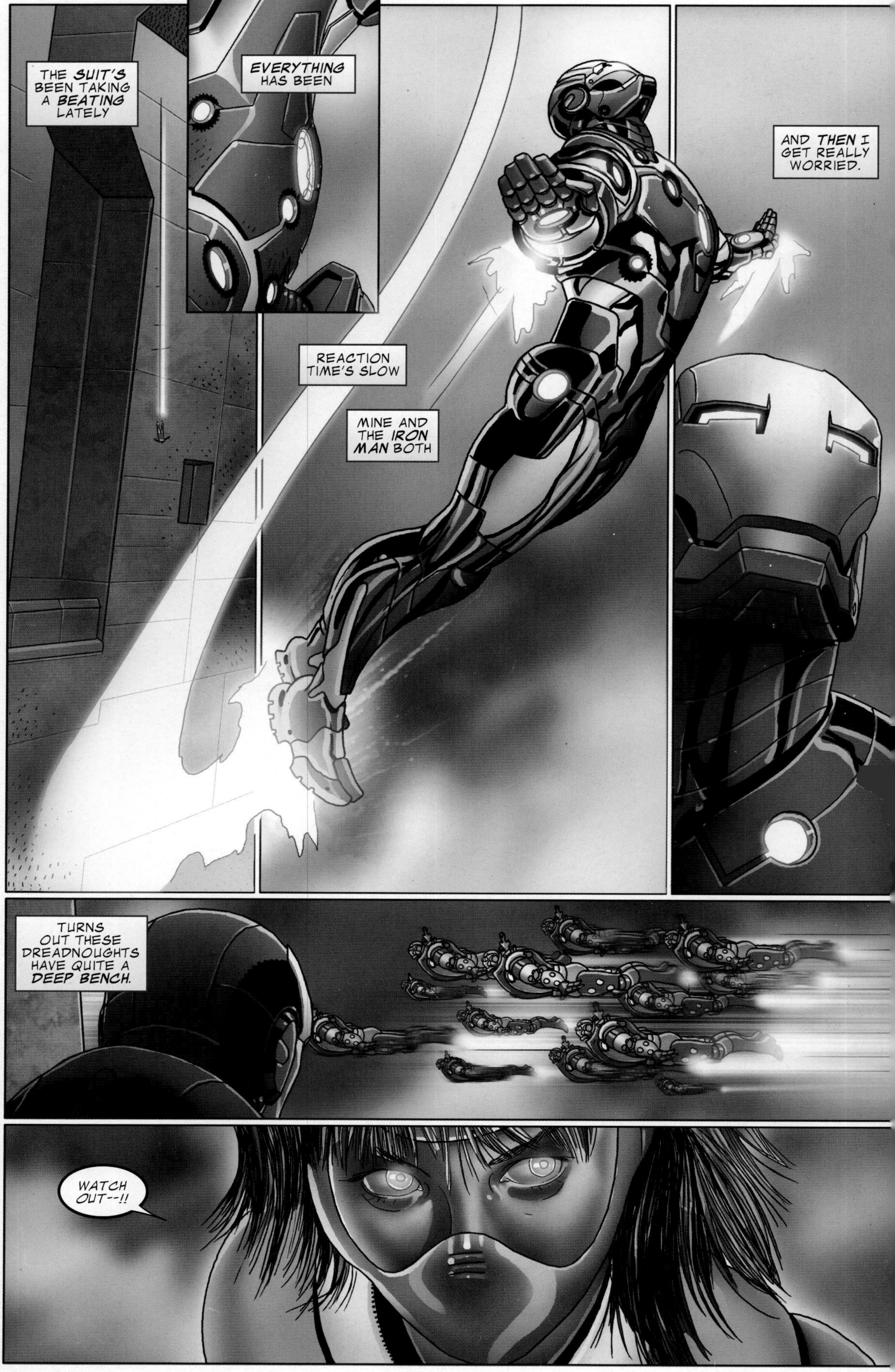
THE SUIT'S BEEN TAKING A BEATING LATELY
EVERYTHING HAS BEEN
REACTION TIME'S SLOW
MINE AND THE IRON MAN BOTH
AND THEN I GET REALLY WORRIED.
TURNS OUT THESE DREADNOUGHTS HAVE QUITE A DEEP BENCH.
WATCH OUT--!!

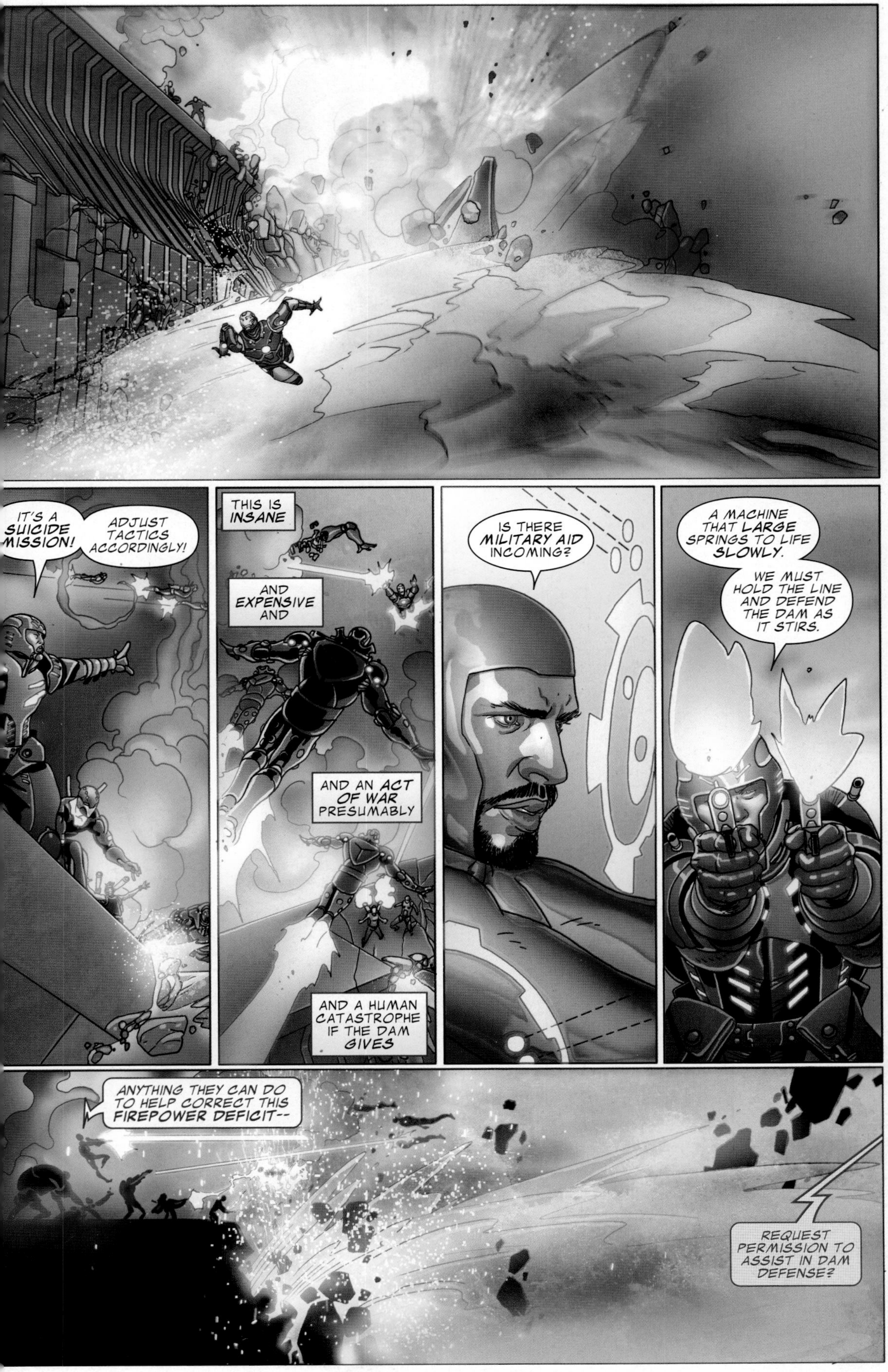
IT'S A SUICIDE MISSION!
ADJUST TACTICS ACCORDINGLY!
THIS IS INSANE
AND EXPENSIVE AND
AND AN ACT OF WAR PRESUMABLY
AND A HUMAN CATASTROPHE IF THE DAM GIVES
IS THERE MILITARY AID INCOMING?
A MACHINE THAT LARGE SPRINGS TO LIFE SLOWLY.
WE MUST HOLD THE LINE AND DEFEND THE DAM AS IT STIRS.
ANYTHING THEY CAN DO TO HELP CORRECT THIS FIREPOWER DEFICIT--
REQUEST PERMISSION TO ASSIST IN DAM DEFENSE?

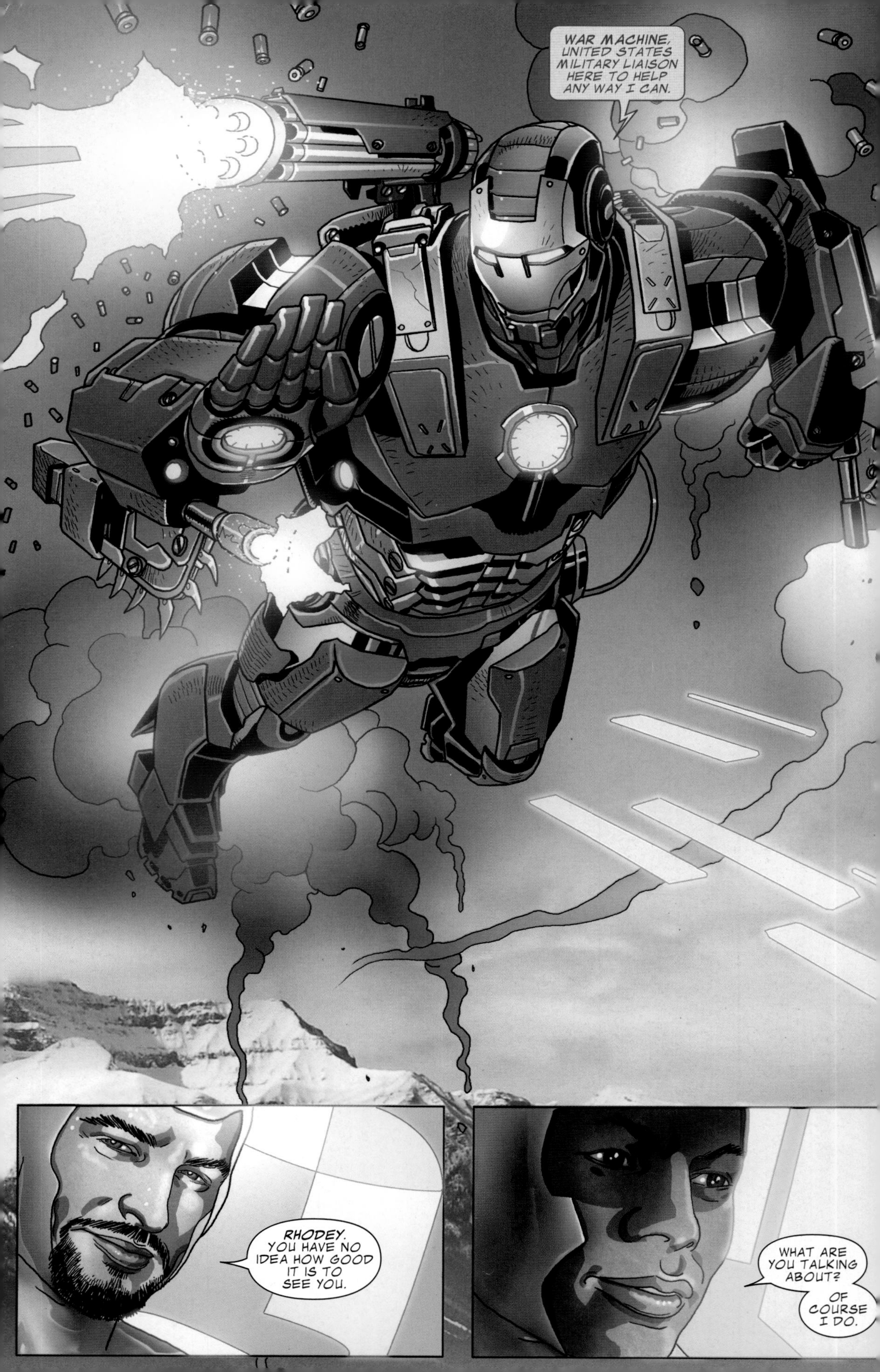
WAR MACHINE, UNITED STATES MILITARY LIAISON HERE TO HELP ANY WAY I CAN.
RHODEY. YOU HAVE NO IDEA HOW GOOD IT IS TO SEE YOU.
WHAT ARE YOU TALKING ABOUT?
OF COURSE I DO.

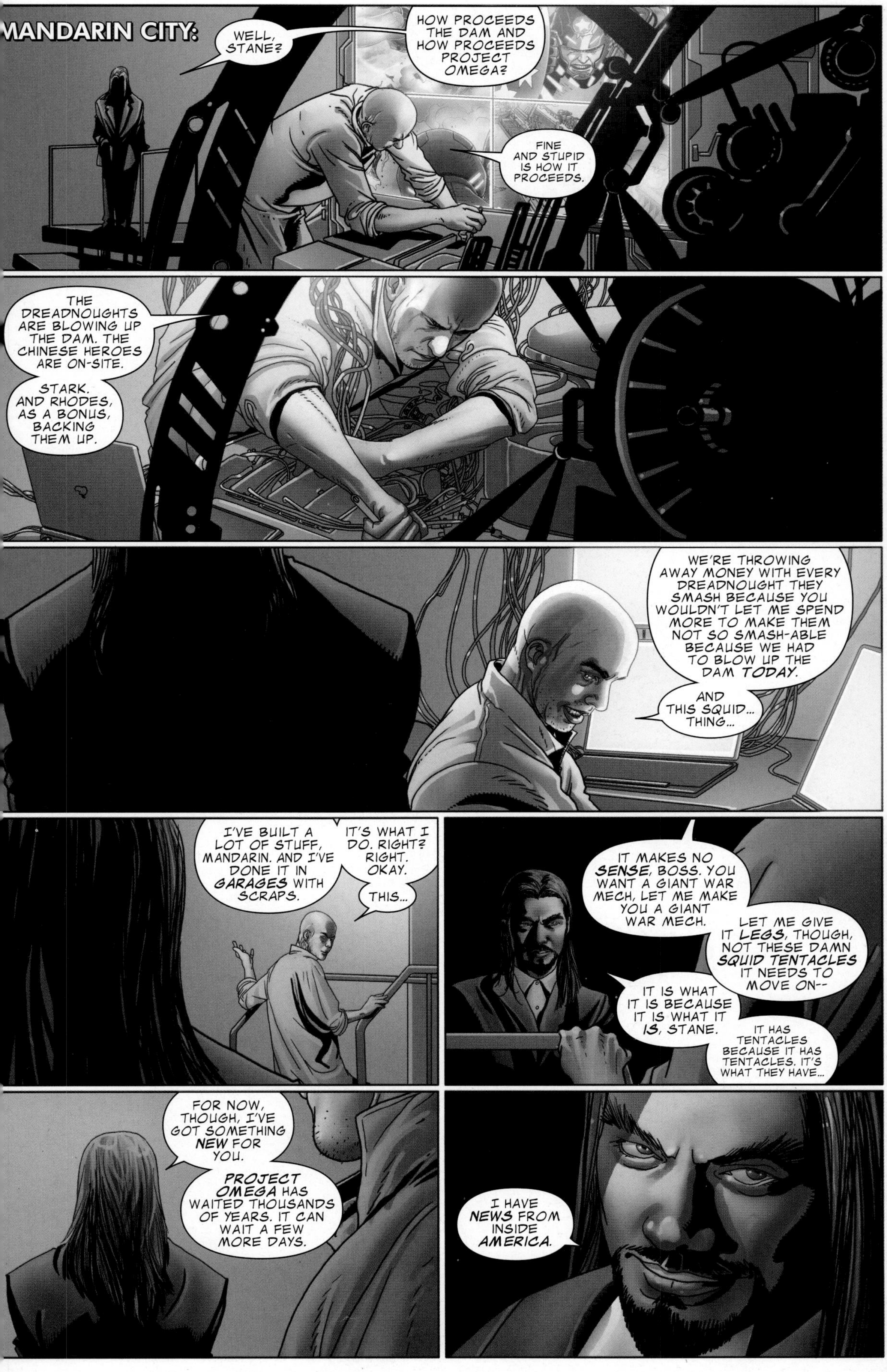
MANDARIN CITY:
WELL, STANE?
HOW PROCEEDS THE DAM AND HOW PROCEEDS PROJECT OMEGA?
FINE AND STUPID IS HOW IT PROCEEDS.
THE DREADNOUGHTS ARE BLOWING UP THE DAM. THE CHINESE HEROES ARE ON-SITE.
STARK. AND RHODES, AS A BONUS, BACKING THEM UP.
WE'RE THROWING AWAY MONEY WITH EVERY DREADNOUGHT THEY SMASH BECAUSE YOU WOULDN'T LET ME SPEND MORE TO MAKE THEM NOT SO SMASH-ABLE BECAUSE WE HAD TO BLOW UP THE DAM TODAY.
AND THIS SQUID... THING...
I'VE BUILT A LOT OF STUFF, MANDARIN. AND I'VE DONE IT IN GARAGES WITH SCRAPS.
IT'S WHAT I DO. RIGHT? RIGHT. OKAY.
THIS...
IT MAKES NO SENSE, BOSS. YOU WANT A GIANT WAR MECH, LET ME MAKE YOU A GIANT WAR MECH.
LET ME GIVE IT LEGS, THOUGH, NOT THESE DAMN SQUID TENTACLES IT NEEDS TO MOVE ON--
IT IS WHAT IT IS BECAUSE IT IS WHAT IT IS, STANE.
IT HAS TENTACLES BECAUSE IT HAS TENTACLES. IT'S WHAT THEY HAVE...
FOR NOW, THOUGH, I'VE GOT SOMETHING NEW FOR YOU.
PROJECT OMEGA HAS WAITED THOUSANDS OF YEARS. IT CAN WAIT A FEW MORE DAYS.
I HAVE NEWS FROM INSIDE AMERICA.

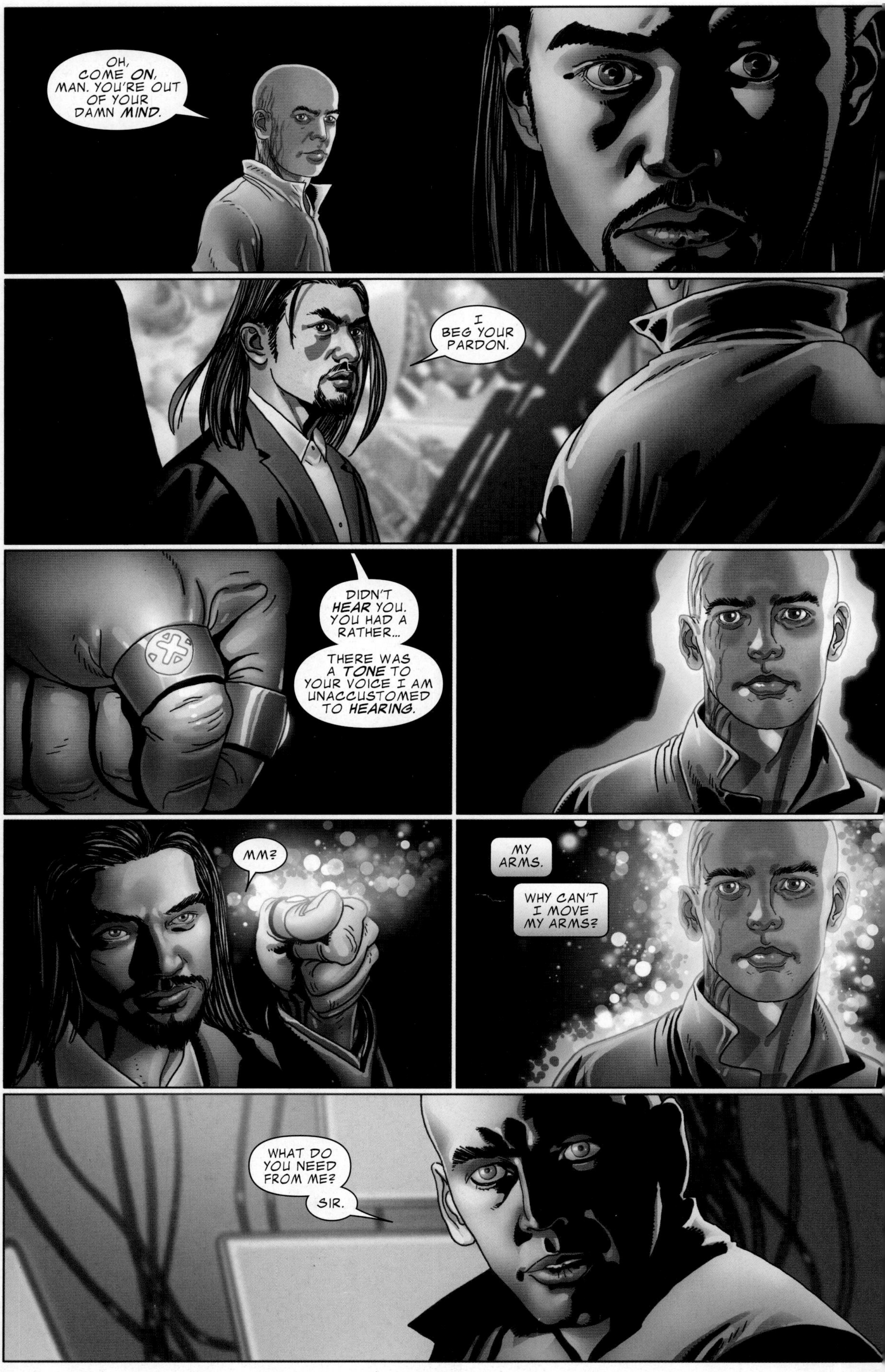
OH, COME ON, MAN. YOU'RE OUT OF YOUR DAMN MIND.
I BEG YOUR PARDON.
DIDN'T HEAR YOU. YOU HAD A RATHER...
THERE WAS A TONE TO YOUR VOICE I AM UNACCUSTOMED TO HEARING.
MM?
MY ARMS.
WHY CAN'T I MOVE MY ARMS?
WHAT DO YOU NEED FROM ME?
SIR.

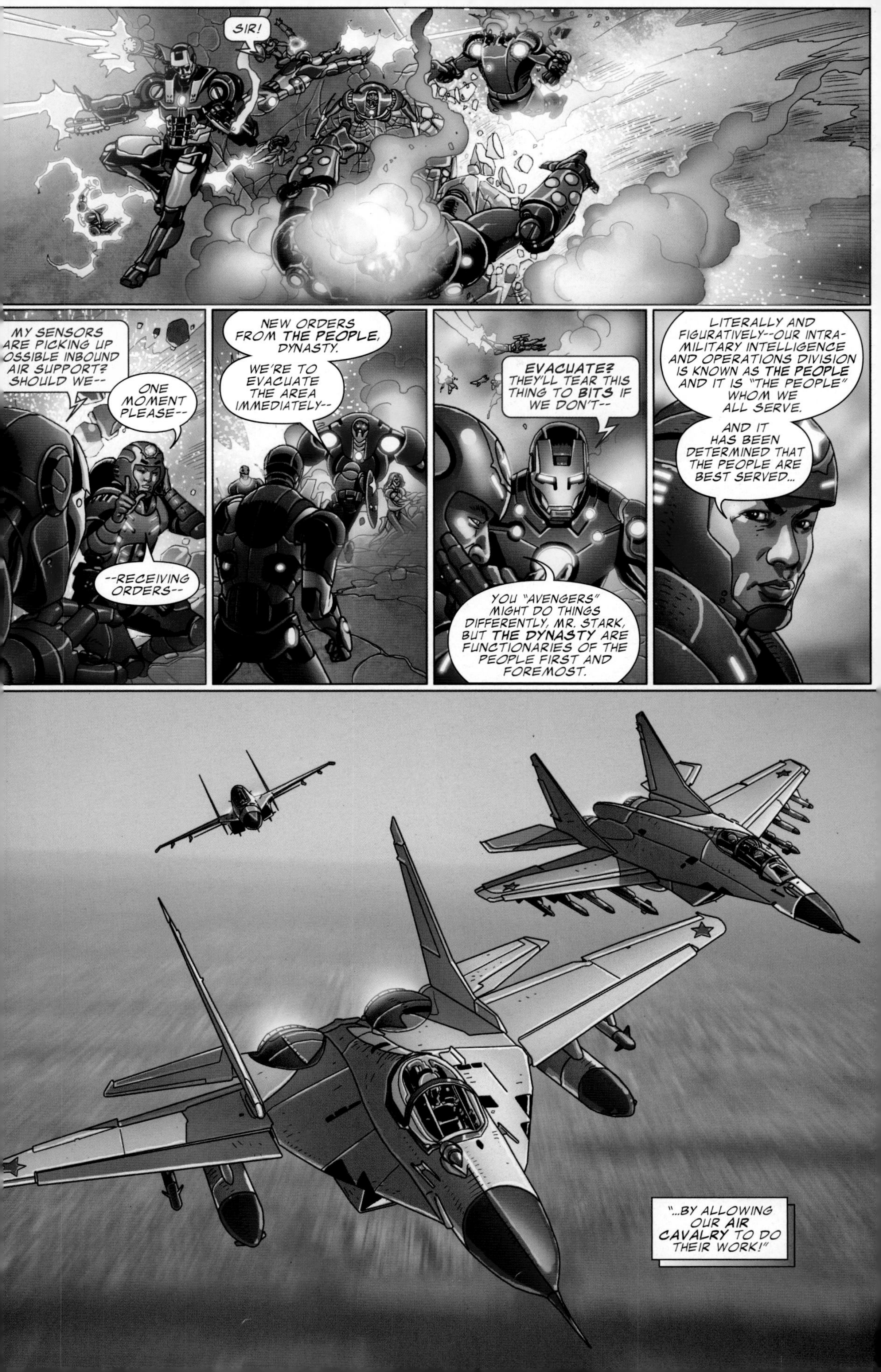
SIR!
MY SENSORS ARE PICKING UP POSSIBLE INBOUND AIR SUPPORT? SHOULD WE--
ONE MOMENT PLEASE--
--RECEIVING ORDERS--
NEW ORDERS FROM THE PEOPLE, DYNASTY.
WE'RE TO EVACUATE THE AREA IMMEDIATELY--
EVACUATE? THEY'LL TEAR THIS THING TO BITS IF WE DON'T--
YOU "AVENGERS" MIGHT DO THINGS DIFFERENTLY, MR. STARK, BUT THE DYNASTY ARE FUNCTIONARIES OF THE PEOPLE FIRST AND FOREMOST.
LITERALLY AND FIGURATIVELY--OUR INTRA-MILITARY INTELLIGENCE AND OPERATIONS DIVISION IS KNOWN AS THE PEOPLE AND IT IS "THE PEOPLE" WHOM WE ALL SERVE.
AND IT HAS BEEN DETERMINED THAT THE PEOPLE ARE BEST SERVED...
"...BY ALLOWING OUR AIR CAVALRY TO DO THEIR WORK!"

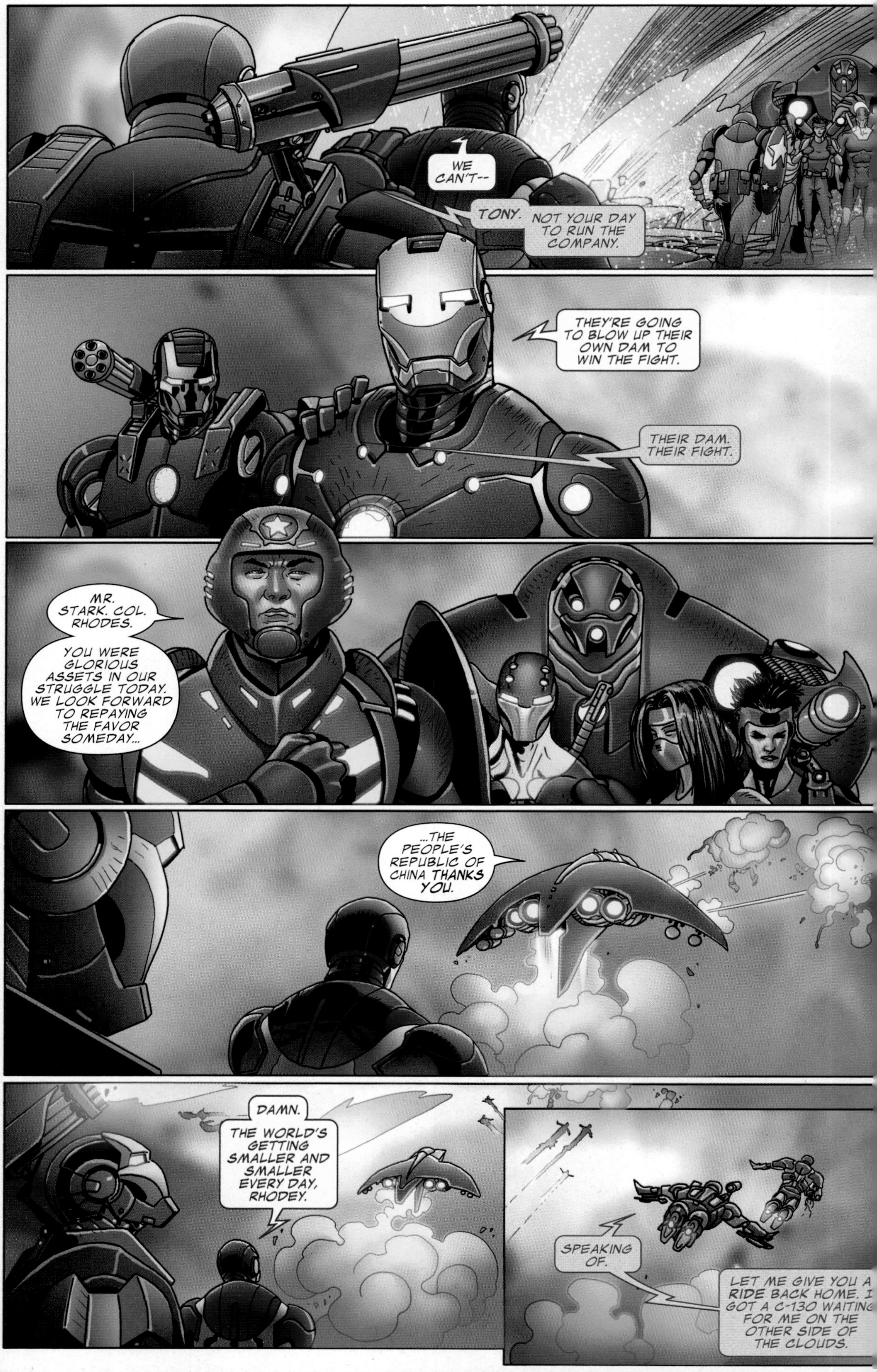
WE CAN'T--
TONY.
NOT YOUR DAY TO RUN THE COMPANY.
THEY'RE GOING TO BLOW UP THEIR OWN DAM TO WIN THE FIGHT.
THEIR DAM. THEIR FIGHT.
MR. STARK. COL. RHODES.
YOU WERE GLORIOUS ASSETS IN OUR STRUGGLE TODAY. WE LOOK FORWARD TO REPAYING THE FAVOR SOMEDAY...
...THE PEOPLE'S REPUBLIC OF CHINA THANKS YOU.
DAMN.
THE WORLD'S GETTING SMALLER AND SMALLER EVERY DAY, RHODEY.
SPEAKING OF.
LET ME GIVE YOU A RIDE BACK HOME. I GOT A C-130 WAITING FOR ME ON THE OTHER SIDE OF THE CLOUDS.

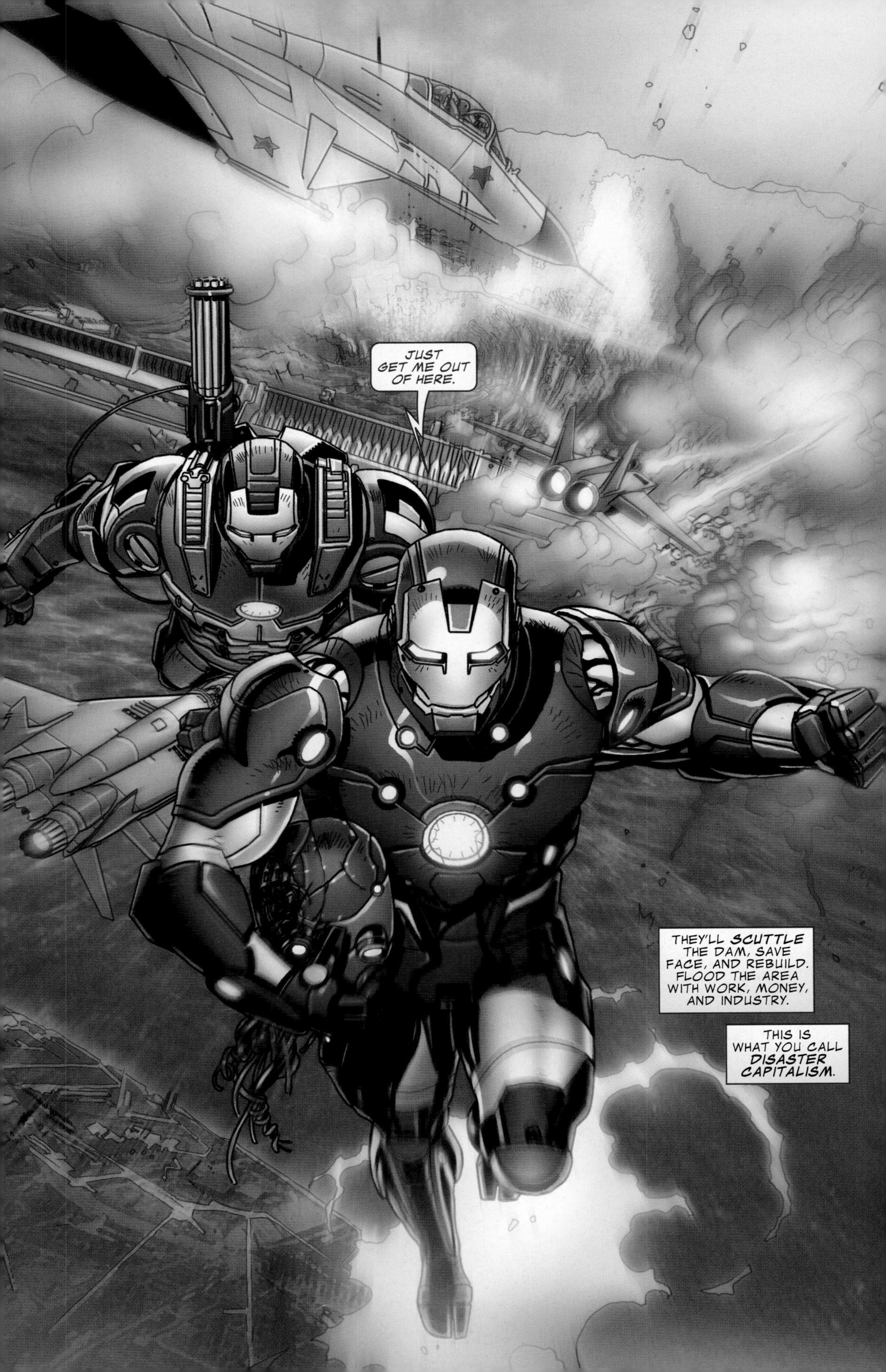
JUST GET ME OUT OF HERE.
THEY'LL SCUTTLE THE DAM, SAVE FACE, AND REBUILD. FLOOD THE AREA WITH WORK, MONEY, AND INDUSTRY.
THIS IS WHAT YOU CALL DISASTER CAPITALISM.

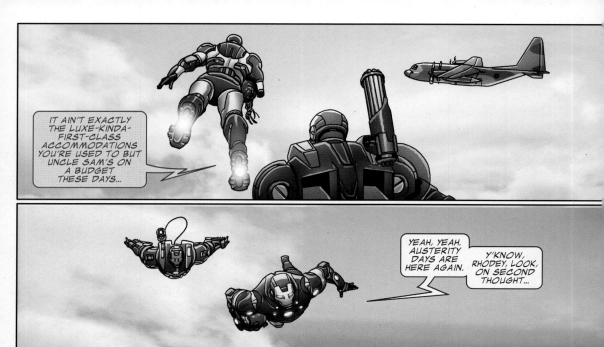

IT AIN'T EXACTLY THE LUXE-KINDA-FIRST-CLASS ACCOMMODATIONS YOU'RE USED TO BUT UNCLE SAM'S ON A BUDGET THESE DAYS...

YEAH, YEAH. AUSTERITY DAYS ARE HERE AGAIN.

Y'KNOW, RHODEY, LOOK, ON SECOND THOUGHT...

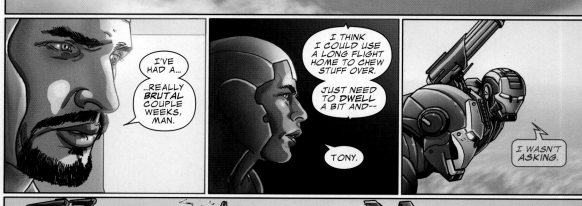

I'VE HAD A...

...REALLY BRUTAL COUPLE WEEKS, MAN.

I THINK I COULD USE A LONG FLIGHT HOME TO CHEW STUFF OVER.

JUST NEED TO DWELL A BIT AND--

TONY.

I WASN'T ASKING.

THE UNITED STATES GOVERNMENT WOULD LIKE TO ESCORT YOU HOME.

RHODEY, WHAT THE HELL, MAN...?

TONY. THE DETROIT STEEL CORPS AND I WERE DISPATCHED TO BRING YOU HOME.

WE ALL NEED TO TALK. DO THE SMART THING.

BUT I'M SO GOOD AT BEING DUMB...

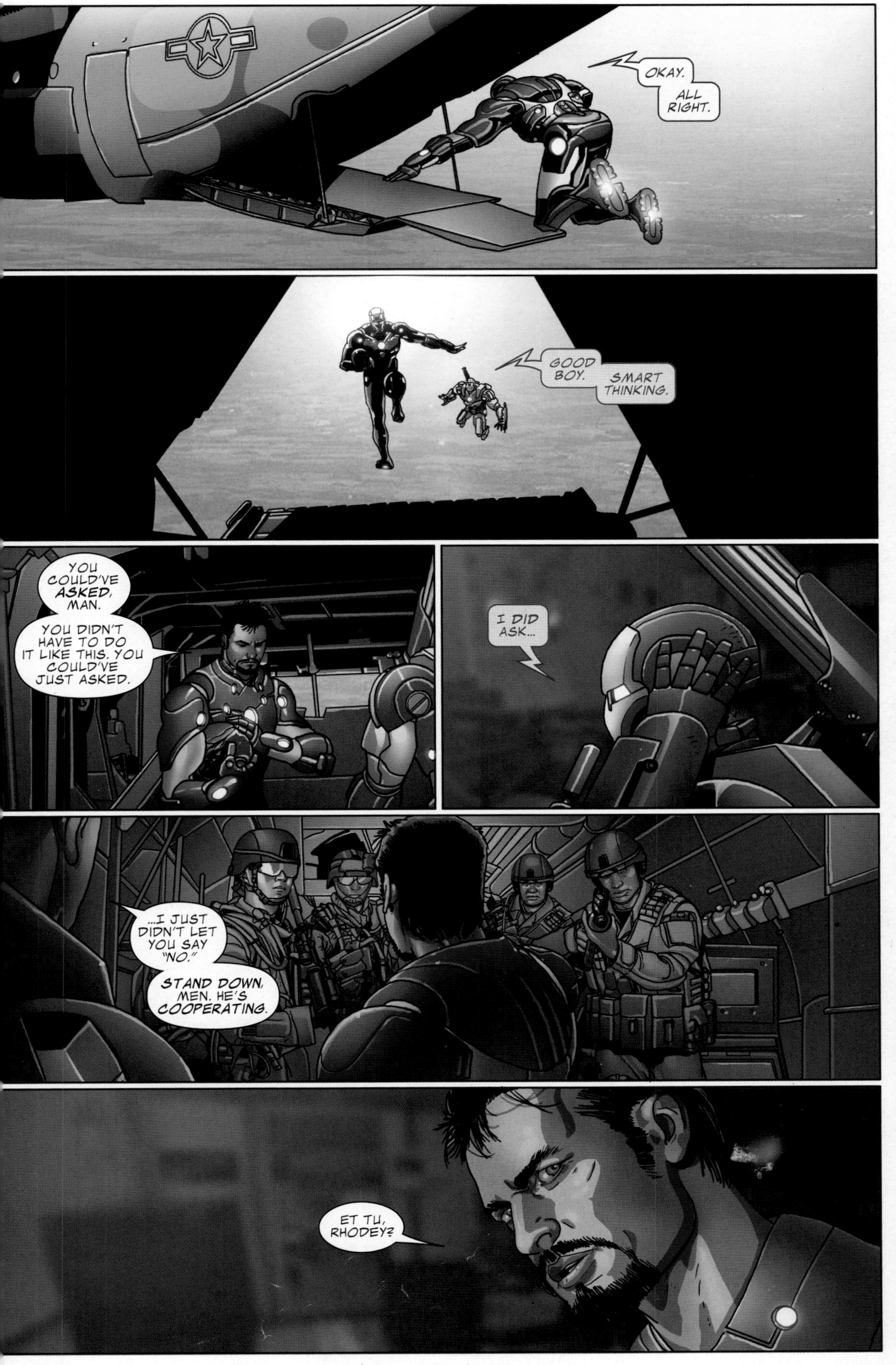
OKAY.
ALL RIGHT.
GOOD BOY.
SMART THINKING.
YOU COULD'VE ASKED, MAN.
YOU DIDN'T HAVE TO DO IT LIKE THIS. YOU COULD'VE JUST ASKED.
I DID ASK...
...I JUST DIDN'T LET YOU SAY "NO."
STAND DOWN, MEN. HE'S COOPERATING.
ET TU, RHODEY?

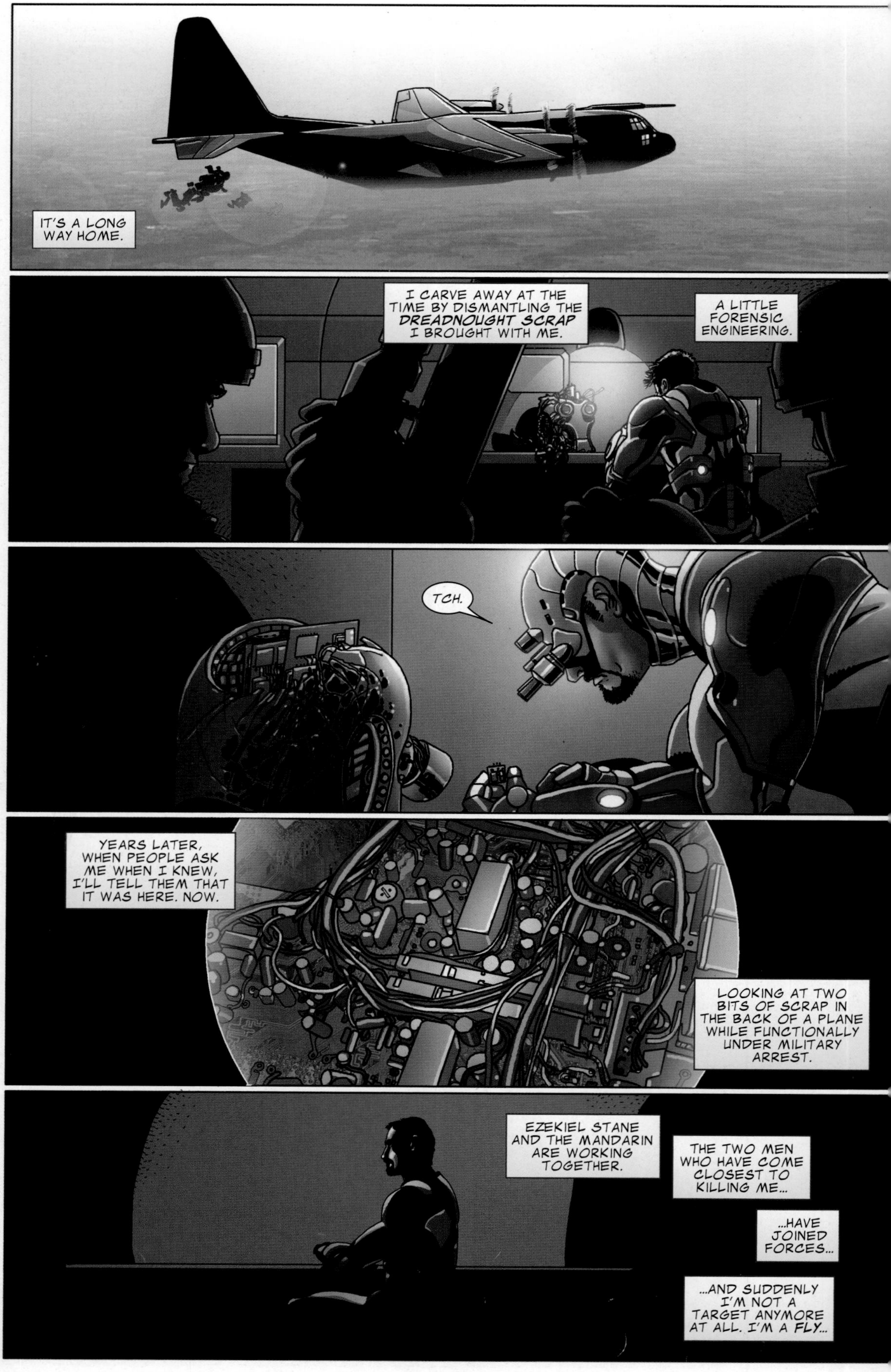
IT'S A LONG WAY HOME.
I CARVE AWAY AT THE TIME BY DISMANTLING THE DREADNOUGHT SCRAP I BROUGHT WITH ME.
A LITTLE FORENSIC ENGINEERING.
TCH.
YEARS LATER, WHEN PEOPLE ASK ME WHEN I KNEW, I'LL TELL THEM THAT IT WAS HERE. NOW.
LOOKING AT TWO BITS OF SCRAP IN THE BACK OF A PLANE WHILE FUNCTIONALLY UNDER MILITARY ARREST.
EZEKIEL STANE AND THE MANDARIN ARE WORKING TOGETHER.
THE TWO MEN WHO HAVE COME CLOSEST TO KILLING ME...
...HAVE JOINED FORCES...
...AND SUDDENLY I'M NOT A TARGET ANYMORE AT ALL. I'M A FLY...

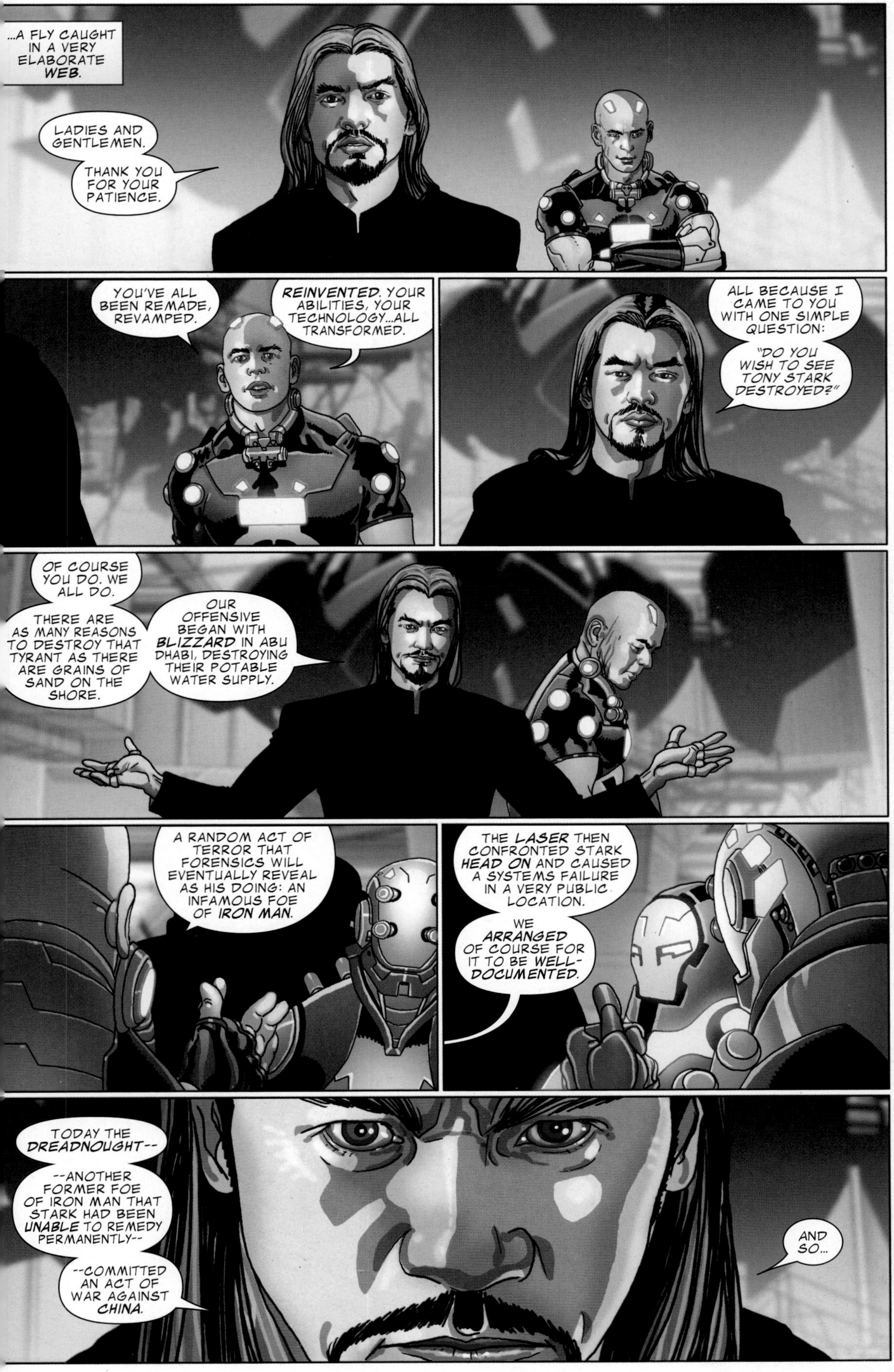
...A FLY CAUGHT IN A VERY ELABORATE WEB.
LADIES AND GENTLEMEN.
THANK YOU FOR YOUR PATIENCE.
YOU'VE ALL BEEN REMADE, REVAMPED.
REINVENTED. YOUR ABILITIES, YOUR TECHNOLOGY...ALL TRANSFORMED.
ALL BECAUSE I CAME TO YOU WITH ONE SIMPLE QUESTION:
"DO YOU WISH TO SEE TONY STARK DESTROYED?"
OF COURSE YOU DO. WE ALL DO.
THERE ARE AS MANY REASONS TO DESTROY THAT TYRANT AS THERE ARE GRAINS OF SAND ON THE SHORE.
OUR OFFENSIVE BEGAN WITH BLIZZARD IN ABU DHABI, DESTROYING THEIR POTABLE WATER SUPPLY.
A RANDOM ACT OF TERROR THAT FORENSICS WILL EVENTUALLY REVEAL AS HIS DOING: AN INFAMOUS FOE OF IRON MAN.
THE LASER THEN CONFRONTED STARK HEAD ON AND CAUSED A SYSTEMS FAILURE IN A VERY PUBLIC LOCATION.
WE ARRANGED OF COURSE FOR IT TO BE WELL-DOCUMENTED.
TODAY THE DREADNOUGHT--
--ANOTHER FORMER FOE OF IRON MAN THAT STARK HAD BEEN UNABLE TO REMEDY PERMANENTLY--
--COMMITTED AN ACT OF WAR AGAINST CHINA.
AND SO...

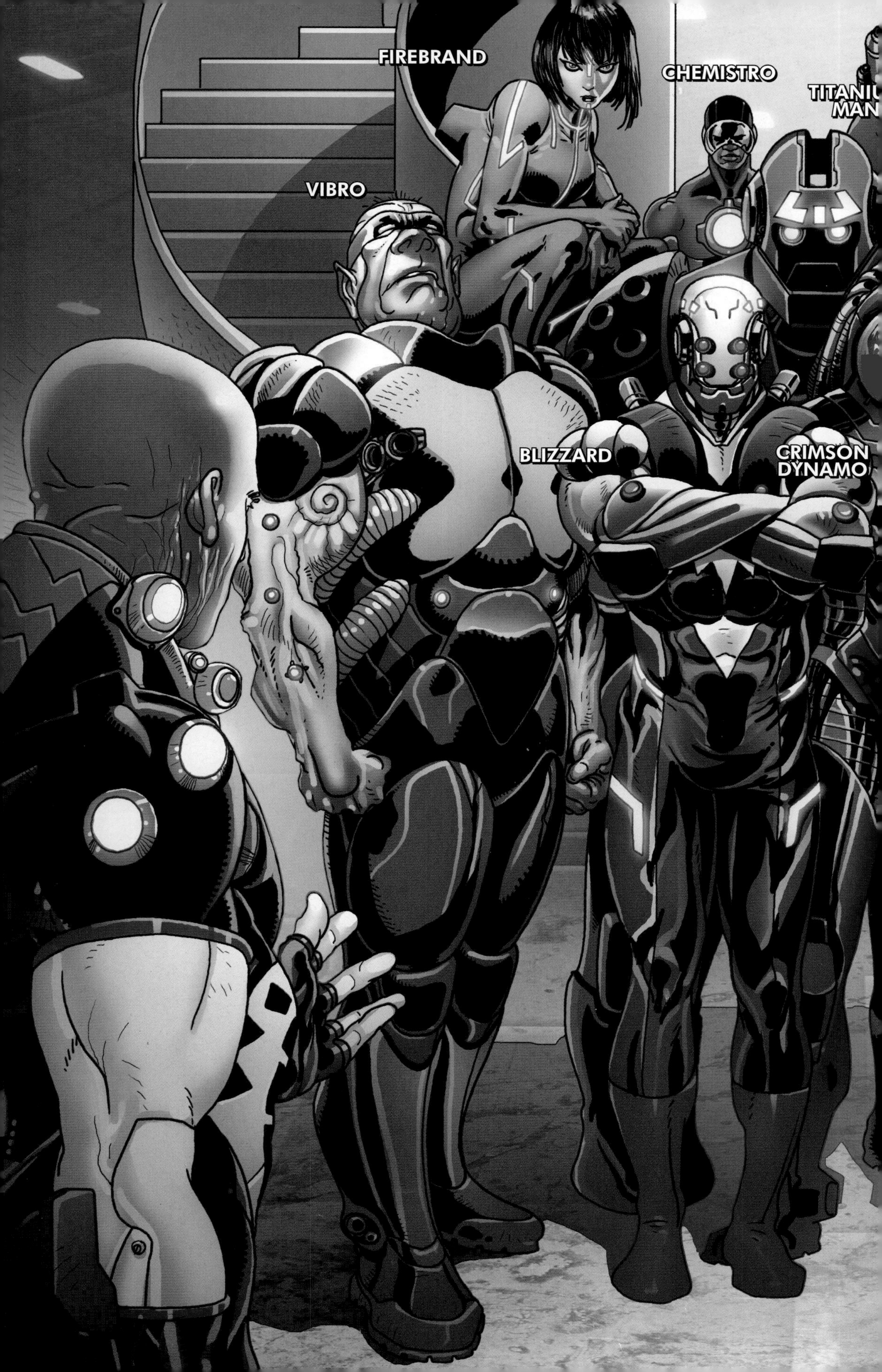
FIREBRAND
CHEMISTRO
TITANIU
MAN
VIBRO
BLIZZARD
CRIMSON
DYNAMO

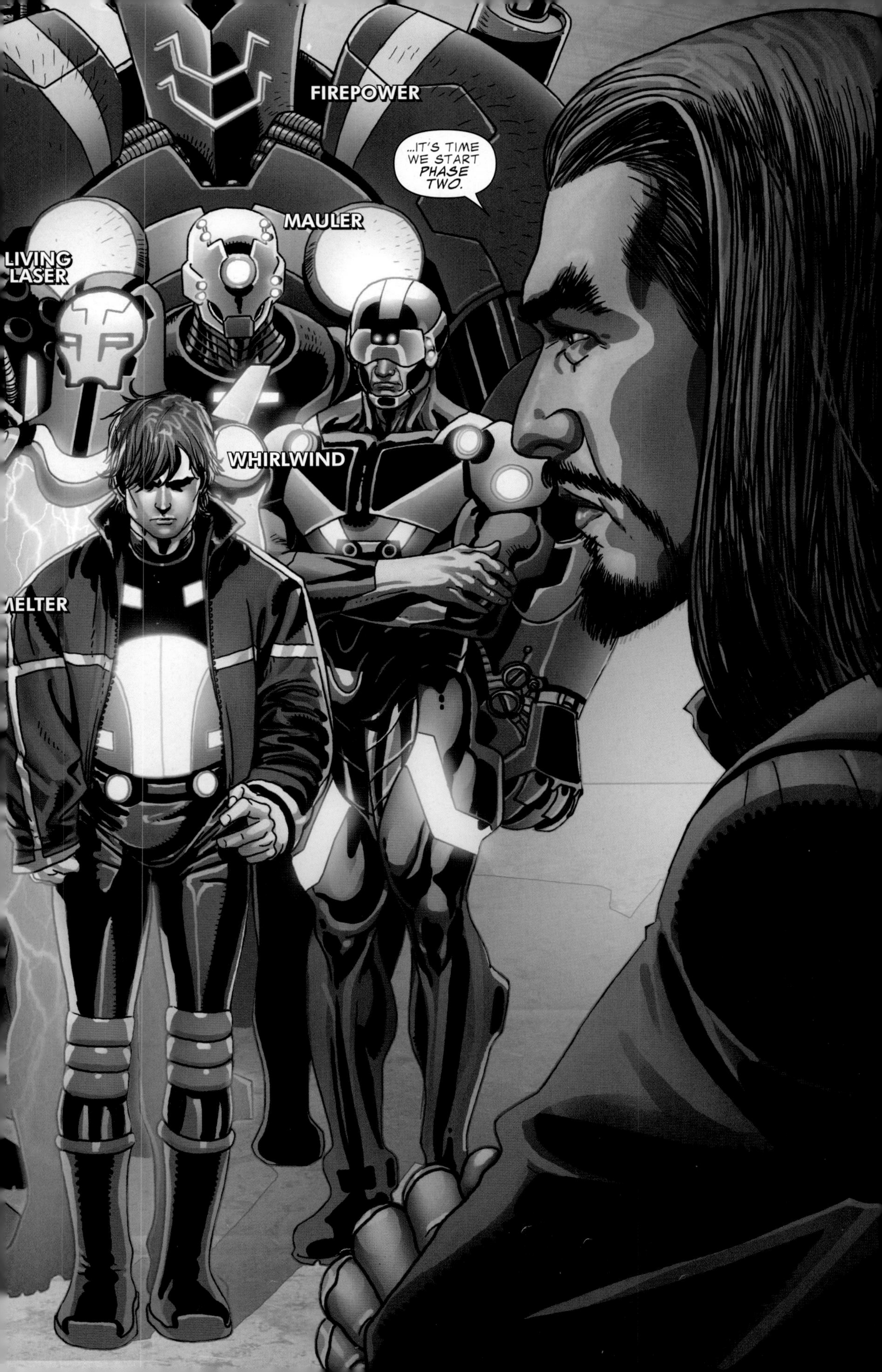
FIREPOWER
...IT'S TIME WE START PHASE TWO.
MAULER
LIVING LASER
WHIRLWIND
MELTER

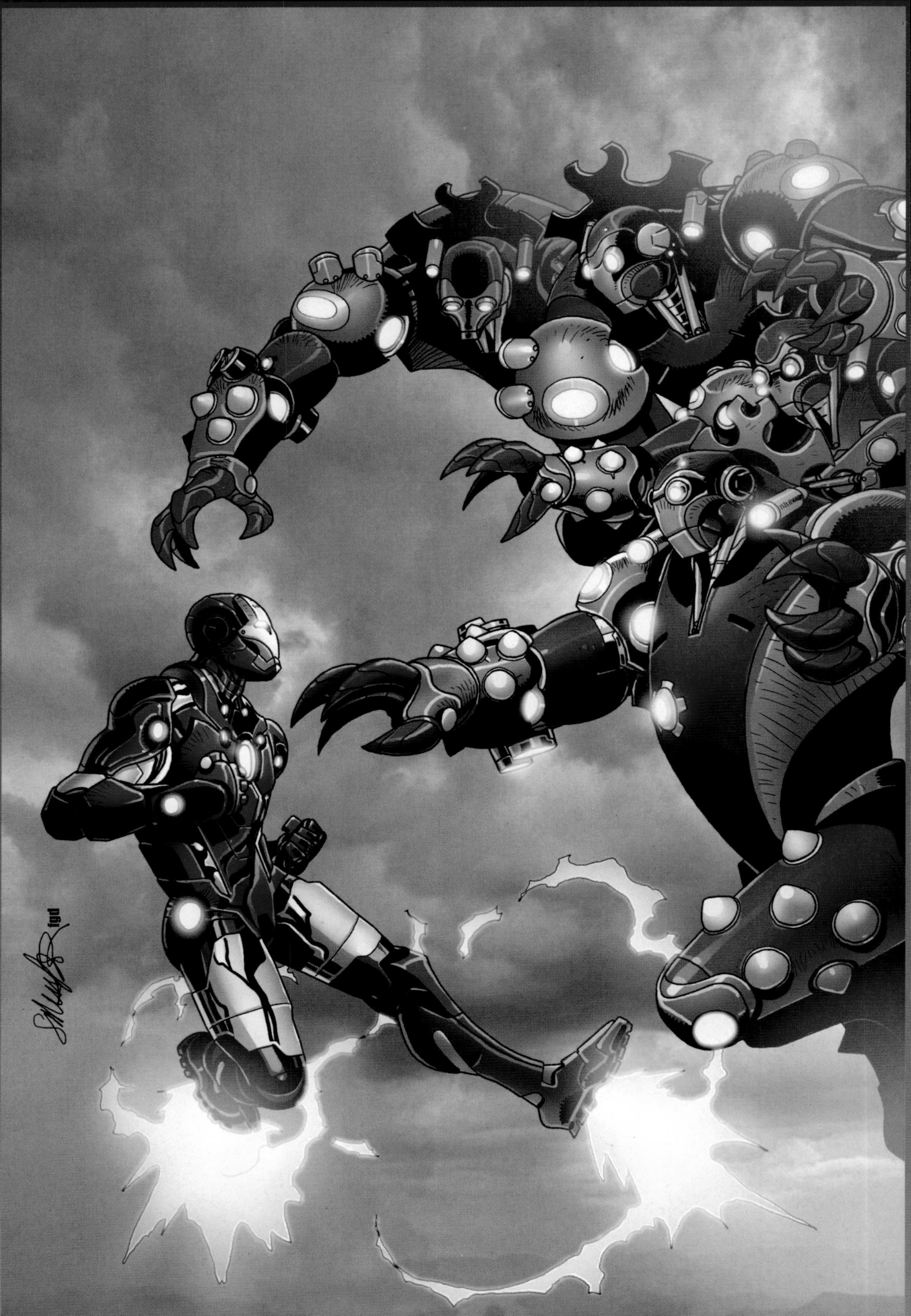

514 PART FIVE: MELT

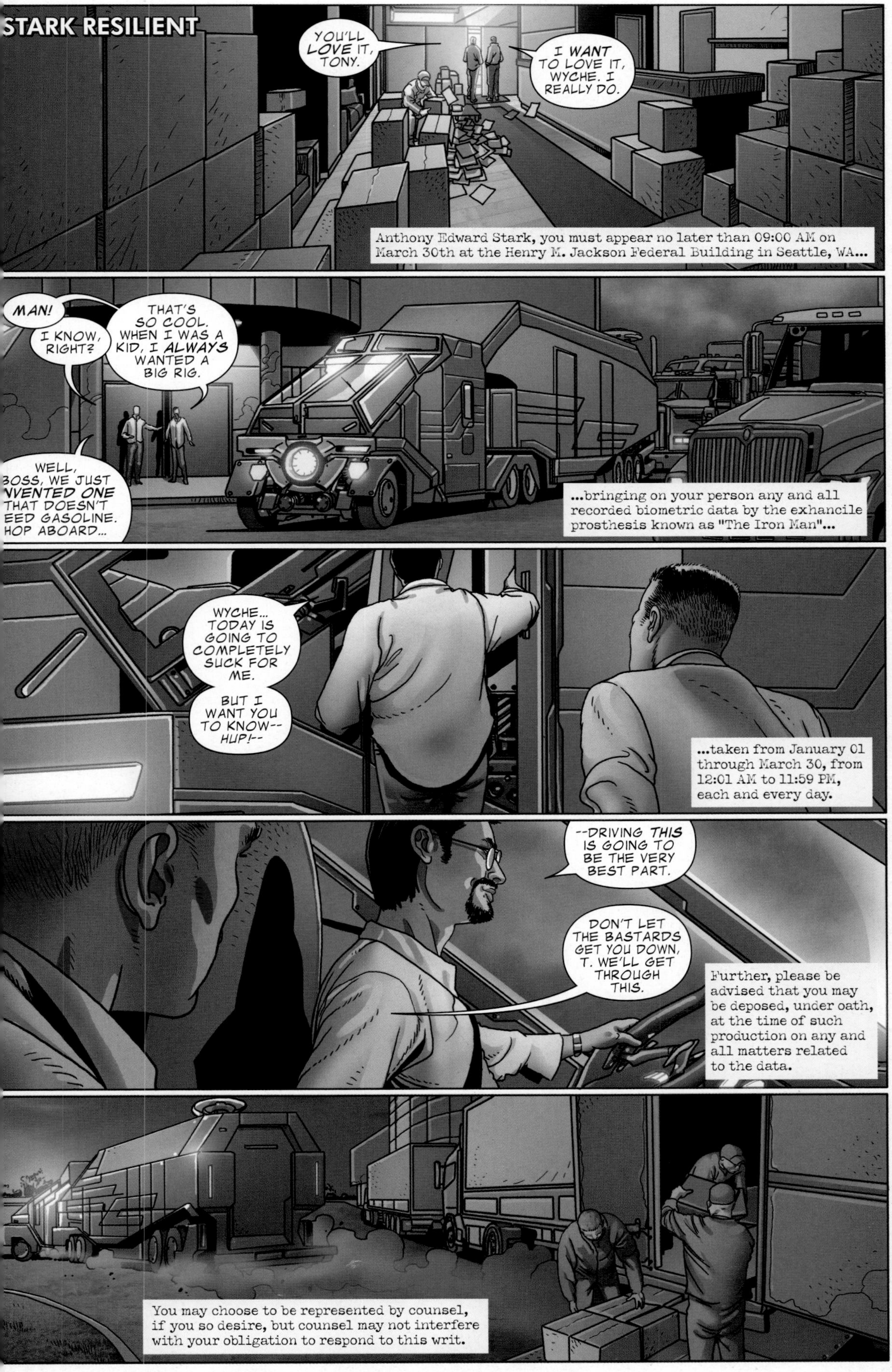
STARK RESILIENT
YOU'LL LOVE IT, TONY.
I WANT TO LOVE IT, WYCHE. I REALLY DO.
Anthony Edward Stark, you must appear no later than 09:00 AM on March 30th at the Henry M. Jackson Federal Building in Seattle, WA...
MAN!
I KNOW, RIGHT?
THAT'S SO COOL. WHEN I WAS A KID, I ALWAYS WANTED A BIG RIG.
WELL, BOSS, WE JUST INVENTED ONE THAT DOESN'T NEED GASOLINE. HOP ABOARD...
...bringing on your person any and all recorded biometric data by the exhancile prosthesis known as "The Iron Man"...
WYCHE... TODAY IS GOING TO COMPLETELY SUCK FOR ME.
BUT I WANT YOU TO KNOW-- HUP!--
...taken from January 01 through March 30, from 12:01 AM to 11:59 PM, each and every day.
--DRIVING THIS IS GOING TO BE THE VERY BEST PART.
DON'T LET THE BASTARDS GET YOU DOWN, T. WE'LL GET THROUGH THIS.
Further, please be advised that you may be deposed, under oath, at the time of such production on any and all matters related to the data.
You may choose to be represented by counsel, if you so desire, but counsel may not interfere with your obligation to respond to this writ.

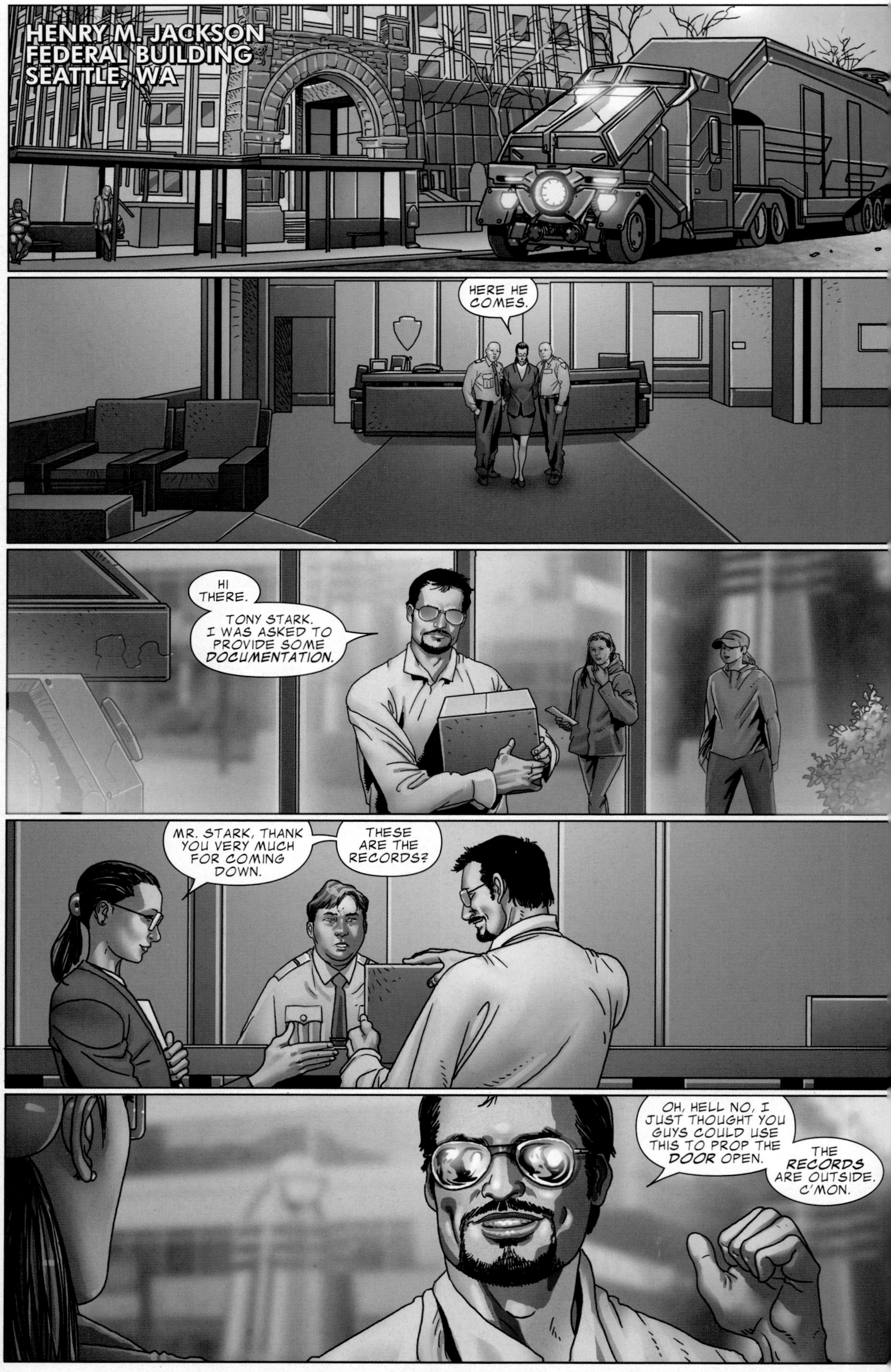
HENRY M. JACKSON FEDERAL BUILDING SEATTLE, WA
HERE HE COMES.
HI THERE.
TONY STARK. I WAS ASKED TO PROVIDE SOME DOCUMENTATION.
MR. STARK, THANK YOU VERY MUCH FOR COMING DOWN.
THESE ARE THE RECORDS?
OH, HELL NO, I JUST THOUGHT YOU GUYS COULD USE THIS TO PROP THE DOOR OPEN.
THE RECORDS ARE OUTSIDE. C'MON.

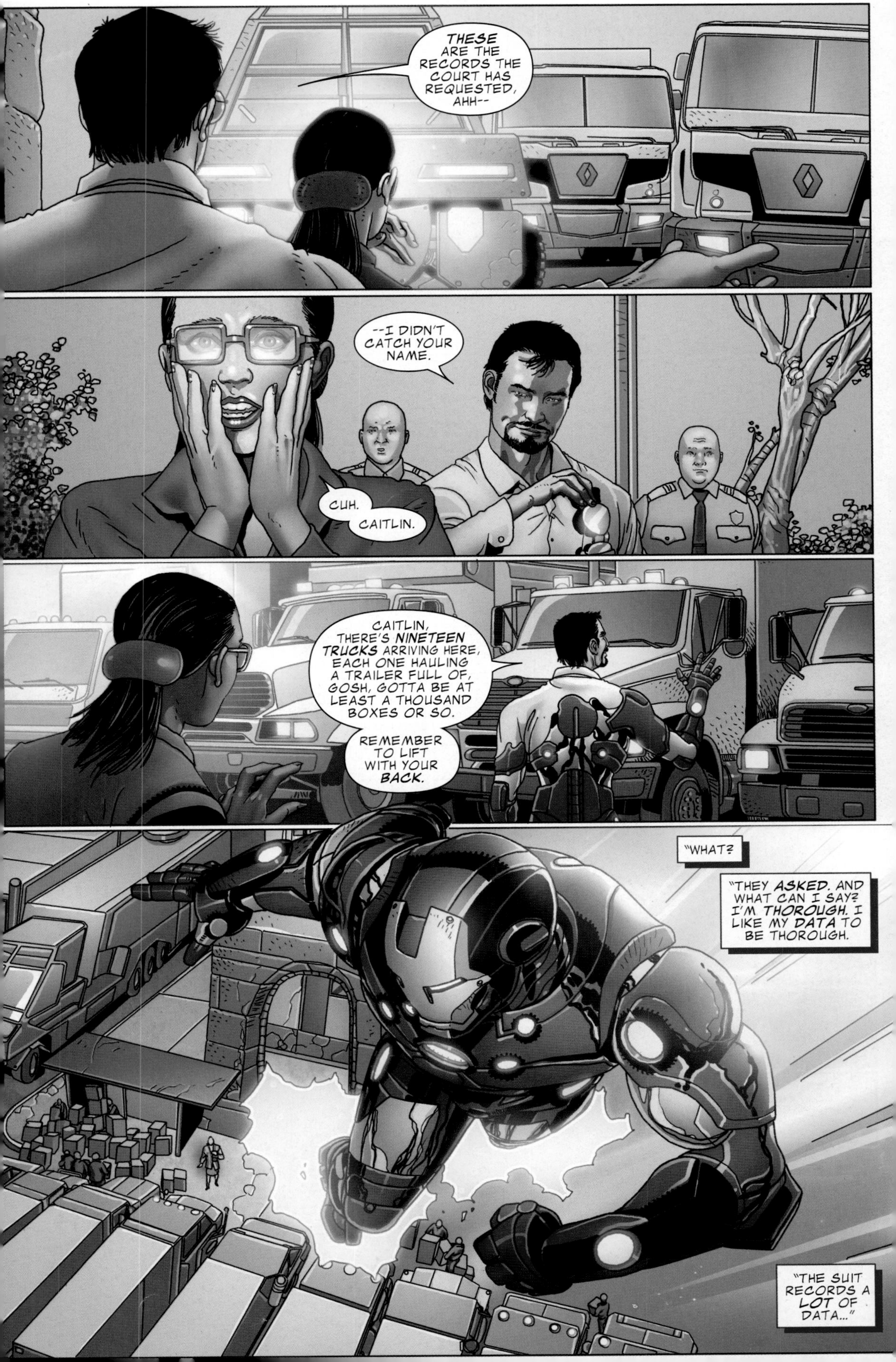
THESE ARE THE RECORDS THE COURT HAS REQUESTED, AHH--
--I DIDN'T CATCH YOUR NAME.
CUH.
CAITLIN.
CAITLIN, THERE'S NINETEEN TRUCKS ARRIVING HERE, EACH ONE HAULING A TRAILER FULL OF, GOSH, GOTTA BE AT LEAST A THOUSAND BOXES OR SO.
REMEMBER TO LIFT WITH YOUR BACK.
"WHAT?
"THEY ASKED. AND WHAT CAN I SAY? I'M THOROUGH. I LIKE MY DATA TO BE THOROUGH.
"THE SUIT RECORDS A LOT OF DATA..."

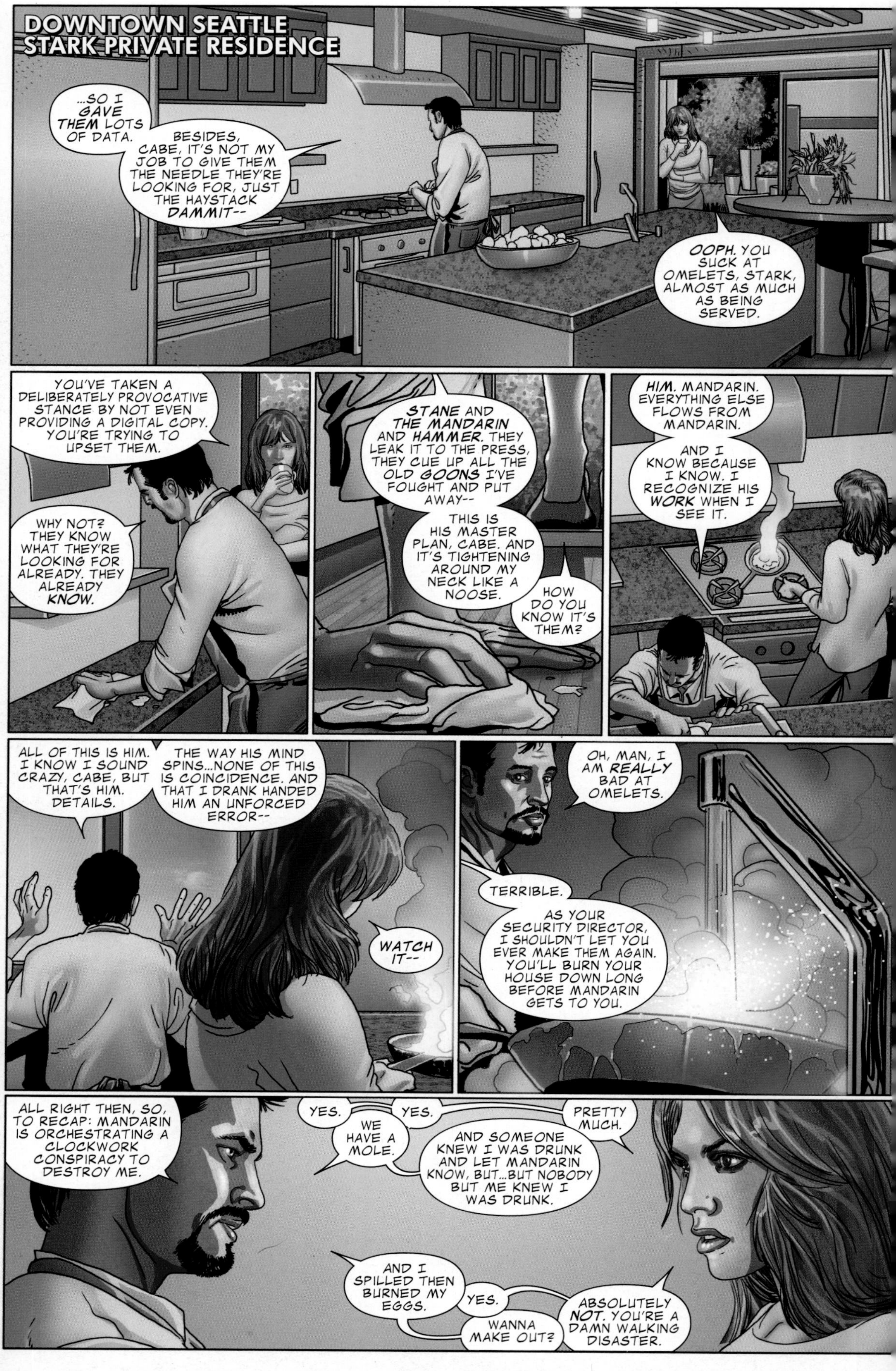
DOWNTOWN SEATTLE
STARK PRIVATE RESIDENCE
...SO I GAVE THEM LOTS OF DATA.
BESIDES, CABE, IT'S NOT MY JOB TO GIVE THEM THE NEEDLE THEY'RE LOOKING FOR, JUST THE HAYSTACK DAMMIT--
OOPH. YOU SUCK AT OMELETS, STARK, ALMOST AS MUCH AS BEING SERVED.
YOU'VE TAKEN A DELIBERATELY PROVOCATIVE STANCE BY NOT EVEN PROVIDING A DIGITAL COPY. YOU'RE TRYING TO UPSET THEM.
WHY NOT? THEY KNOW WHAT THEY'RE LOOKING FOR ALREADY. THEY ALREADY KNOW.
STANE AND THE MANDARIN AND HAMMER. THEY LEAK IT TO THE PRESS, THEY CUE UP ALL THE OLD GOONS I'VE FOUGHT AND PUT AWAY--
THIS IS HIS MASTER PLAN, CABE. AND IT'S TIGHTENING AROUND MY NECK LIKE A NOOSE.
HOW DO YOU KNOW IT'S THEM?
HIM. MANDARIN. EVERYTHING ELSE FLOWS FROM MANDARIN.
AND I KNOW BECAUSE I KNOW. I RECOGNIZE HIS WORK WHEN I SEE IT.
ALL OF THIS IS HIM. I KNOW I SOUND CRAZY, CABE, BUT THAT'S HIM. DETAILS.
THE WAY HIS MIND SPINS...NONE OF THIS IS COINCIDENCE. AND THAT I DRANK HANDED HIM AN UNFORCED ERROR--
WATCH IT--
OH, MAN, I AM REALLY BAD AT OMELETS.
TERRIBLE.
AS YOUR SECURITY DIRECTOR, I SHOULDN'T LET YOU EVER MAKE THEM AGAIN. YOU'LL BURN YOUR HOUSE DOWN LONG BEFORE MANDARIN GETS TO YOU.
ALL RIGHT THEN, SO, TO RECAP: MANDARIN IS ORCHESTRATING A CLOCKWORK CONSPIRACY TO DESTROY ME.
YES.
WE HAVE A MOLE.
YES.
AND SOMEONE KNEW I WAS DRUNK AND LET MANDARIN KNOW, BUT...BUT NOBODY BUT ME KNEW I WAS DRUNK.
PRETTY MUCH.
AND I SPILLED THEN BURNED MY EGGS.
YES.
WANNA MAKE OUT?
ABSOLUTELY NOT. YOU'RE A DAMN WALKING DISASTER.

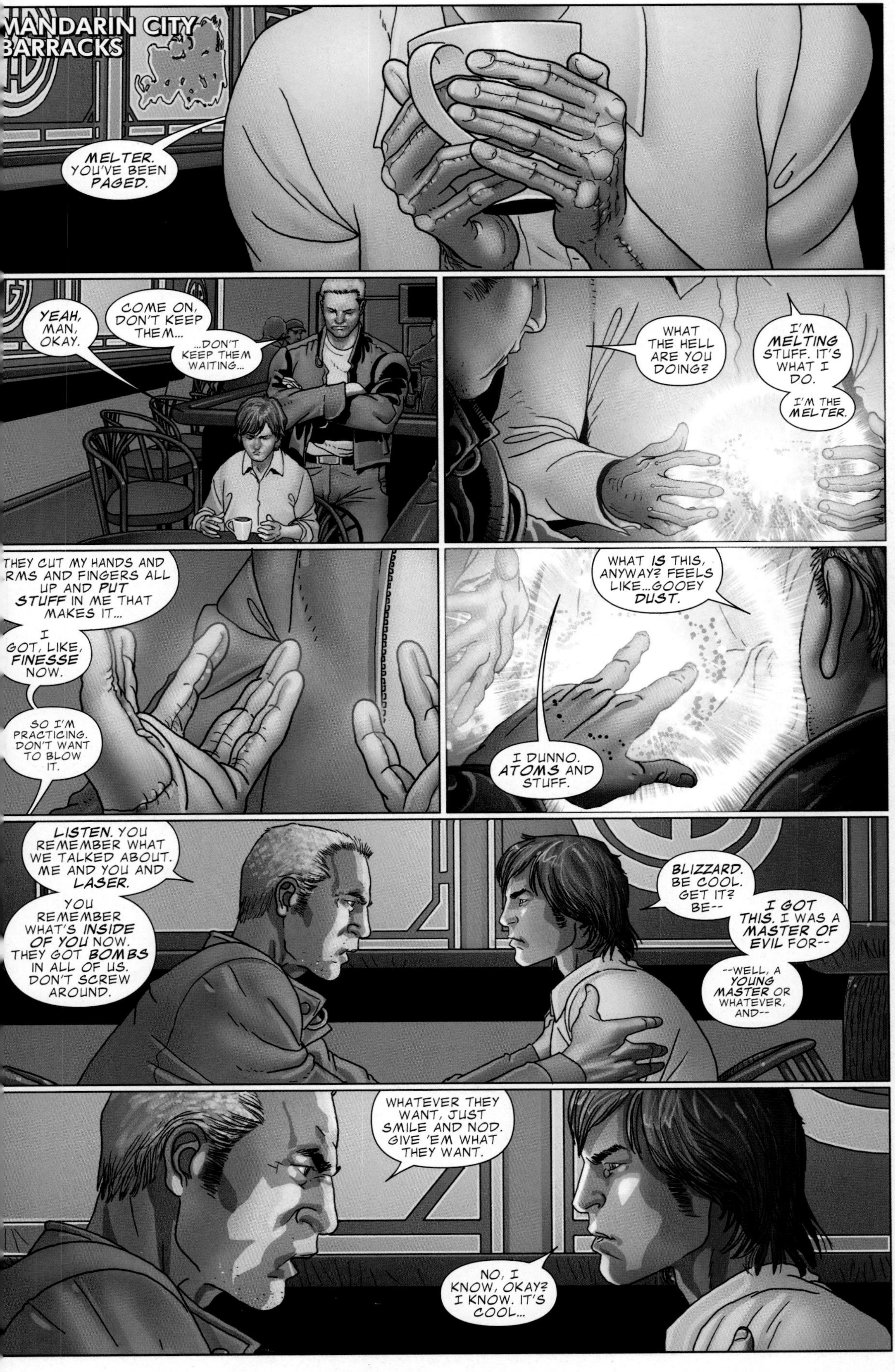

MANDARIN CITY BARRACKS
MELTER. YOU'VE BEEN PAGED.
YEAH, MAN, OKAY.
COME ON, DON'T KEEP THEM...
...DON'T KEEP THEM WAITING...
WHAT THE HELL ARE YOU DOING?
I'M MELTING STUFF. IT'S WHAT I DO.
I'M THE MELTER.
THEY CUT MY HANDS AND RMS AND FINGERS ALL UP AND PUT STUFF IN ME THAT MAKES IT...
I GOT, LIKE, FINESSE NOW.
SO I'M PRACTICING. DON'T WANT TO BLOW IT.
WHAT IS THIS, ANYWAY? FEELS LIKE...GOOEY DUST.
I DUNNO. ATOMS AND STUFF.
LISTEN. YOU REMEMBER WHAT WE TALKED ABOUT. ME AND YOU AND LASER.
YOU REMEMBER WHAT'S INSIDE OF YOU NOW. THEY GOT BOMBS IN ALL OF US. DON'T SCREW AROUND.
BLIZZARD. BE COOL. GET IT? BE--
I GOT THIS. I WAS A MASTER OF EVIL FOR--
--WELL, A YOUNG MASTER OR WHATEVER, AND--
WHATEVER THEY WANT, JUST SMILE AND NOD. GIVE 'EM WHAT THEY WANT.
NO, I KNOW, OKAY? I KNOW. IT'S COOL...

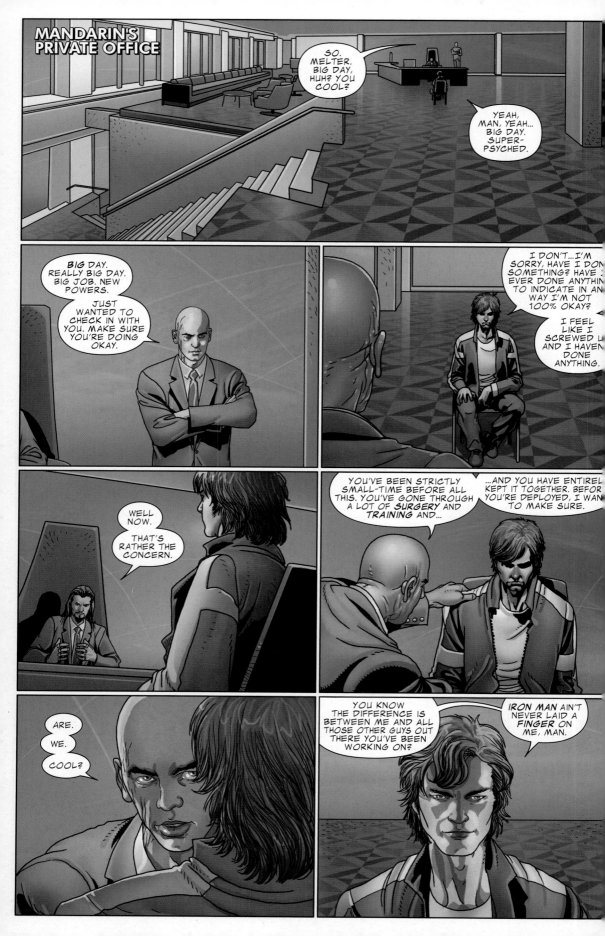

SO. MELTER. BIG DAY, HUH? YOU COOL?

YEAH, MAN, YEAH... BIG DAY. SUPER-PSYCHED.

BIG DAY. REALLY BIG DAY. BIG JOB. NEW POWERS.

JUST WANTED TO CHECK IN WITH YOU. MAKE SURE YOU'RE DOING OKAY.

I DON'T...I'M SORRY, HAVE I DON[E] SOMETHING? HAVE [I] EVER DONE ANYTHIN[G] TO INDICATE IN AN[Y] WAY I'M NOT 100% OKAY?

I FEEL LIKE I SCREWED U[P] AND I HAVEN'[T] DONE ANYTHING.

WELL NOW. THAT'S RATHER THE CONCERN.

YOU'VE BEEN STRICTLY SMALL-TIME BEFORE ALL THIS. YOU'VE GONE THROUGH A LOT OF *SURGERY* AND *TRAINING* AND...

...AND YOU HAVE ENTIREL[Y] KEPT IT TOGETHER. BEFOR[E] YOU'RE DEPLOYED, I WAN[T] TO MAKE SURE.

ARE. WE. COOL?

YOU KNOW THE DIFFERENCE IS BETWEEN ME AND ALL THOSE OTHER GUYS OUT THERE YOU'VE BEEN WORKING ON?

IRON MAN AIN'T NEVER LAID A *FINGER* ON ME, MAN.

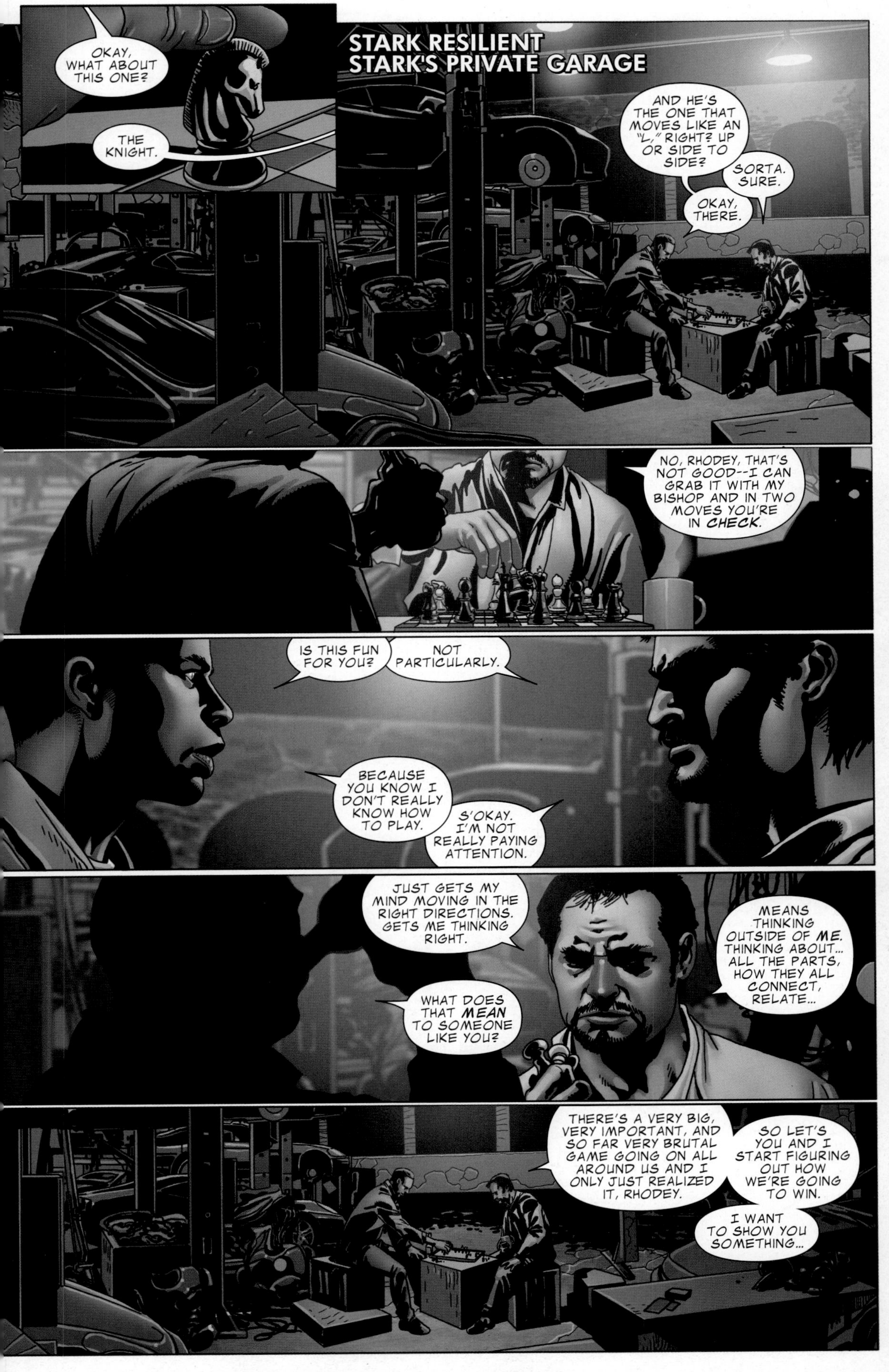

OKAY, WHAT ABOUT THIS ONE?
STARK RESILIENT STARK'S PRIVATE GARAGE
THE KNIGHT.
AND HE'S THE ONE THAT MOVES LIKE AN "L," RIGHT? UP OR SIDE TO SIDE?
SORTA. SURE.
OKAY, THERE.
NO, RHODEY, THAT'S NOT GOOD--I CAN GRAB IT WITH MY BISHOP AND IN TWO MOVES YOU'RE IN CHECK.
IS THIS FUN FOR YOU?
NOT PARTICULARLY.
BECAUSE YOU KNOW I DON'T REALLY KNOW HOW TO PLAY.
S'OKAY. I'M NOT REALLY PAYING ATTENTION.
JUST GETS MY MIND MOVING IN THE RIGHT DIRECTIONS. GETS ME THINKING RIGHT.
WHAT DOES THAT MEAN TO SOMEONE LIKE YOU?
MEANS THINKING OUTSIDE OF ME. THINKING ABOUT... ALL THE PARTS, HOW THEY ALL CONNECT, RELATE...
THERE'S A VERY BIG, VERY IMPORTANT, AND SO FAR VERY BRUTAL GAME GOING ON ALL AROUND US AND I ONLY JUST REALIZED IT, RHODEY.
SO LET'S YOU AND I START FIGURING OUT HOW WE'RE GOING TO WIN.
I WANT TO SHOW YOU SOMETHING...

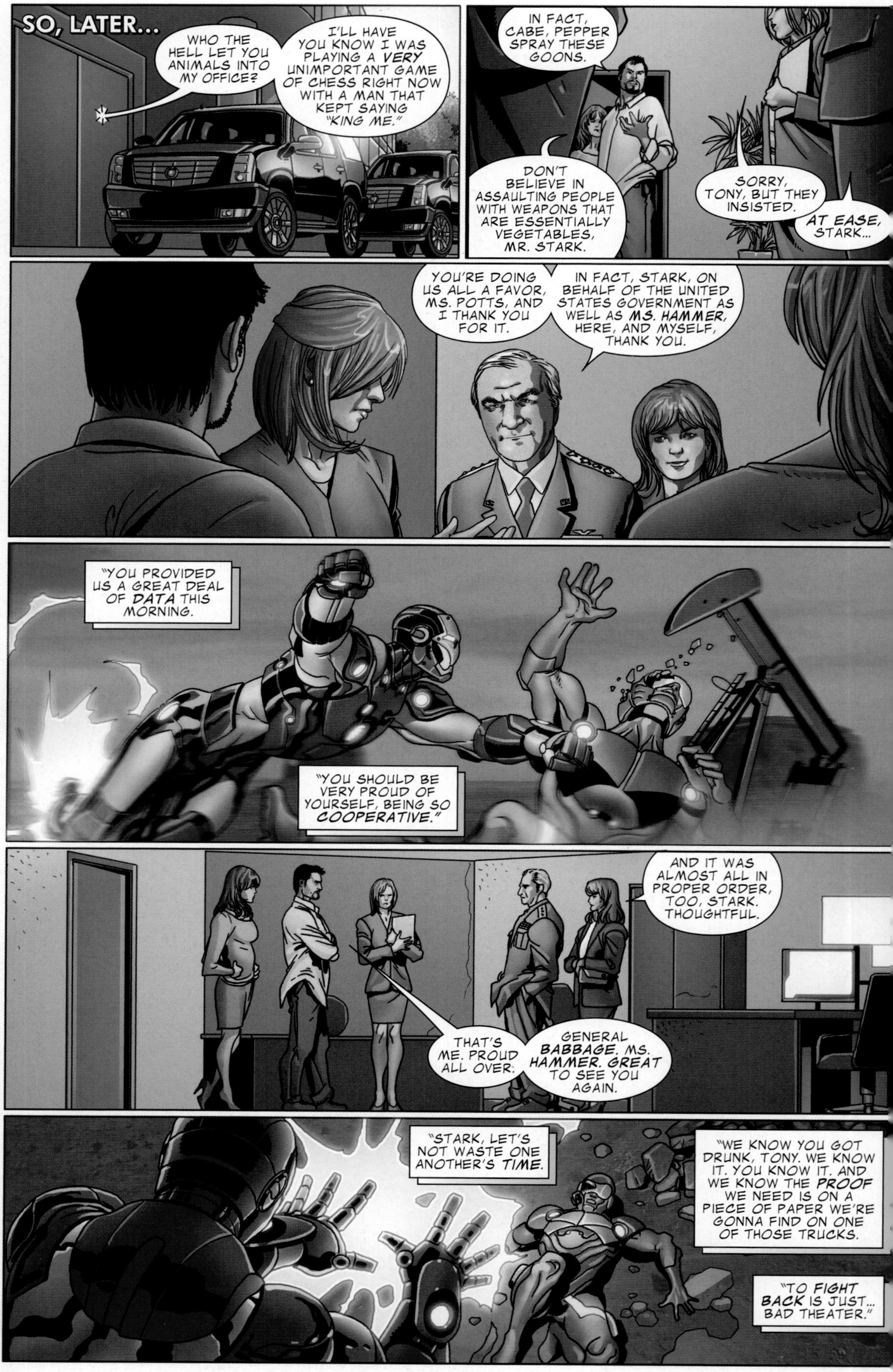
SO, LATER...
WHO THE HELL LET YOU ANIMALS INTO MY OFFICE?
I'LL HAVE YOU KNOW I WAS PLAYING A VERY UNIMPORTANT GAME OF CHESS RIGHT NOW WITH A MAN THAT KEPT SAYING "KING ME."
IN FACT, CABE, PEPPER SPRAY THESE GOONS.
DON'T BELIEVE IN ASSAULTING PEOPLE WITH WEAPONS THAT ARE ESSENTIALLY VEGETABLES, MR. STARK.
SORRY, TONY, BUT THEY INSISTED.
AT EASE, STARK...
YOU'RE DOING US ALL A FAVOR, MS. POTTS, AND I THANK YOU FOR IT.
IN FACT, STARK, ON BEHALF OF THE UNITED STATES GOVERNMENT AS WELL AS MS. HAMMER, HERE, AND MYSELF, THANK YOU.
"YOU PROVIDED US A GREAT DEAL OF DATA THIS MORNING.
"YOU SHOULD BE VERY PROUD OF YOURSELF, BEING SO COOPERATIVE."
AND IT WAS ALMOST ALL IN PROPER ORDER, TOO, STARK. THOUGHTFUL.
THAT'S ME. PROUD ALL OVER.
GENERAL BABBAGE. MS. HAMMER. GREAT TO SEE YOU AGAIN.
"STARK, LET'S NOT WASTE ONE ANOTHER'S TIME.
"WE KNOW YOU GOT DRUNK, TONY. WE KNOW IT. YOU KNOW IT. AND WE KNOW THE PROOF WE NEED IS ON A PIECE OF PAPER WE'RE GONNA FIND ON ONE OF THOSE TRUCKS.
"TO FIGHT BACK IS JUST... BAD THEATER."

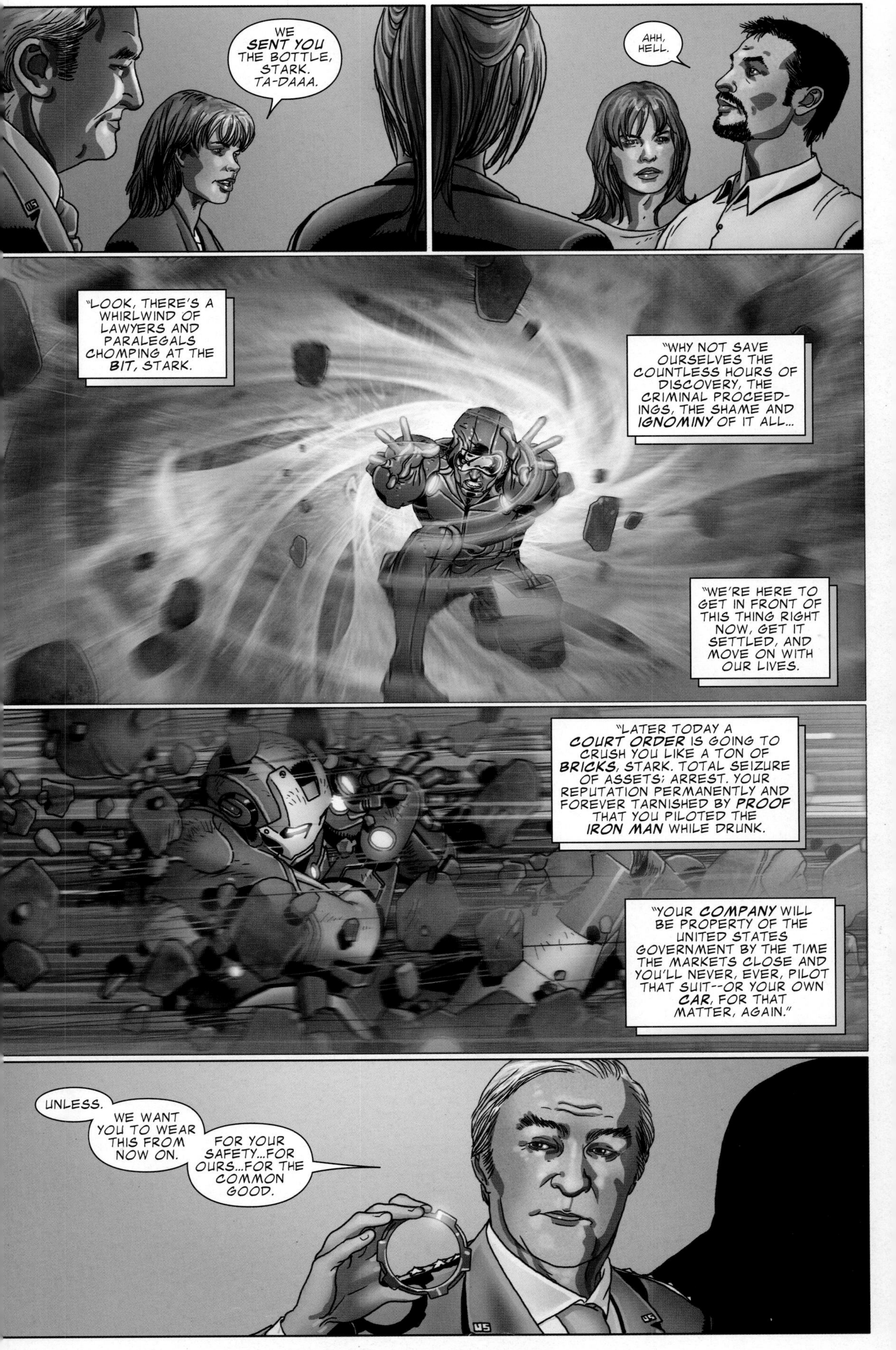

WE SENT YOU THE BOTTLE, STARK. TA-DAAA.
AHH, HELL.
"LOOK, THERE'S A WHIRLWIND OF LAWYERS AND PARALEGALS CHOMPING AT THE BIT, STARK.
"WHY NOT SAVE OURSELVES THE COUNTLESS HOURS OF DISCOVERY, THE CRIMINAL PROCEEDINGS, THE SHAME AND IGNOMINY OF IT ALL...
"WE'RE HERE TO GET IN FRONT OF THIS THING RIGHT NOW, GET IT SETTLED, AND MOVE ON WITH OUR LIVES.
"LATER TODAY A COURT ORDER IS GOING TO CRUSH YOU LIKE A TON OF BRICKS, STARK. TOTAL SEIZURE OF ASSETS; ARREST. YOUR REPUTATION PERMANENTLY AND FOREVER TARNISHED BY PROOF THAT YOU PILOTED THE IRON MAN WHILE DRUNK.
"YOUR COMPANY WILL BE PROPERTY OF THE UNITED STATES GOVERNMENT BY THE TIME THE MARKETS CLOSE AND YOU'LL NEVER, EVER, PILOT THAT SUIT--OR YOUR OWN CAR, FOR THAT MATTER, AGAIN."
UNLESS.
WE WANT YOU TO WEAR THIS FROM NOW ON.
FOR YOUR SAFETY...FOR OURS...FOR THE COMMON GOOD.

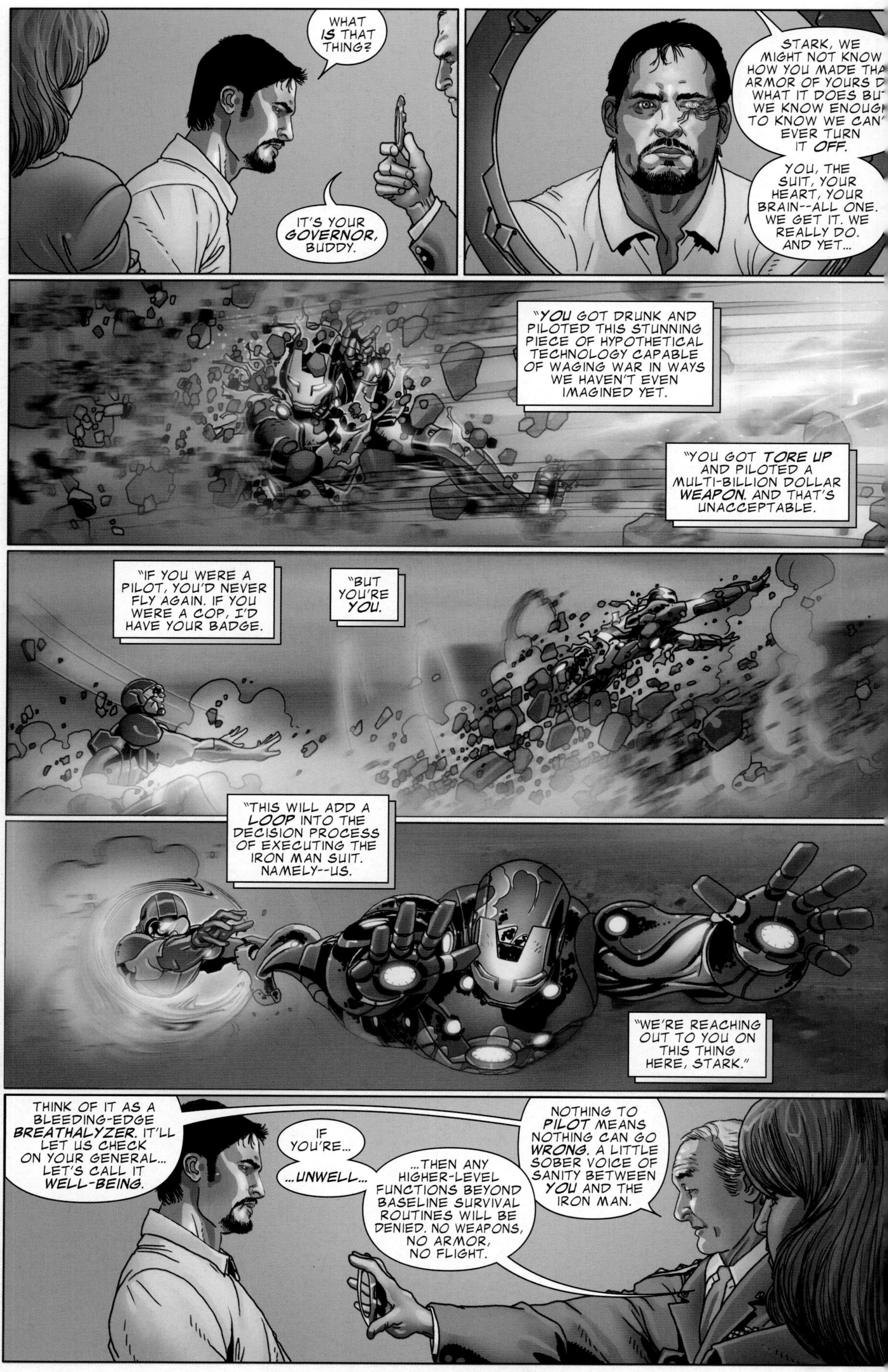
WHAT IS THAT THING?
IT'S YOUR GOVERNOR, BUDDY.
STARK, WE MIGHT NOT KNOW HOW YOU MADE THA ARMOR OF YOURS D WHAT IT DOES BU WE KNOW ENOUG TO KNOW WE CAN' EVER TURN IT OFF.
YOU, THE SUIT, YOUR HEART, YOUR BRAIN--ALL ONE. WE GET IT. WE REALLY DO. AND YET...
"YOU GOT DRUNK AND PILOTED THIS STUNNING PIECE OF HYPOTHETICAL TECHNOLOGY CAPABLE OF WAGING WAR IN WAYS WE HAVEN'T EVEN IMAGINED YET.
"YOU GOT TORE UP AND PILOTED A MULTI-BILLION DOLLAR WEAPON. AND THAT'S UNACCEPTABLE.
"IF YOU WERE A PILOT, YOU'D NEVER FLY AGAIN. IF YOU WERE A COP, I'D HAVE YOUR BADGE.
"BUT YOU'RE YOU.
"THIS WILL ADD A LOOP INTO THE DECISION PROCESS OF EXECUTING THE IRON MAN SUIT. NAMELY--US.
"WE'RE REACHING OUT TO YOU ON THIS THING HERE, STARK."
THINK OF IT AS A BLEEDING-EDGE BREATHALYZER. IT'LL LET US CHECK ON YOUR GENERAL... LET'S CALL IT WELL-BEING.
IF YOU'RE...
...UNWELL...
...THEN ANY HIGHER-LEVEL FUNCTIONS BEYOND BASELINE SURVIVAL ROUTINES WILL BE DENIED. NO WEAPONS, NO ARMOR, NO FLIGHT.
NOTHING TO PILOT MEANS NOTHING CAN GO WRONG. A LITTLE SOBER VOICE OF SANITY BETWEEN YOU AND THE IRON MAN.

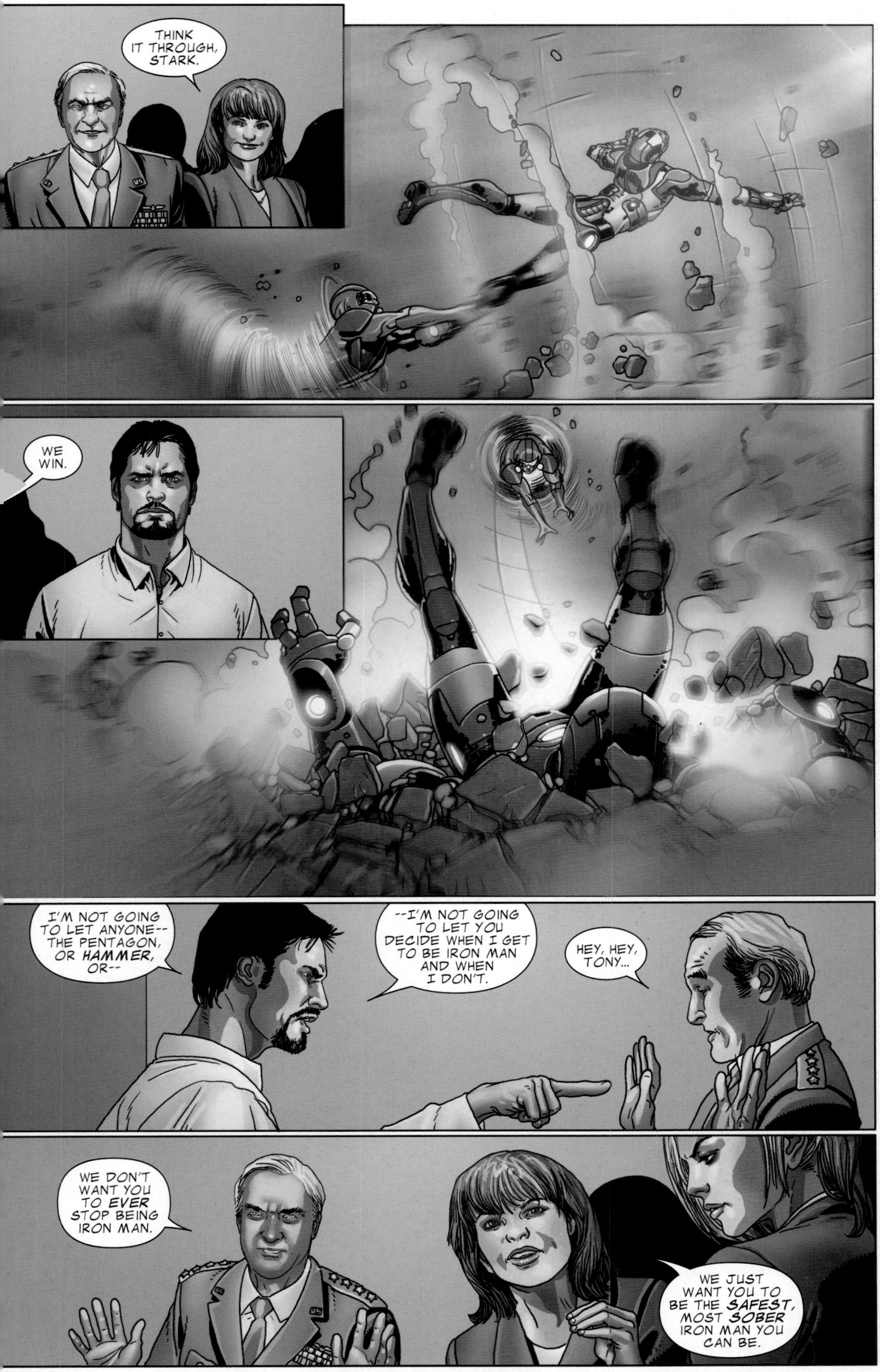
THINK IT THROUGH, STARK.
WE WIN.
I'M NOT GOING TO LET ANYONE-- THE PENTAGON, OR HAMMER, OR--
--I'M NOT GOING TO LET YOU DECIDE WHEN I GET TO BE IRON MAN AND WHEN I DON'T.
HEY, HEY, TONY...
WE DON'T WANT YOU TO EVER STOP BEING IRON MAN.
WE JUST WANT YOU TO BE THE SAFEST, MOST SOBER IRON MAN YOU CAN BE.

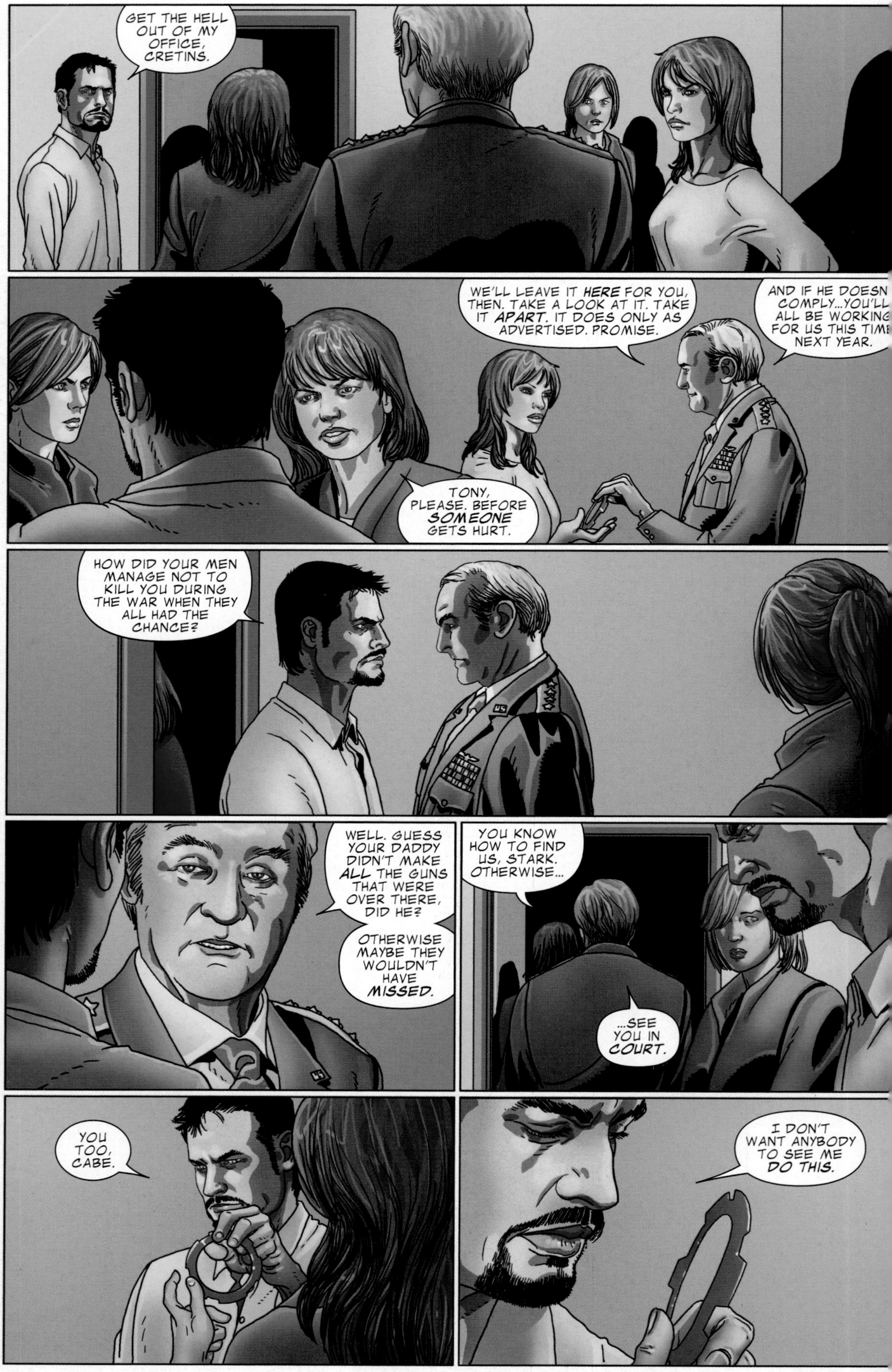
GET THE HELL OUT OF MY OFFICE, CRETINS.
WE'LL LEAVE IT HERE FOR YOU, THEN. TAKE A LOOK AT IT. TAKE IT APART. IT DOES ONLY AS ADVERTISED. PROMISE.
AND IF HE DOESN COMPLY...YOU'LL ALL BE WORKING FOR US THIS TIME NEXT YEAR.
TONY, PLEASE. BEFORE SOMEONE GETS HURT.
HOW DID YOUR MEN MANAGE NOT TO KILL YOU DURING THE WAR WHEN THEY ALL HAD THE CHANCE?
WELL. GUESS YOUR DADDY DIDN'T MAKE ALL THE GUNS THAT WERE OVER THERE, DID HE?
OTHERWISE MAYBE THEY WOULDN'T HAVE MISSED.
YOU KNOW HOW TO FIND US, STARK. OTHERWISE...
...SEE YOU IN COURT.
YOU TOO, CABE.
I DON'T WANT ANYBODY TO SEE ME DO THIS.

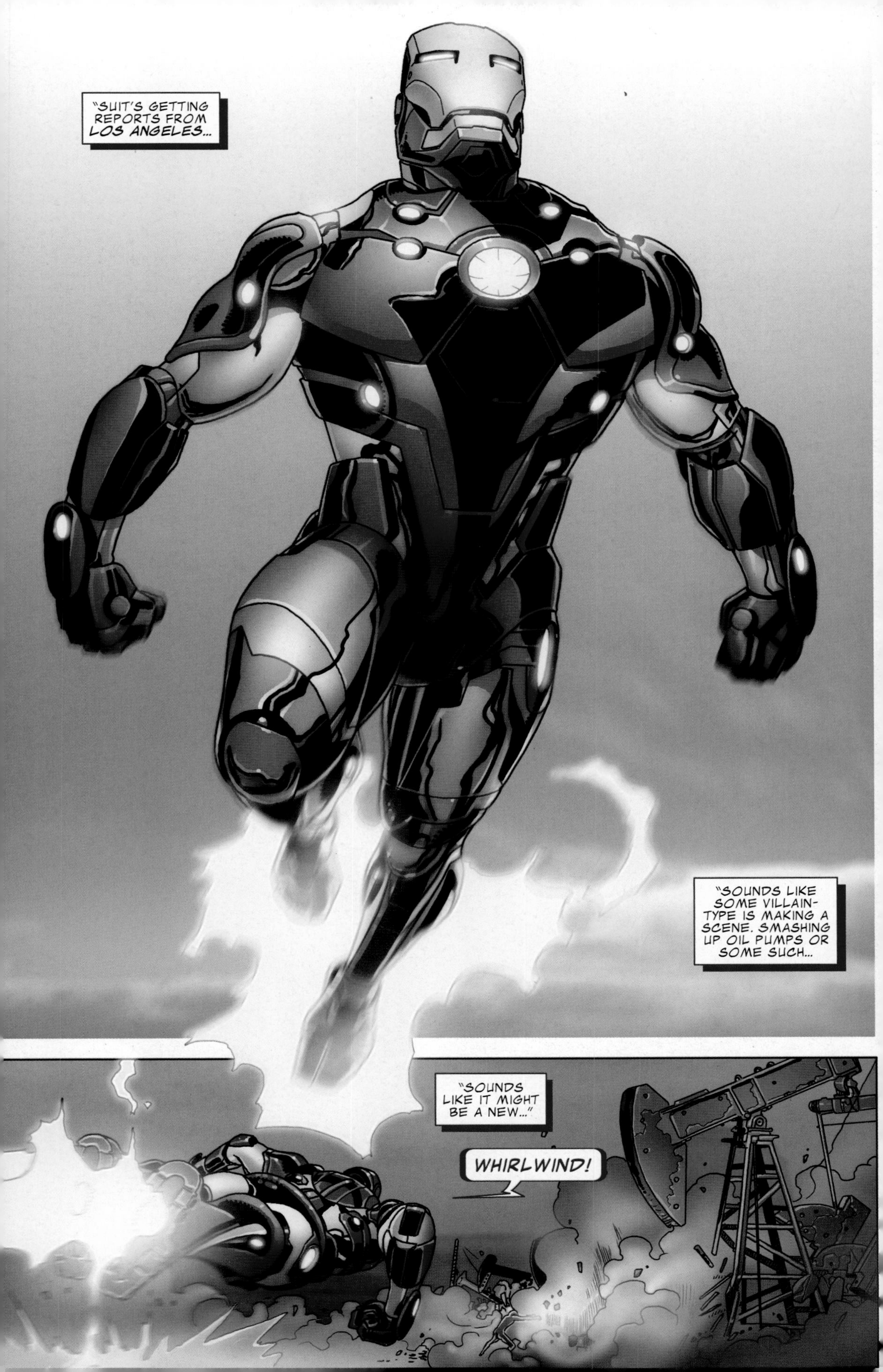
"SUIT'S GETTING REPORTS FROM LOS ANGELES...
"SOUNDS LIKE SOME VILLAIN-TYPE IS MAKING A SCENE. SMASHING UP OIL PUMPS OR SOME SUCH...
"SOUNDS LIKE IT MIGHT BE A NEW..."
WHIRLWIND!

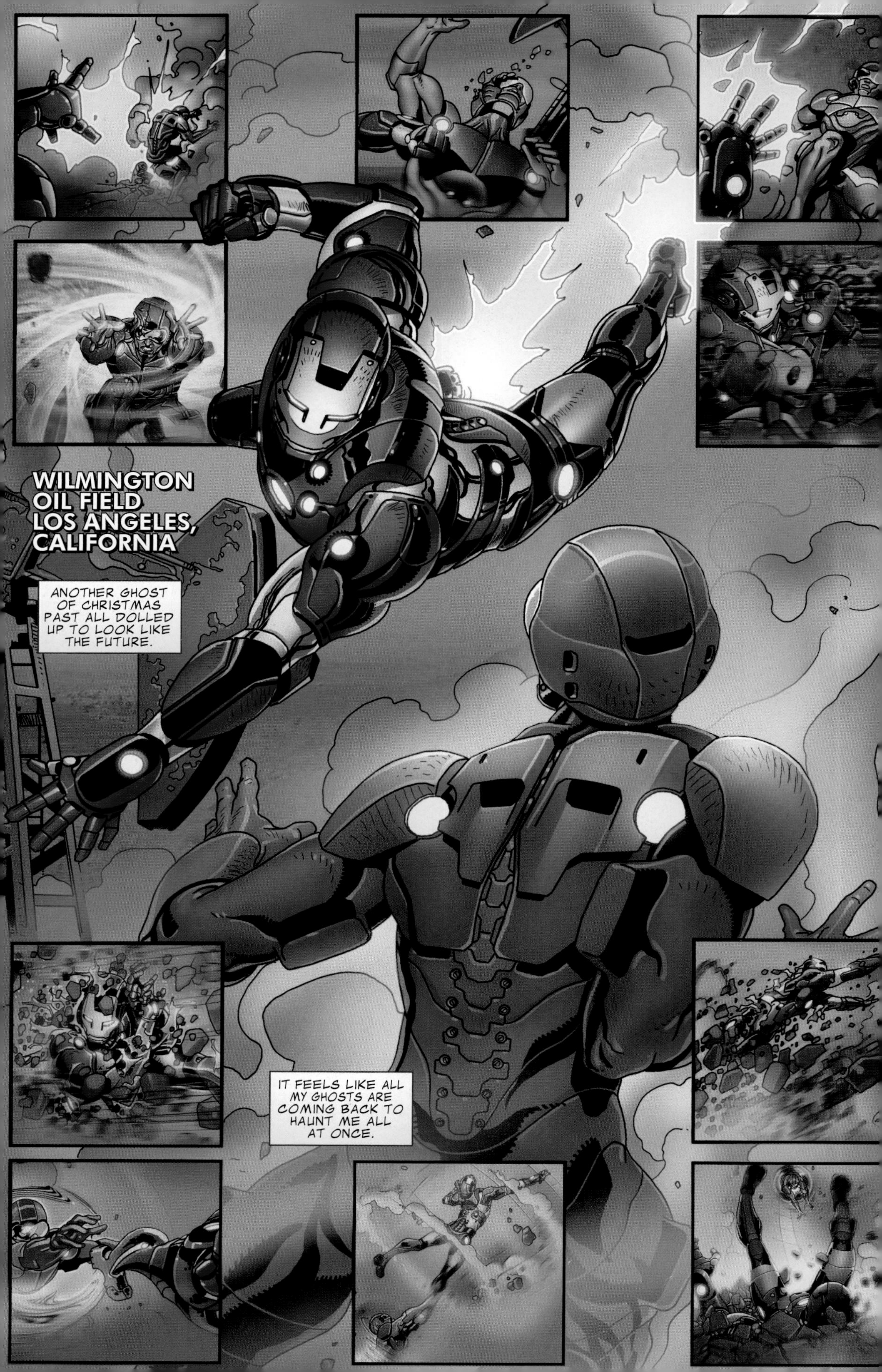
WILMINGTON OIL FIELD LOS ANGELES, CALIFORNIA
ANOTHER GHOST OF CHRISTMAS PAST ALL DOLLED UP TO LOOK LIKE THE FUTURE.
IT FEELS LIKE ALL MY GHOSTS ARE COMING BACK TO HAUNT ME ALL AT ONCE.

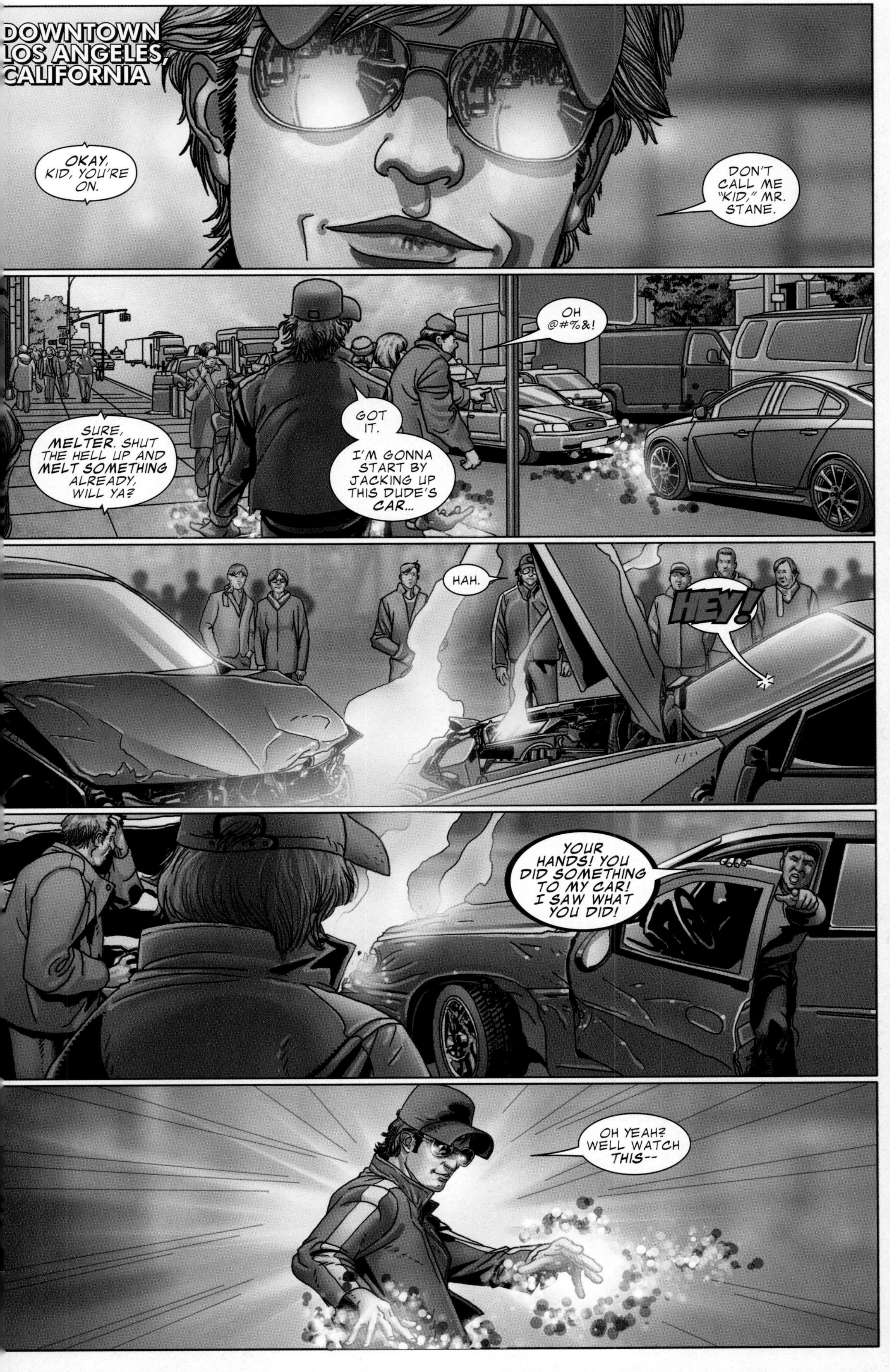
DOWNTOWN LOS ANGELES, CALIFORNIA
OKAY, KID, YOU'RE ON.
DON'T CALL ME "KID," MR. STANE.
SURE, MELTER. SHUT THE HELL UP AND MELT SOMETHING ALREADY, WILL YA?
GOT IT.
I'M GONNA START BY JACKING UP THIS DUDE'S CAR...
OH @#%&!
HAH.
HEY!
YOUR HANDS! YOU DID SOMETHING TO MY CAR! I SAW WHAT YOU DID!
OH YEAH? WELL WATCH THIS--

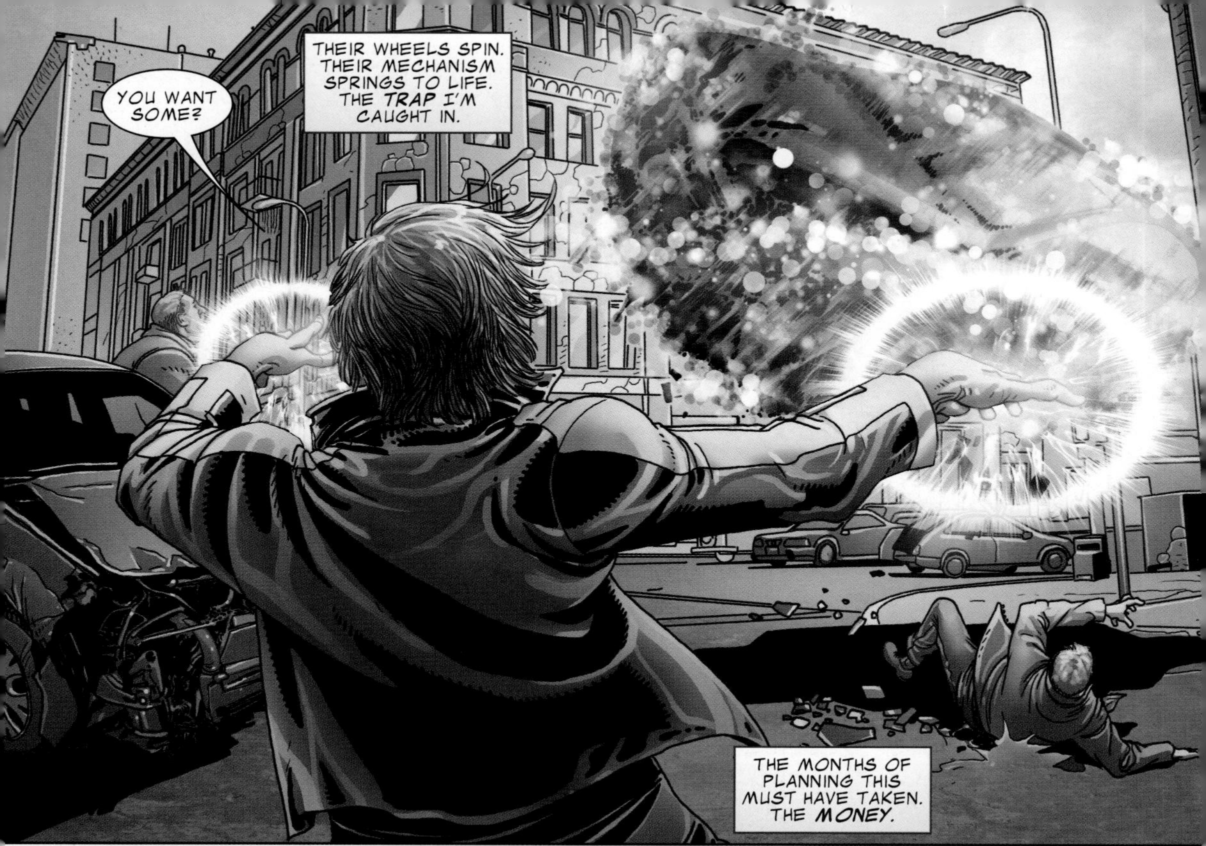
THEIR WHEELS SPIN. THEIR MECHANISM SPRINGS TO LIFE. THE TRAP I'M CAUGHT IN.
YOU WANT SOME?
THE MONTHS OF PLANNING THIS MUST HAVE TAKEN. THE MONEY.
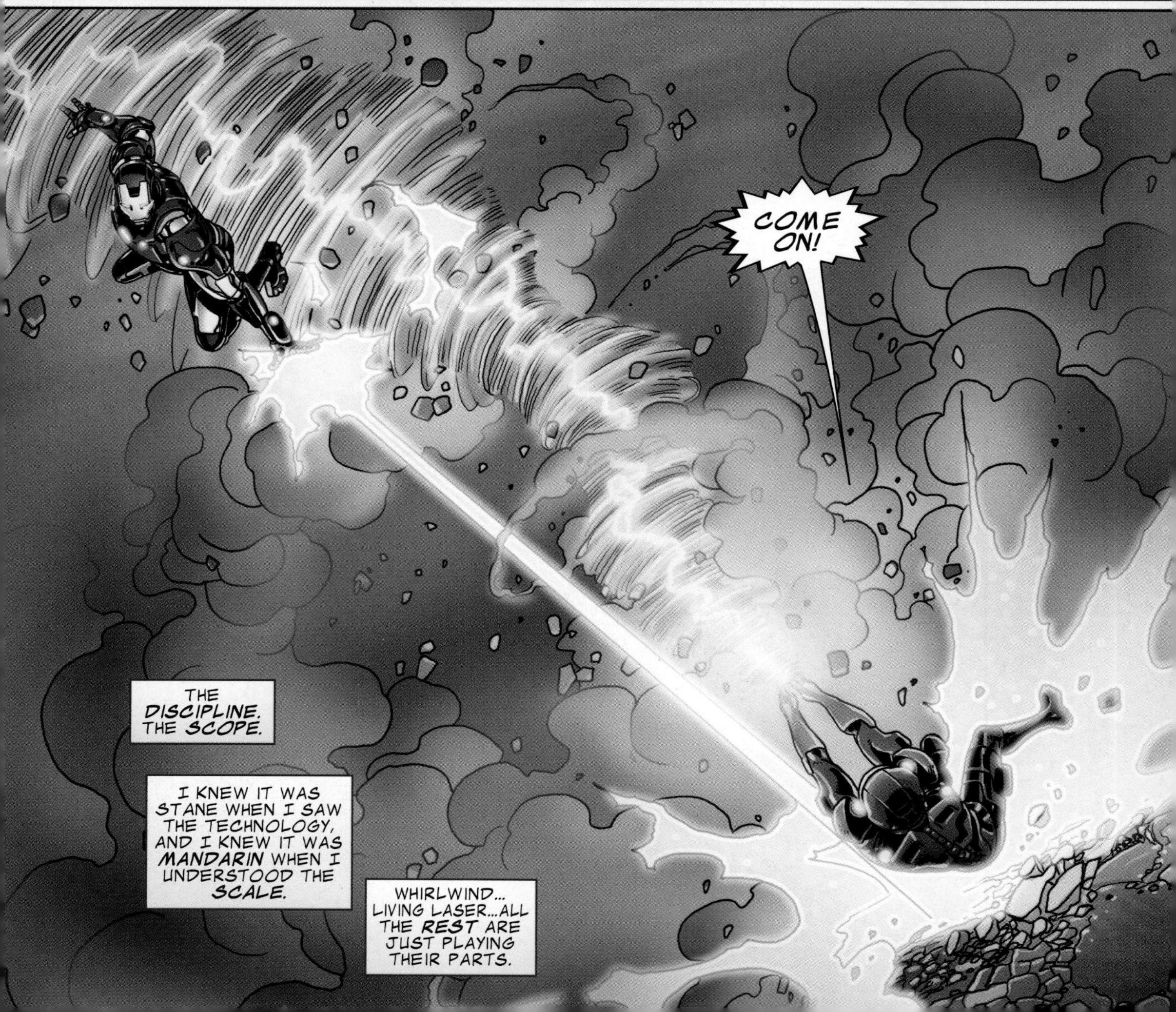
COME ON!
THE DISCIPLINE. THE SCOPE.
I KNEW IT WAS STANE WHEN I SAW THE TECHNOLOGY, AND I KNEW IT WAS MANDARIN WHEN I UNDERSTOOD THE SCALE.
WHIRLWIND... LIVING LASER...ALL THE REST ARE JUST PLAYING THEIR PARTS.

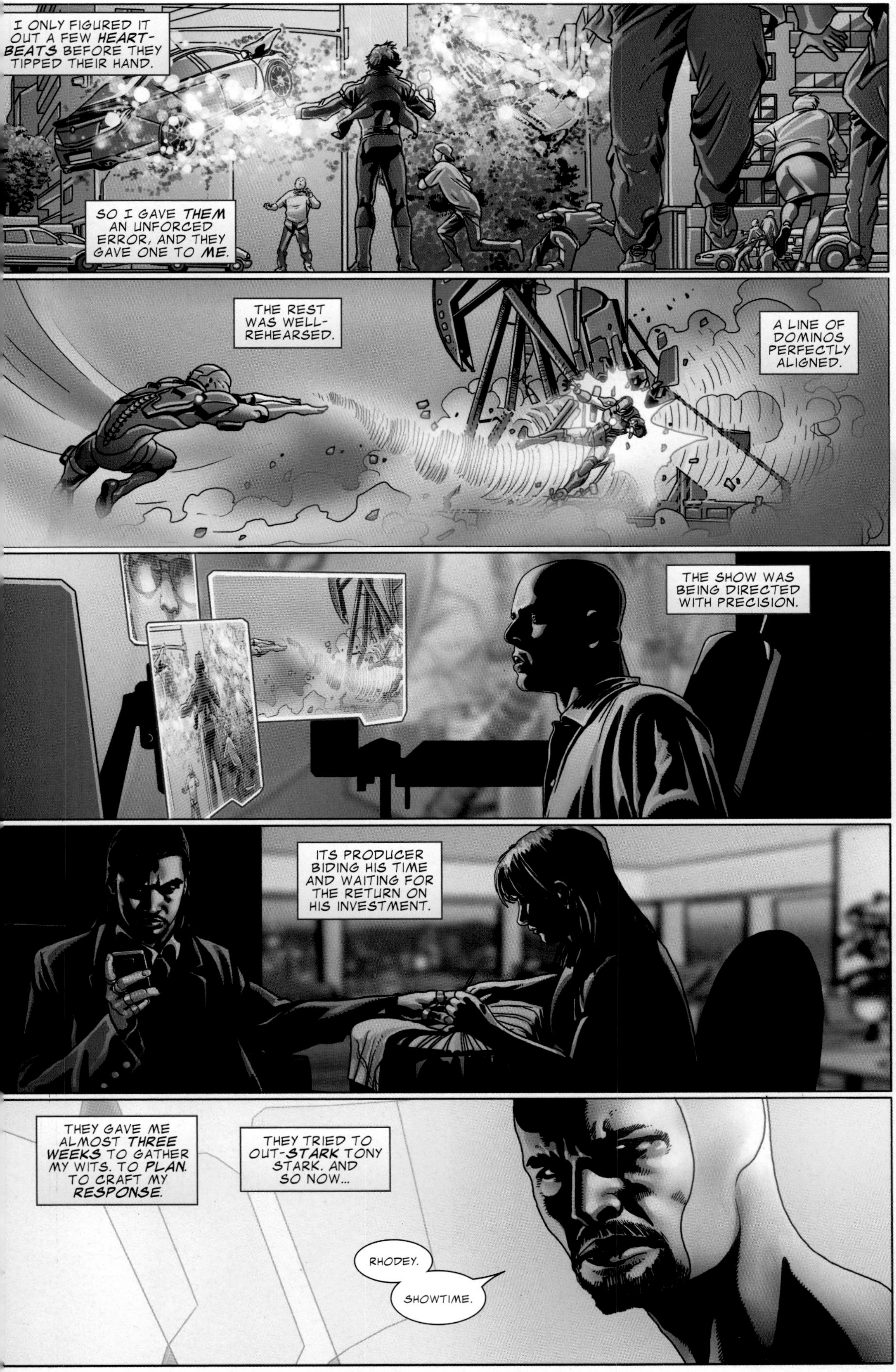
I ONLY FIGURED IT OUT A FEW HEART-BEATS BEFORE THEY TIPPED THEIR HAND.
SO I GAVE THEM AN UNFORCED ERROR, AND THEY GAVE ONE TO ME.
THE REST WAS WELL-REHEARSED.
A LINE OF DOMINOS PERFECTLY ALIGNED.
THE SHOW WAS BEING DIRECTED WITH PRECISION.
ITS PRODUCER BIDING HIS TIME AND WAITING FOR THE RETURN ON HIS INVESTMENT.
THEY GAVE ME ALMOST THREE WEEKS TO GATHER MY WITS. TO PLAN. TO CRAFT MY RESPONSE.
THEY TRIED TO OUT-STARK TONY STARK. AND SO NOW...
RHODEY.
SHOWTIME.

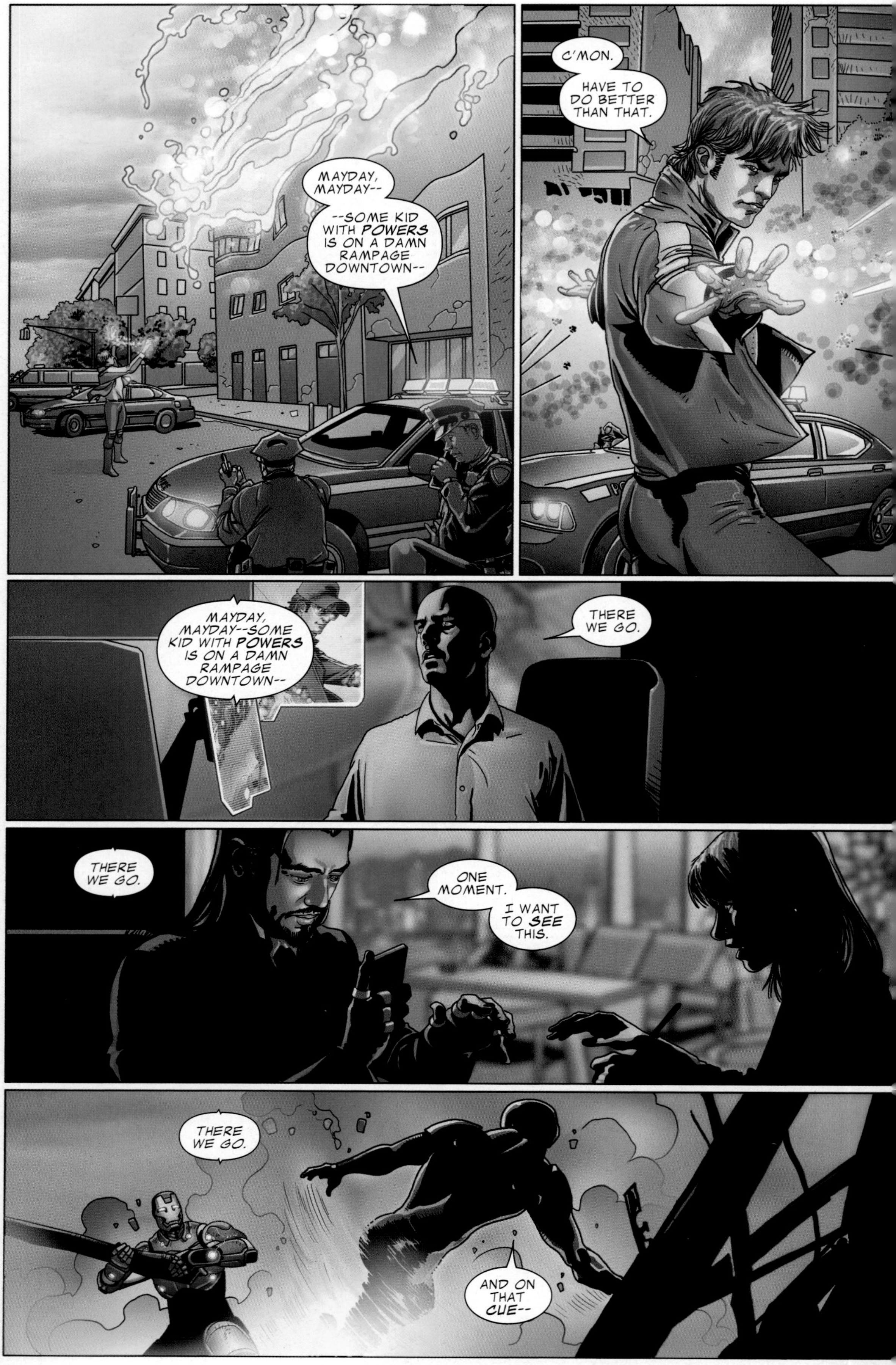
MAYDAY, MAYDAY--
--SOME KID WITH POWERS IS ON A DAMN RAMPAGE DOWNTOWN--
C'MON.
HAVE TO DO BETTER THAN THAT.
MAYDAY, MAYDAY--SOME KID WITH POWERS IS ON A DAMN RAMPAGE DOWNTOWN--
THERE WE GO.
THERE WE GO.
ONE MOMENT.
I WANT TO SEE THIS.
THERE WE GO.
AND ON THAT CUE--

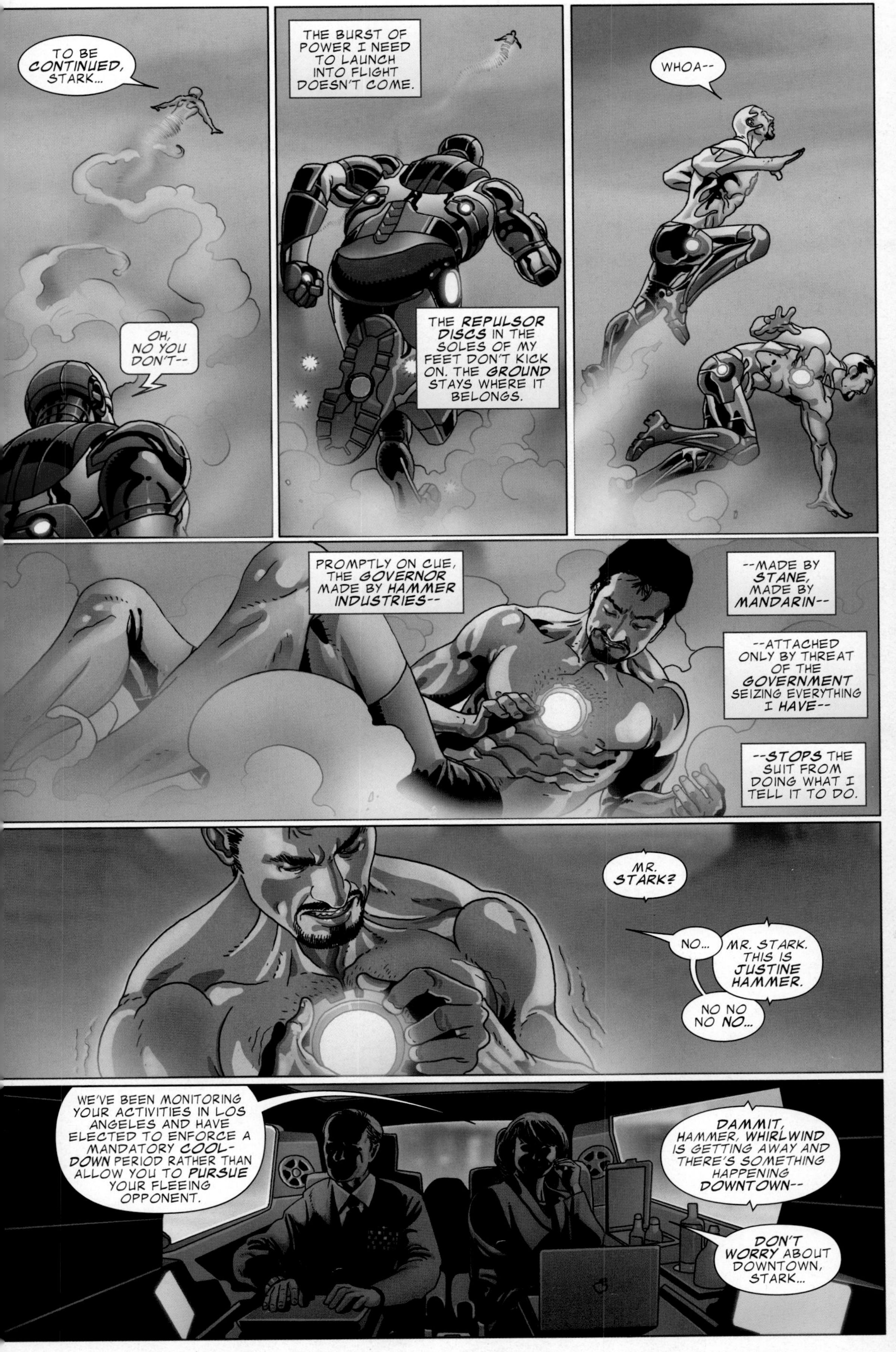
TO BE CONTINUED, STARK...
OH, NO YOU DON'T--
THE BURST OF POWER I NEED TO LAUNCH INTO FLIGHT DOESN'T COME.
THE REPULSOR DISCS IN THE SOLES OF MY FEET DON'T KICK ON. THE GROUND STAYS WHERE IT BELONGS.
WHOA--
PROMPTLY ON CUE, THE GOVERNOR MADE BY HAMMER INDUSTRIES--
--MADE BY STANE, MADE BY MANDARIN--
--ATTACHED ONLY BY THREAT OF THE GOVERNMENT SEIZING EVERYTHING I HAVE--
--STOPS THE SUIT FROM DOING WHAT I TELL IT TO DO.
MR. STARK?
NO...
MR. STARK. THIS IS JUSTINE HAMMER.
NO NO NO NO...
WE'VE BEEN MONITORING YOUR ACTIVITIES IN LOS ANGELES AND HAVE ELECTED TO ENFORCE A MANDATORY COOL-DOWN PERIOD RATHER THAN ALLOW YOU TO PURSUE YOUR FLEEING OPPONENT.
DAMMIT, HAMMER, WHIRLWIND IS GETTING AWAY AND THERE'S SOMETHING HAPPENING DOWNTOWN--
DON'T WORRY ABOUT DOWNTOWN, STARK...

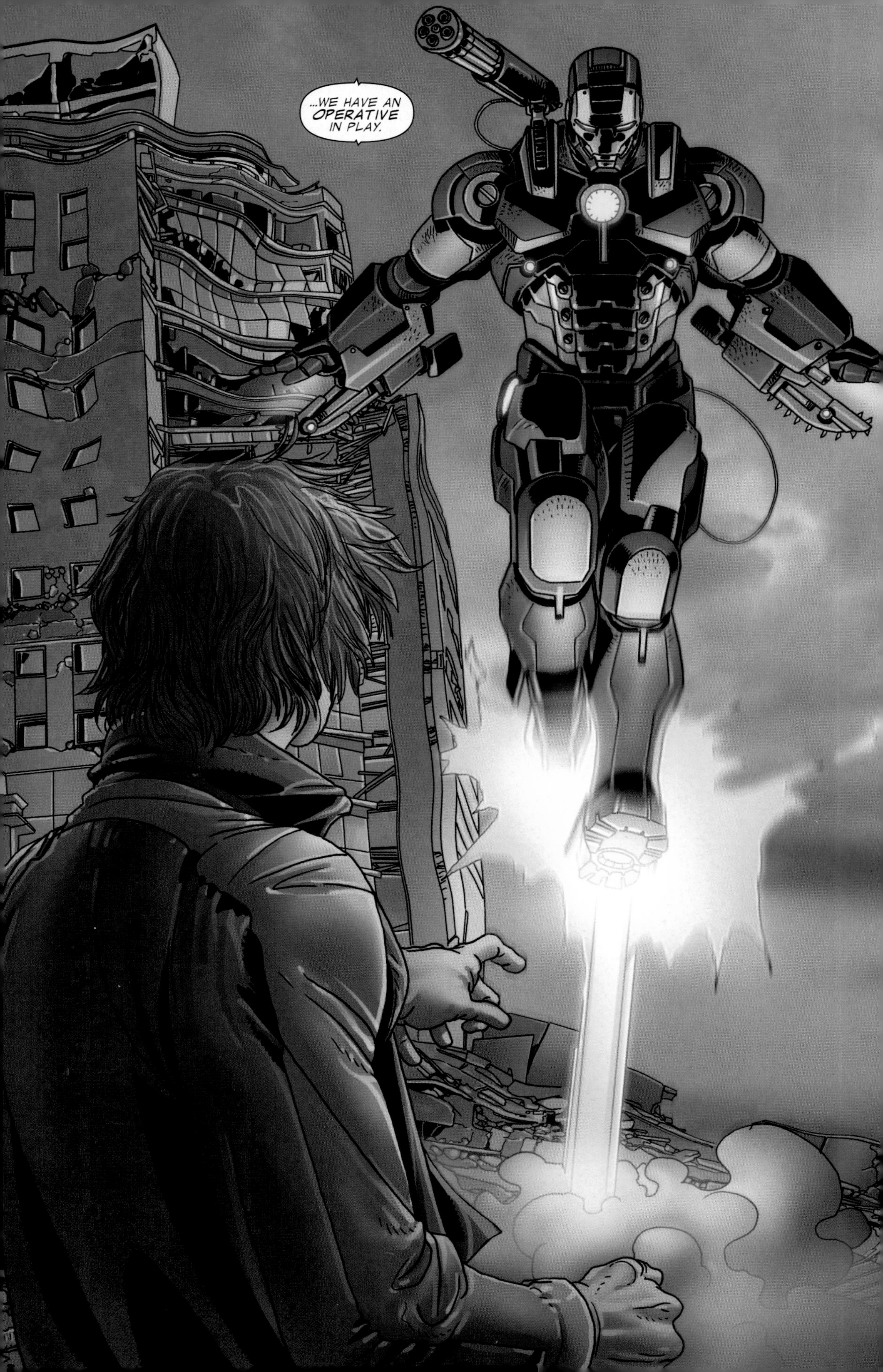
...WE HAVE AN OPERATIVE IN PLAY.

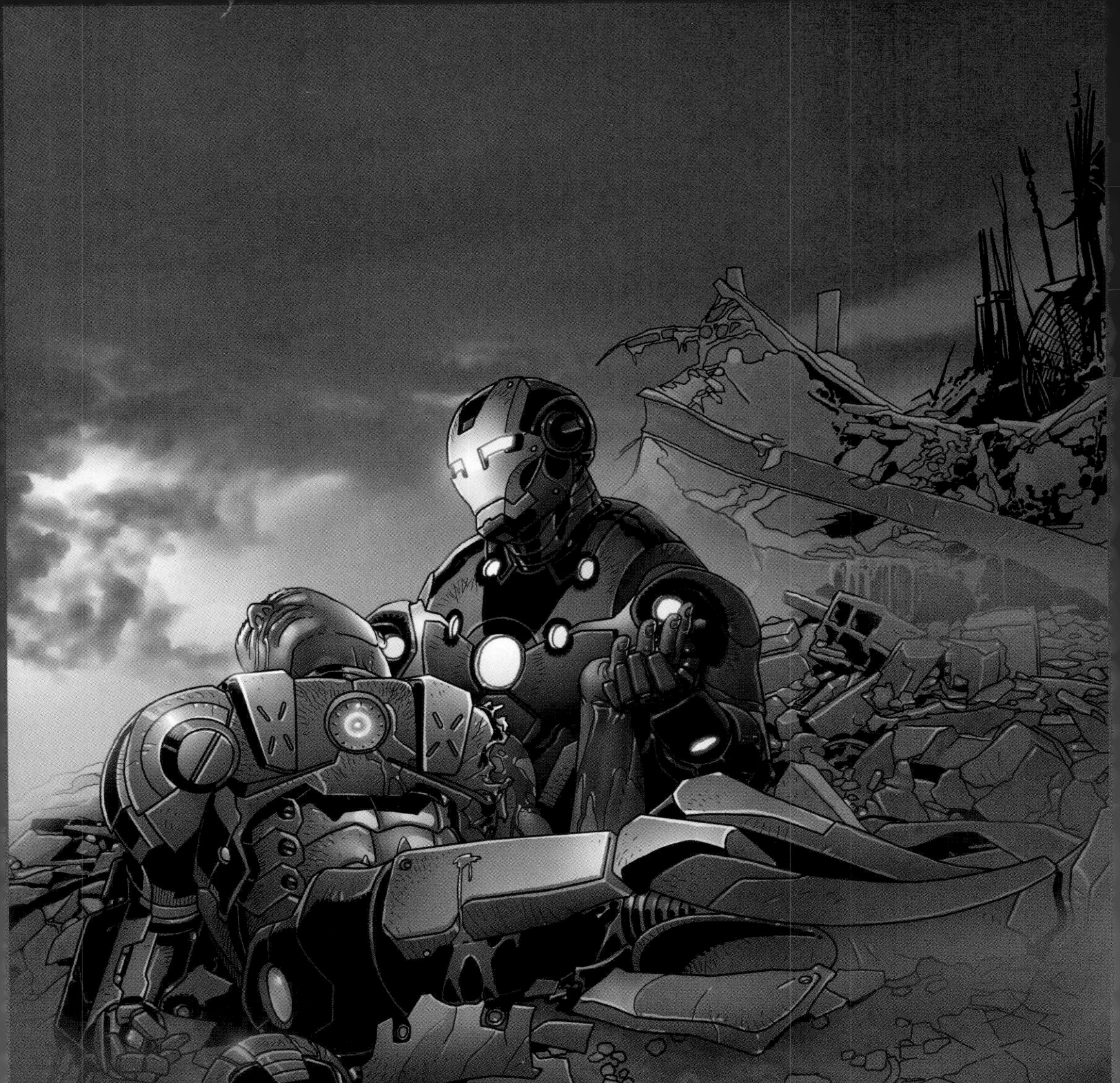

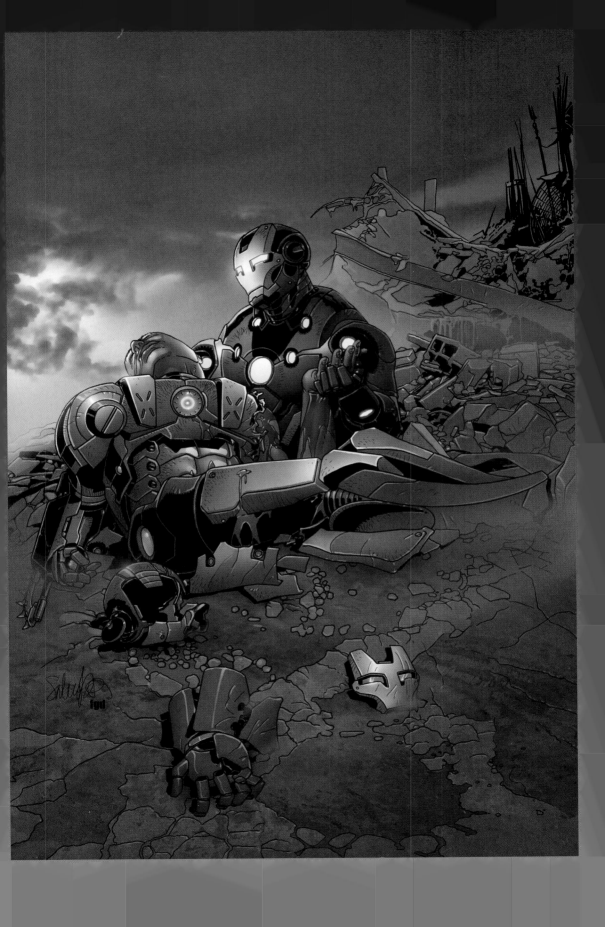

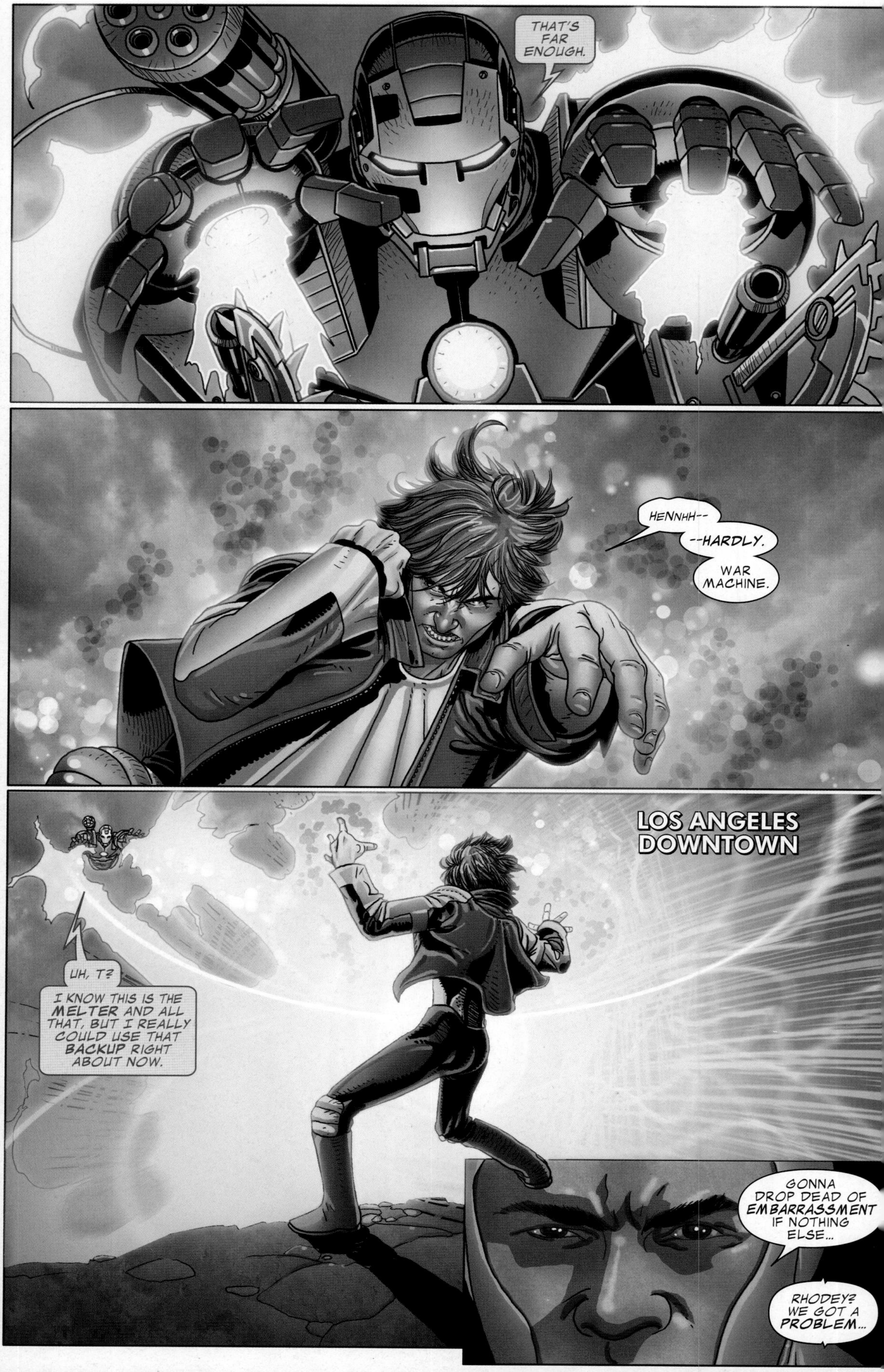
THAT'S FAR ENOUGH.
HENNHH--
--HARDLY.
WAR MACHINE.
LOS ANGELES DOWNTOWN
UH, T?
I KNOW THIS IS THE MELTER AND ALL THAT, BUT I REALLY COULD USE THAT BACKUP RIGHT ABOUT NOW.
GONNA DROP DEAD OF EMBARRASSMENT IF NOTHING ELSE...
RHODEY? WE GOT A PROBLEM...

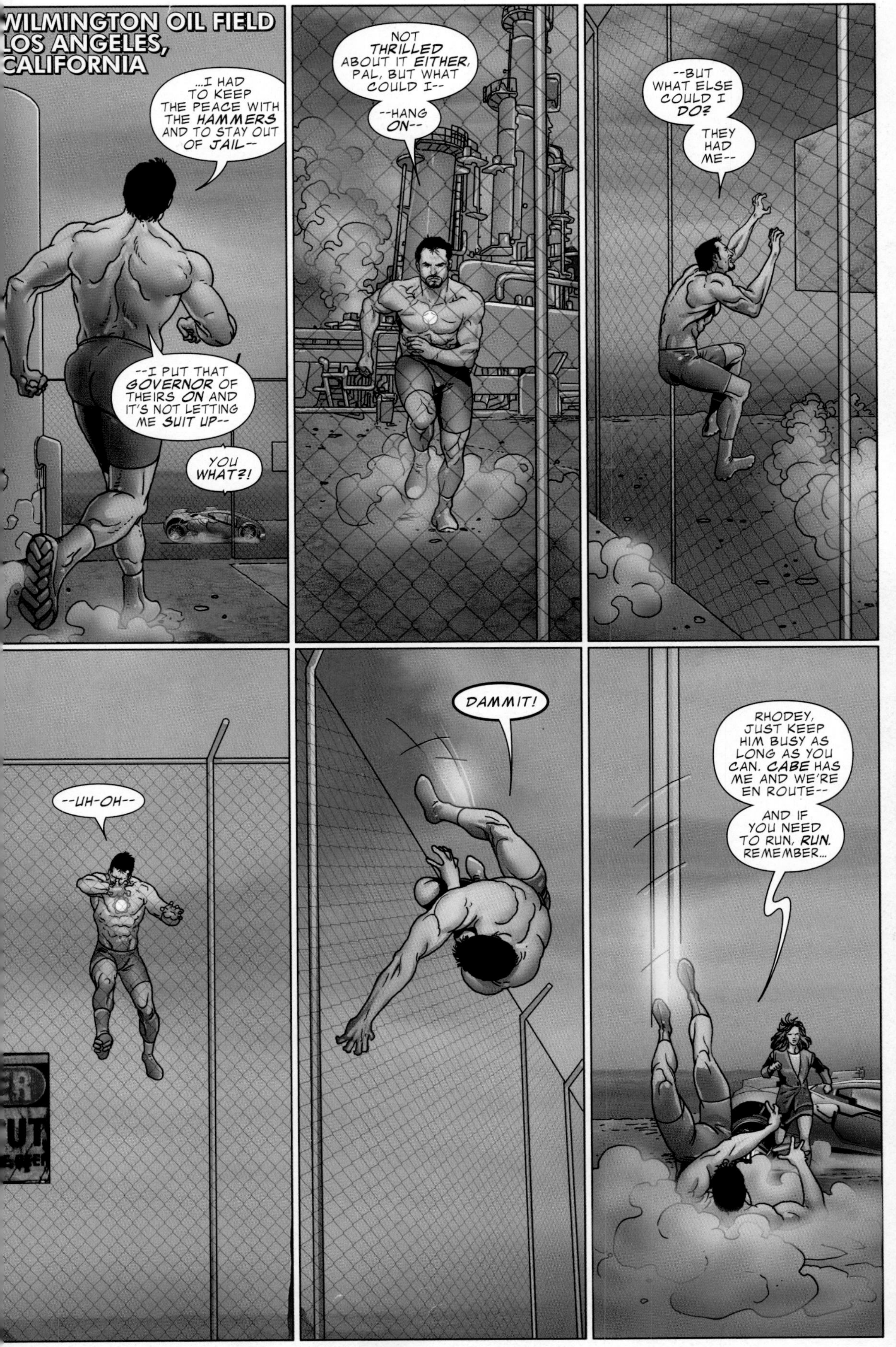
WILMINGTON OIL FIELD LOS ANGELES, CALIFORNIA
...I HAD TO KEEP THE PEACE WITH THE HAMMERS AND TO STAY OUT OF JAIL--
--I PUT THAT GOVERNOR OF THEIRS ON AND IT'S NOT LETTING ME SUIT UP--
YOU WHAT?!
NOT THRILLED ABOUT IT EITHER, PAL, BUT WHAT COULD I--
--HANG ON--
--BUT WHAT ELSE COULD I DO?
THEY HAD ME--
--UH-OH--
DAMMIT!
RHODEY, JUST KEEP HIM BUSY AS LONG AS YOU CAN. CABE HAS ME AND WE'RE EN ROUTE--
AND IF YOU NEED TO RUN, RUN. REMEMBER...

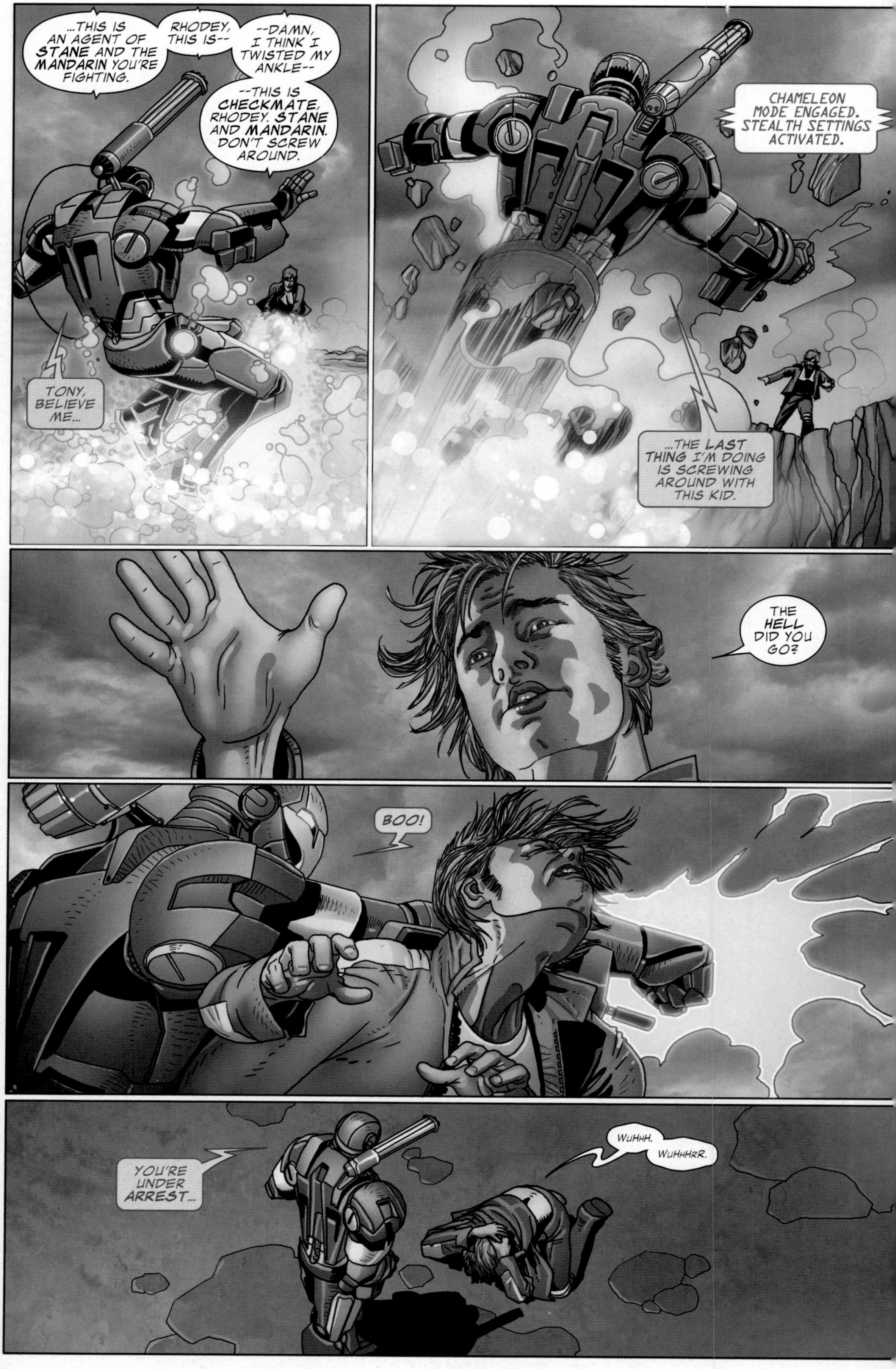
...THIS IS AN AGENT OF STANE AND THE MANDARIN YOU'RE FIGHTING.
RHODEY, THIS IS--
--DAMN, I THINK I TWISTED MY ANKLE--
--THIS IS CHECKMATE, RHODEY. STANE AND MANDARIN. DON'T SCREW AROUND.
TONY, BELIEVE ME...
CHAMELEON MODE ENGAGED. STEALTH SETTINGS ACTIVATED.
...THE LAST THING I'M DOING IS SCREWING AROUND WITH THIS KID.
THE HELL DID YOU GO?
BOO!
YOU'RE UNDER ARREST...
WUHHH.
WUHHHRR.

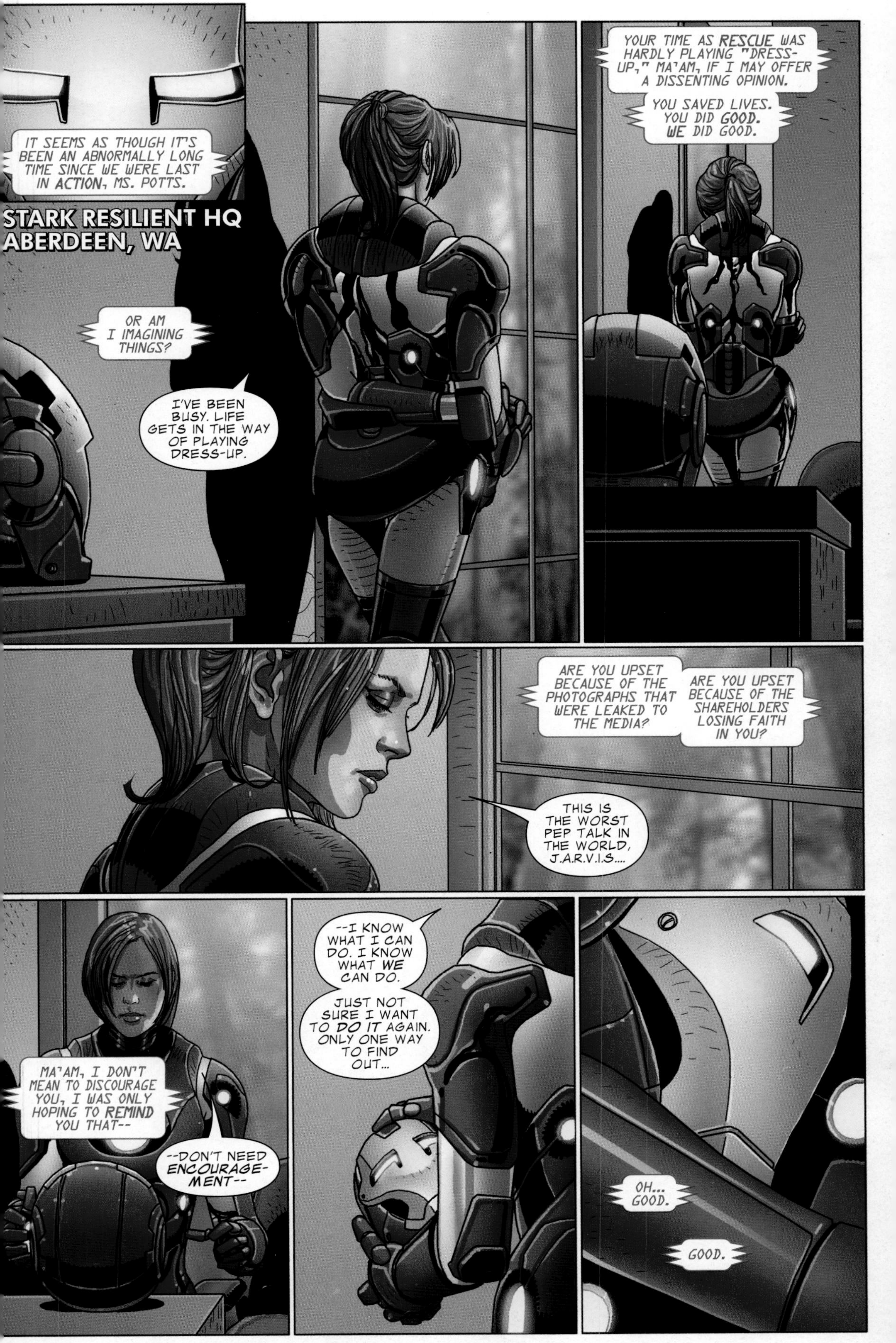
IT SEEMS AS THOUGH IT'S BEEN AN ABNORMALLY LONG TIME SINCE WE WERE LAST IN ACTION, MS. POTTS.
STARK RESILIENT HQ ABERDEEN, WA
OR AM I IMAGINING THINGS?
I'VE BEEN BUSY. LIFE GETS IN THE WAY OF PLAYING DRESS-UP.
YOUR TIME AS RESCUE WAS HARDLY PLAYING "DRESS-UP," MA'AM, IF I MAY OFFER A DISSENTING OPINION.
YOU SAVED LIVES. YOU DID GOOD. WE DID GOOD.
ARE YOU UPSET BECAUSE OF THE PHOTOGRAPHS THAT WERE LEAKED TO THE MEDIA?
ARE YOU UPSET BECAUSE OF THE SHAREHOLDERS LOSING FAITH IN YOU?
THIS IS THE WORST PEP TALK IN THE WORLD, J.A.R.V.I.S....
MA'AM, I DON'T MEAN TO DISCOURAGE YOU, I WAS ONLY HOPING TO REMIND YOU THAT--
--DON'T NEED ENCOURAGE-MENT--
--I KNOW WHAT I CAN DO. I KNOW WHAT WE CAN DO.
JUST NOT SURE I WANT TO DO IT AGAIN. ONLY ONE WAY TO FIND OUT...
OH... GOOD.
GOOD.

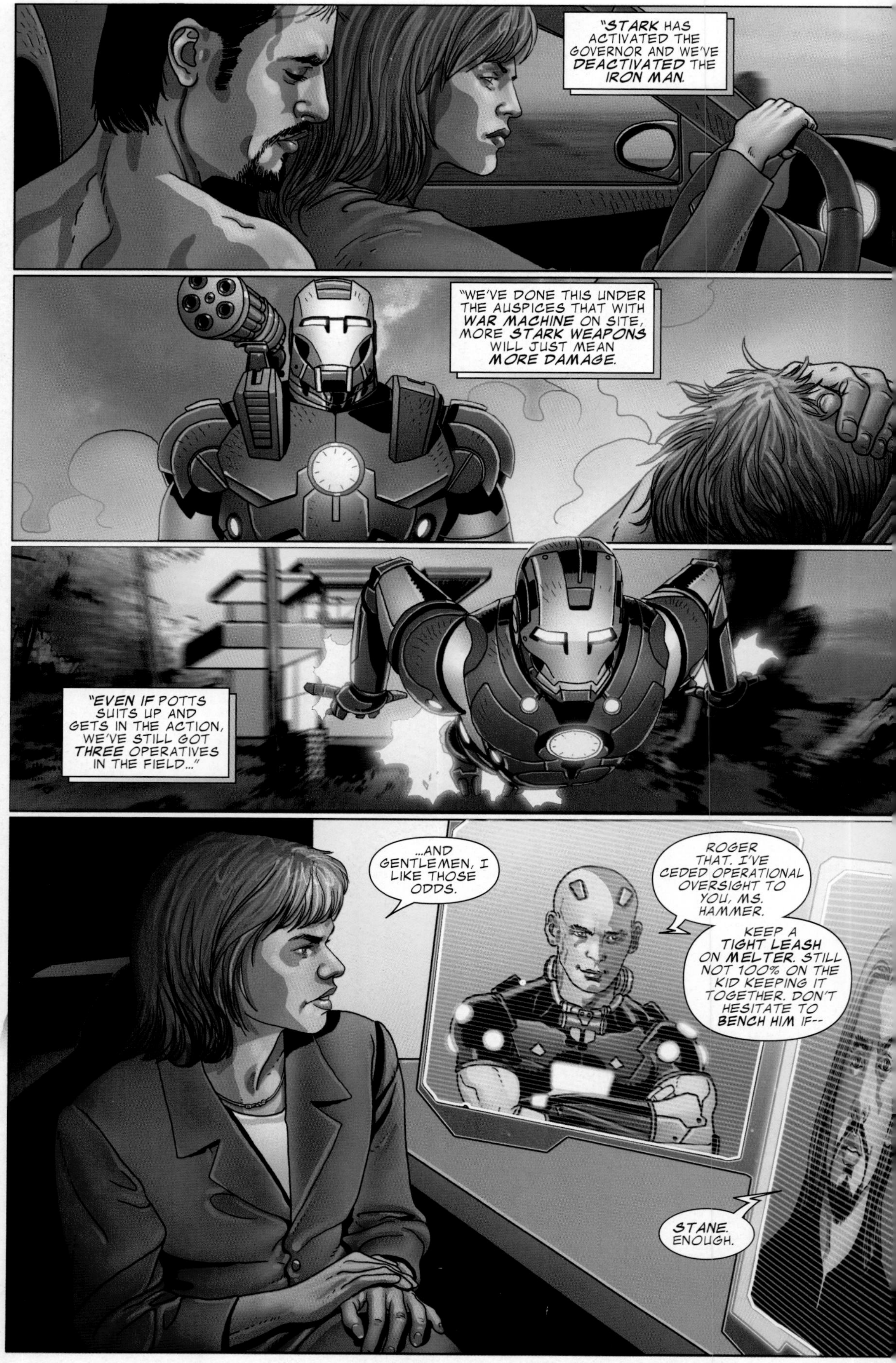
"STARK HAS ACTIVATED THE GOVERNOR AND WE'VE DEACTIVATED THE IRON MAN.
"WE'VE DONE THIS UNDER THE AUSPICES THAT WITH WAR MACHINE ON SITE, MORE STARK WEAPONS WILL JUST MEAN MORE DAMAGE.
"EVEN IF POTTS SUITS UP AND GETS IN THE ACTION, WE'VE STILL GOT THREE OPERATIVES IN THE FIELD..."
...AND GENTLEMEN, I LIKE THOSE ODDS.
ROGER THAT. I'VE CEDED OPERATIONAL OVERSIGHT TO YOU, MS. HAMMER.
KEEP A TIGHT LEASH ON MELTER. STILL NOT 100% ON THE KID KEEPING IT TOGETHER. DON'T HESITATE TO BENCH HIM IF--
STANE. ENOUGH.

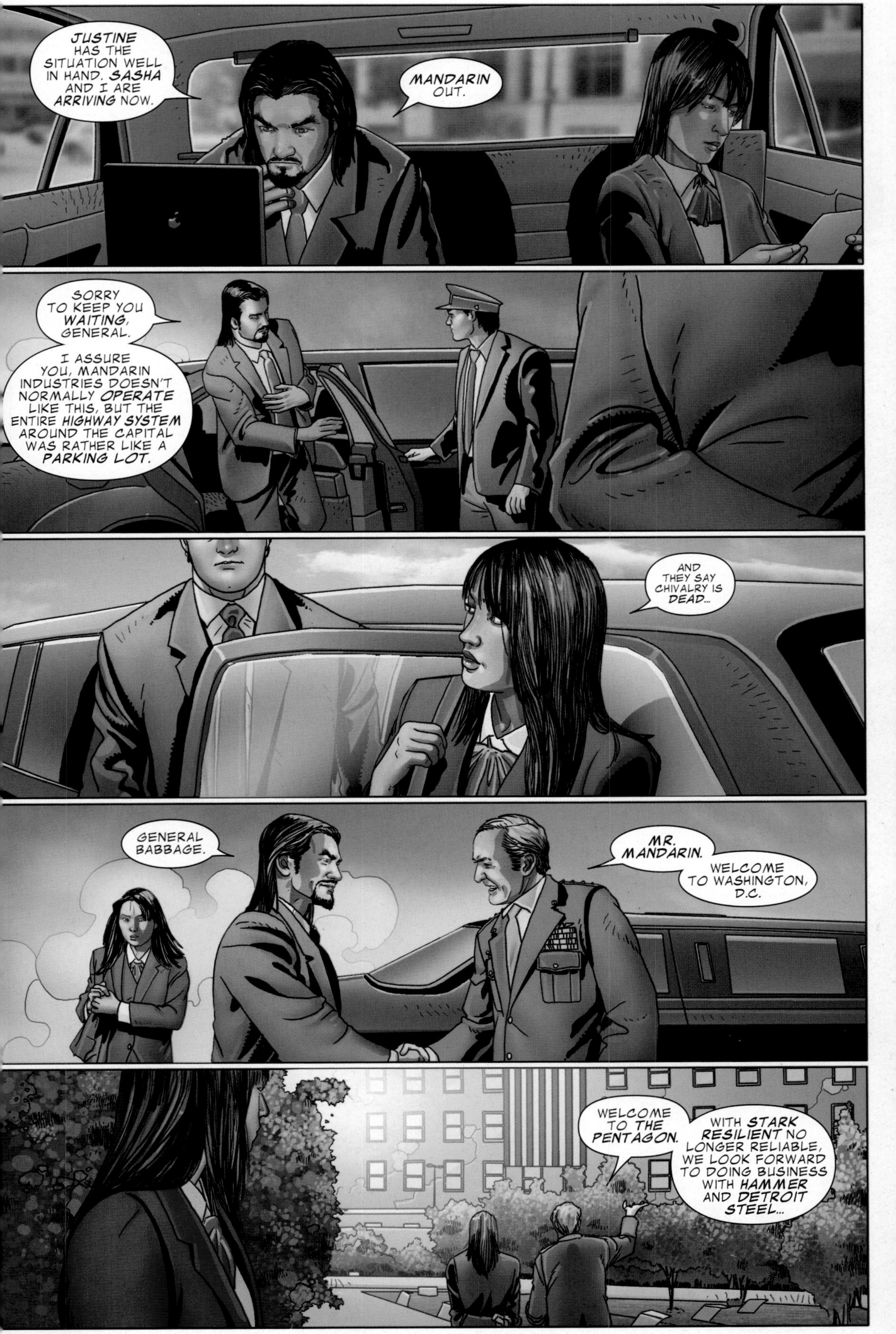
JUSTINE HAS THE SITUATION WELL IN HAND. SASHA AND I ARE ARRIVING NOW.
MANDARIN OUT.
SORRY TO KEEP YOU WAITING, GENERAL.
I ASSURE YOU, MANDARIN INDUSTRIES DOESN'T NORMALLY OPERATE LIKE THIS, BUT THE ENTIRE HIGHWAY SYSTEM AROUND THE CAPITAL WAS RATHER LIKE A PARKING LOT.
AND THEY SAY CHIVALRY IS DEAD...
GENERAL BABBAGE.
MR. MANDARIN.
WELCOME TO WASHINGTON, D.C.
WELCOME TO THE PENTAGON.
WITH STARK RESILIENT NO LONGER RELIABLE, WE LOOK FORWARD TO DOING BUSINESS WITH HAMMER AND DETROIT STEEL...

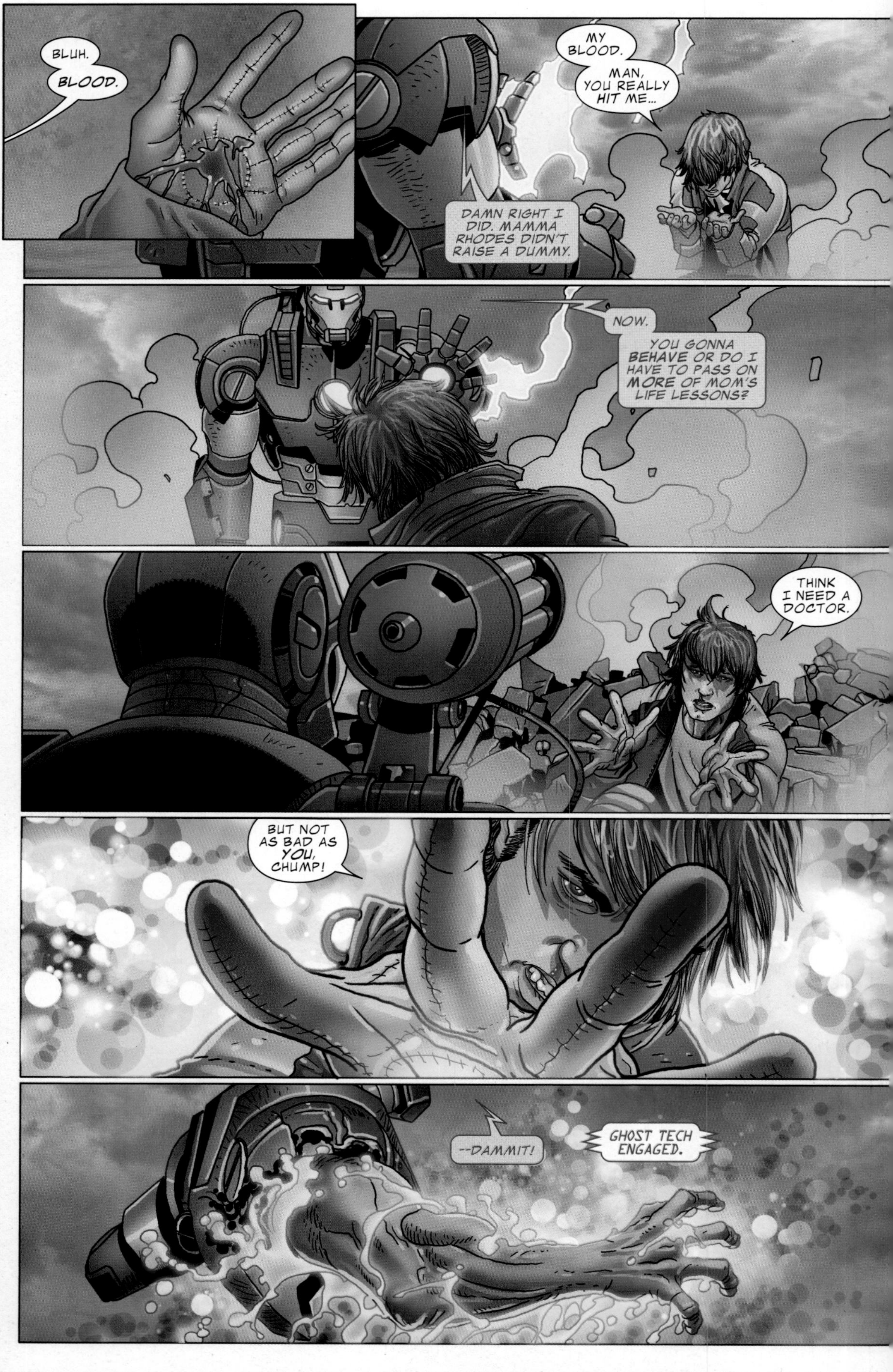
BLUH.
BLOOD.
MY BLOOD.
MAN, YOU REALLY HIT ME...
DAMN RIGHT I DID. MAMMA RHODES DIDN'T RAISE A DUMMY.
NOW.
YOU GONNA BEHAVE OR DO I HAVE TO PASS ON MORE OF MOM'S LIFE LESSONS?
THINK I NEED A DOCTOR.
BUT NOT AS BAD AS YOU, CHUMP!
--DAMMIT!
GHOST TECH ENGAGED.

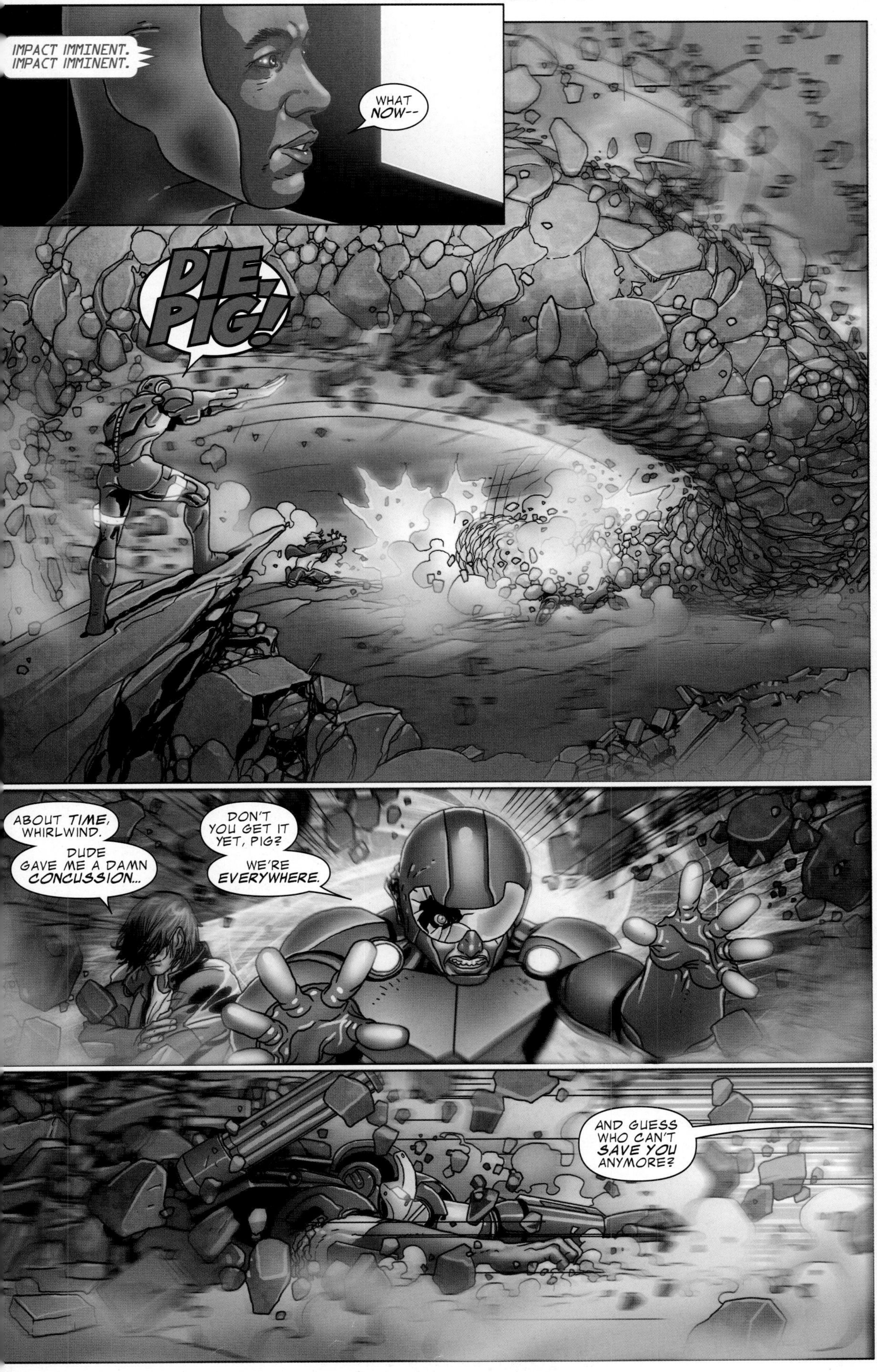
IMPACT IMMINENT.
IMPACT IMMINENT.
WHAT NOW--
DIE, PIG!
ABOUT TIME, WHIRLWIND.
DUDE GAVE ME A DAMN CONCUSSION...
DON'T YOU GET IT YET, PIG?
WE'RE EVERYWHERE.
AND GUESS WHO CAN'T SAVE YOU ANYMORE?

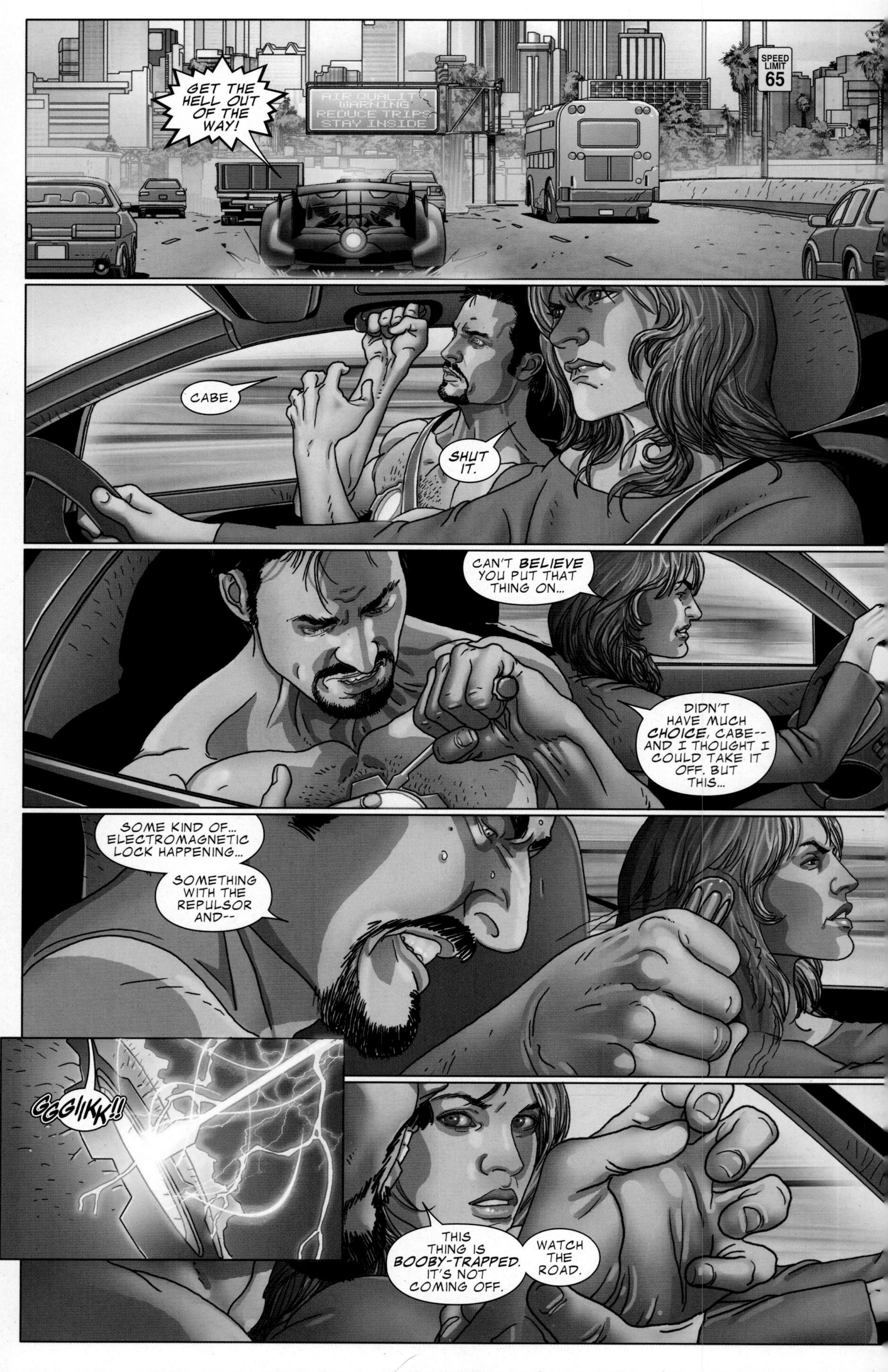
SPEED LIMIT 65
AIR QUALITY WARNING REDUCE TRIPS STAY INSIDE
GET THE HELL OUT OF THE WAY!
CABE.
SHUT IT.
CAN'T BELIEVE YOU PUT THAT THING ON...
DIDN'T HAVE MUCH CHOICE, CABE-- AND I THOUGHT I COULD TAKE IT OFF. BUT THIS...
SOME KIND OF... ELECTROMAGNETIC LOCK HAPPENING...
SOMETHING WITH THE REPULSOR AND--
GGGIIKK!!
THIS THING IS BOOBY-TRAPPED. IT'S NOT COMING OFF.
WATCH THE ROAD.

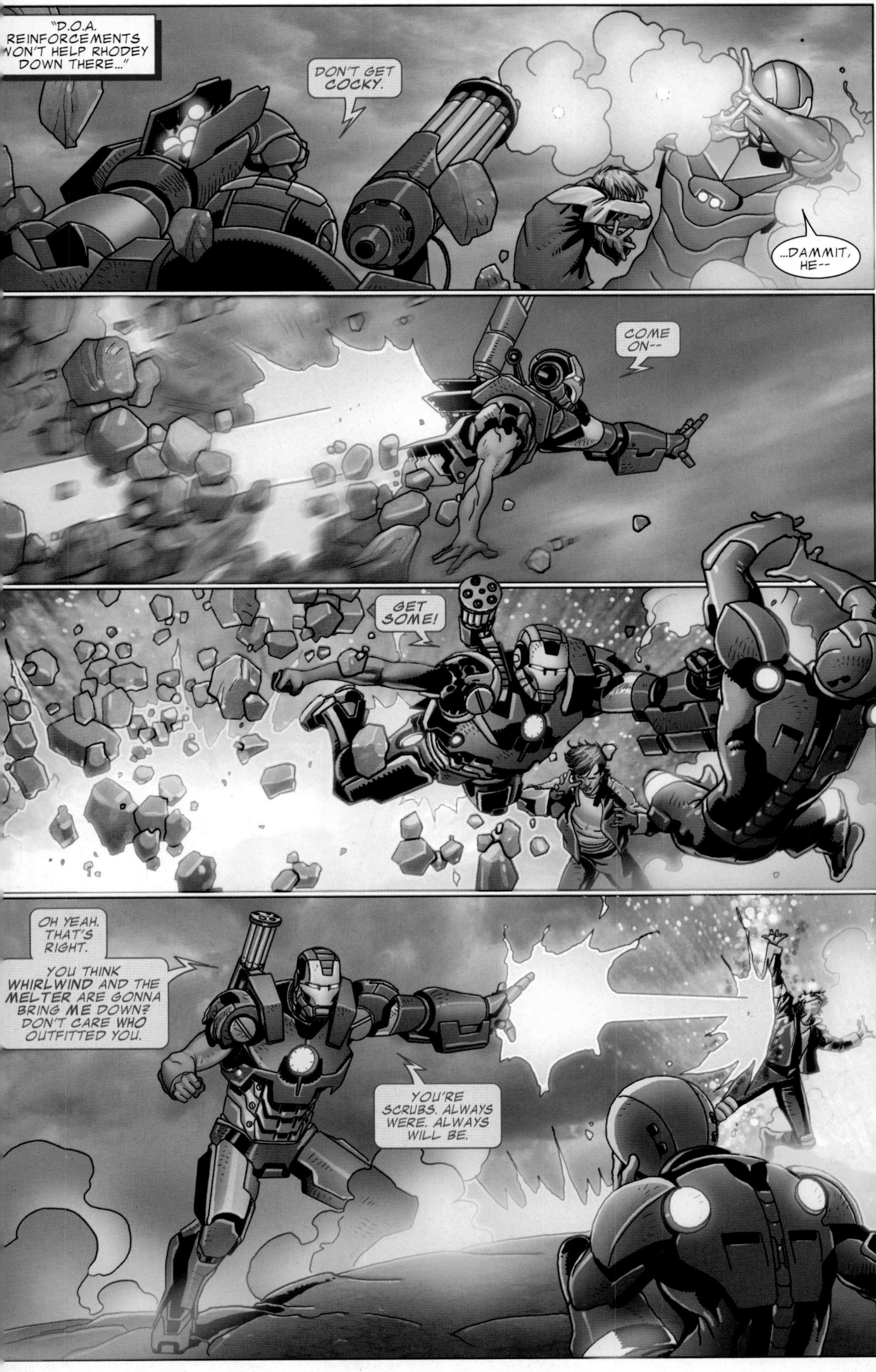
"D.O.A. REINFORCEMENTS WON'T HELP RHODEY DOWN THERE..."
DON'T GET COCKY.
...DAMMIT, HE--
COME ON--
GET SOME!
OH YEAH. THAT'S RIGHT.
YOU THINK WHIRLWIND AND THE MELTER ARE GONNA BRING ME DOWN? DON'T CARE WHO OUTFITTED YOU.
YOU'RE SCRUBS. ALWAYS WERE. ALWAYS WILL BE.

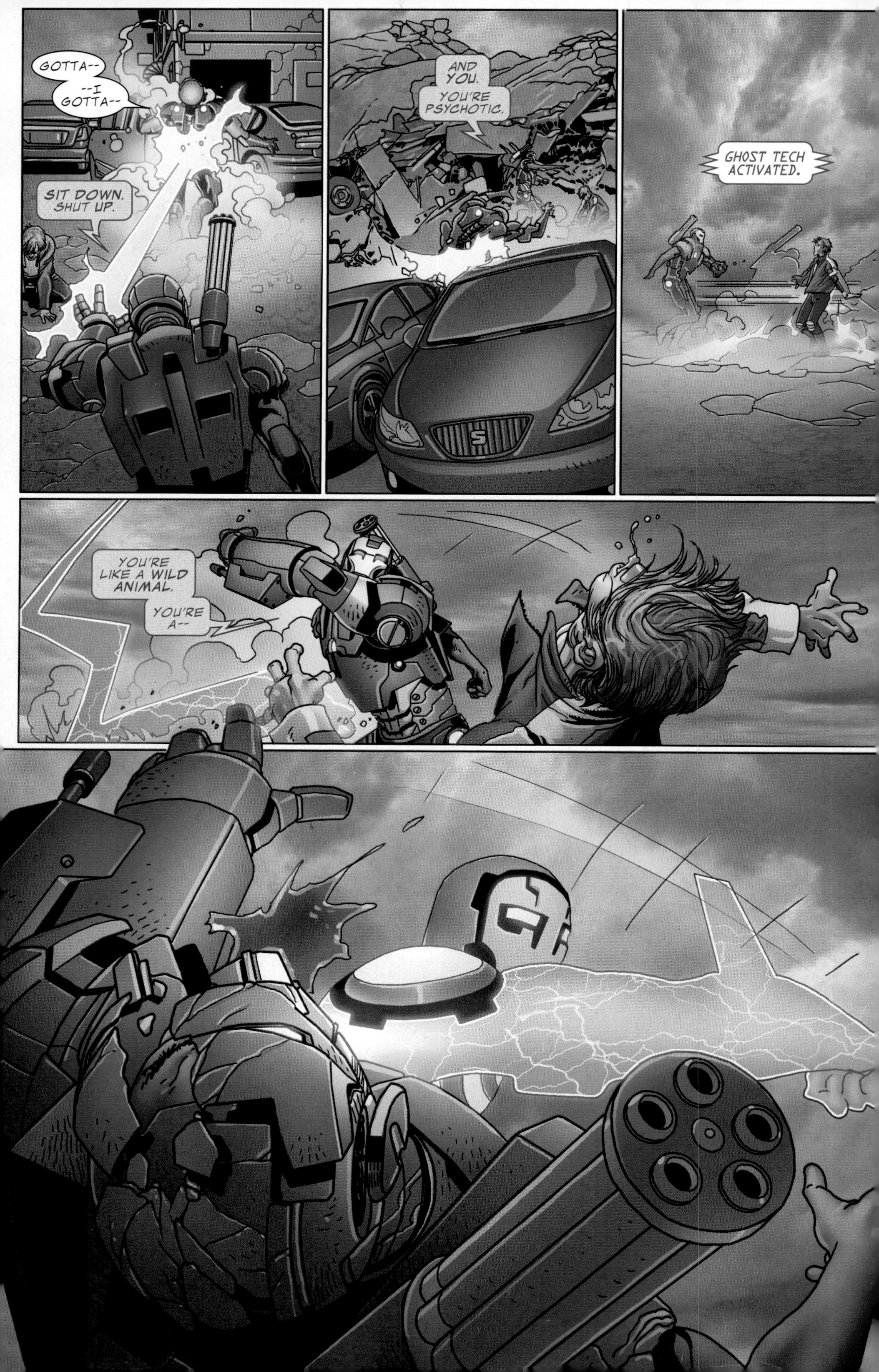
GOTTA--
--I GOTTA--
SIT DOWN. SHUT UP.
AND YOU.
YOU'RE PSYCHOTIC.
GHOST TECH ACTIVATED.
YOU'RE LIKE A WILD ANIMAL.
YOU'RE A--

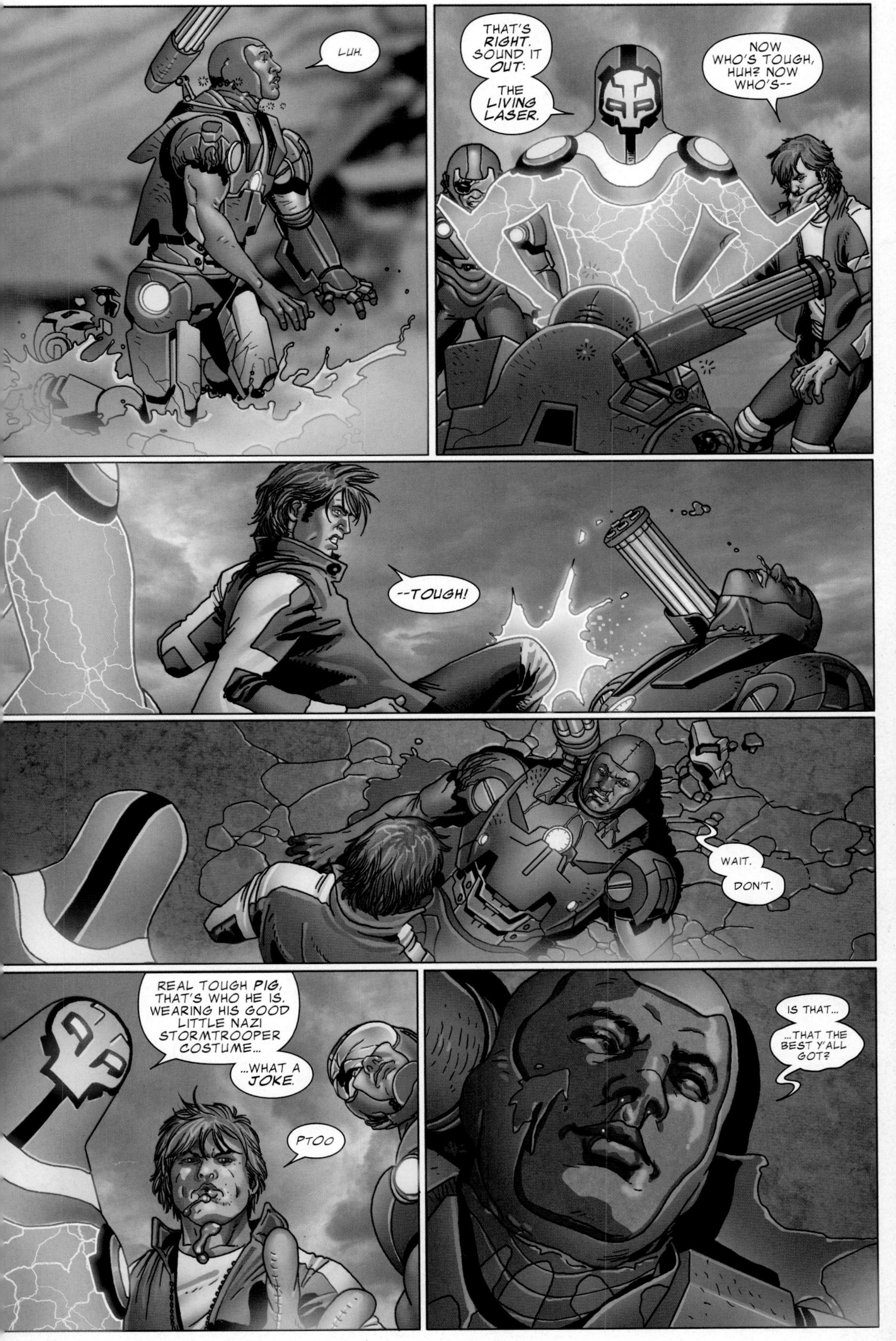
LUH.
THAT'S RIGHT. SOUND IT OUT:
THE LIVING LASER.
NOW WHO'S TOUGH, HUH? NOW WHO'S--
--TOUGH!
WAIT.
DON'T.
REAL TOUGH PIG, THAT'S WHO HE IS. WEARING HIS GOOD LITTLE NAZI STORMTROOPER COSTUME...
...WHAT A JOKE.
PTOO
IS THAT...
...THAT THE BEST Y'ALL GOT?

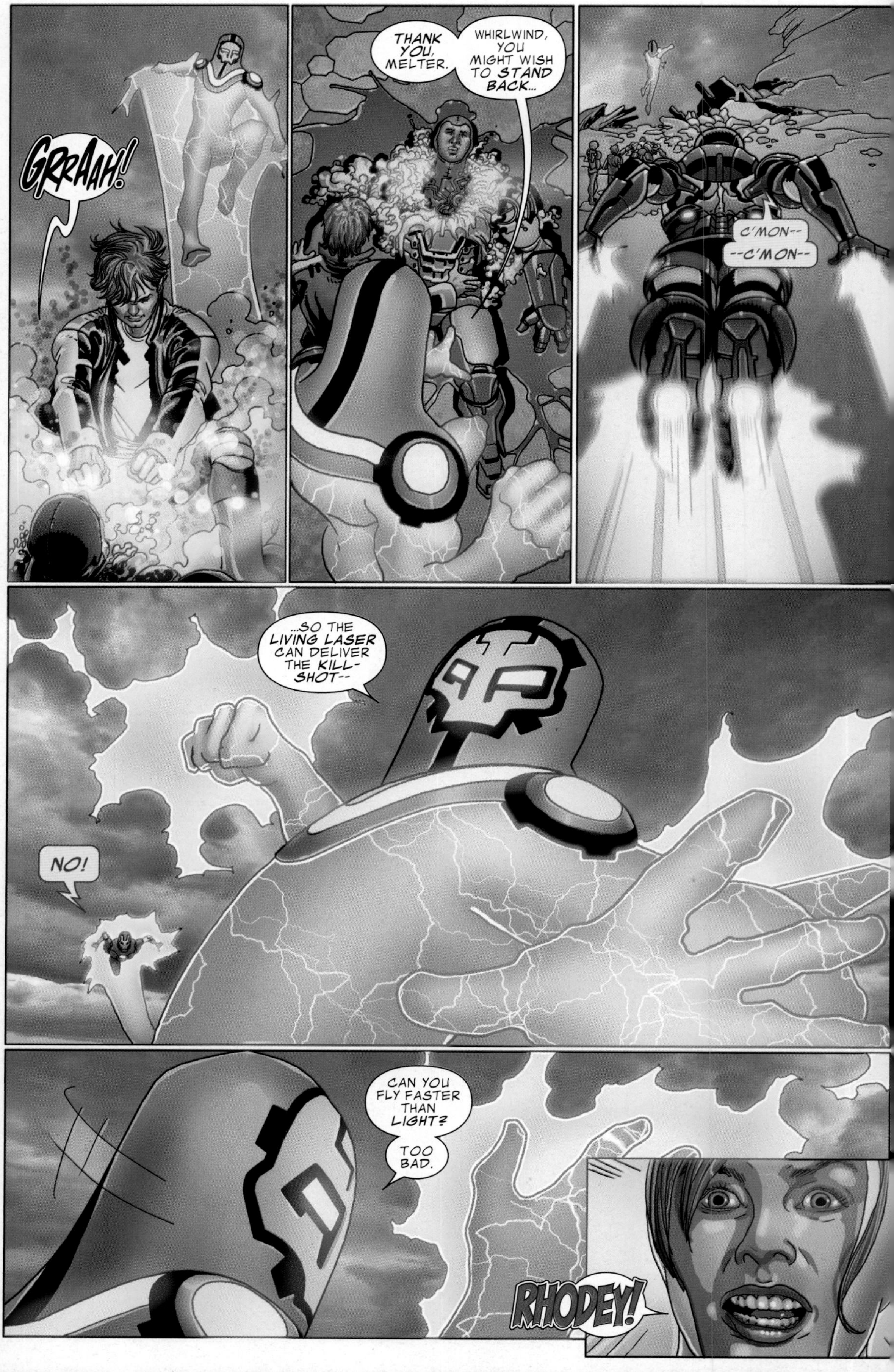
GRRAAH!
THANK YOU, MELTER.
WHIRLWIND, YOU MIGHT WISH TO STAND BACK...
C'MON--
--C'MON--
...SO THE LIVING LASER CAN DELIVER THE KILL-SHOT--
NO!
CAN YOU FLY FASTER THAN LIGHT?
TOO BAD.
RHODEY!

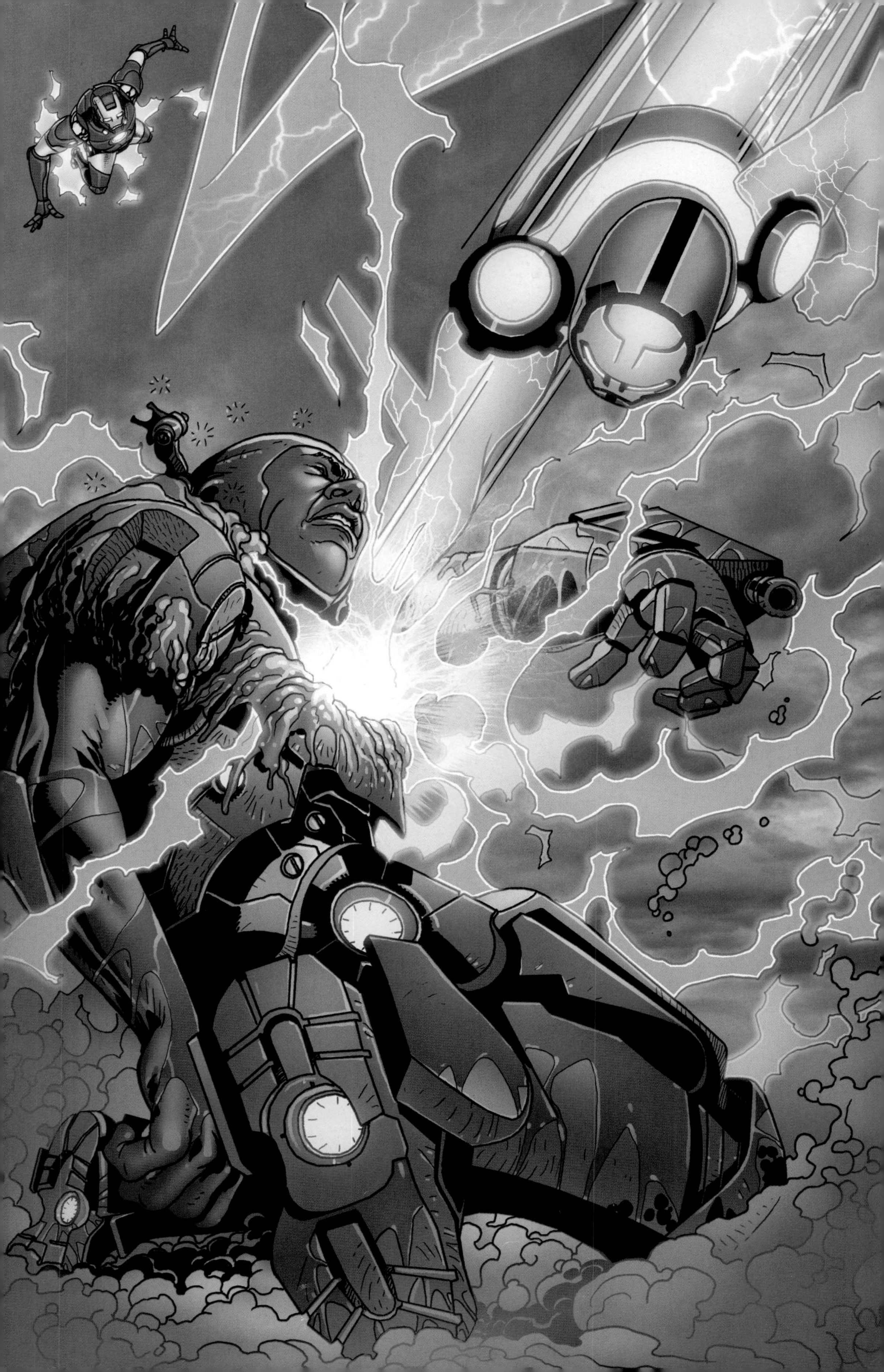

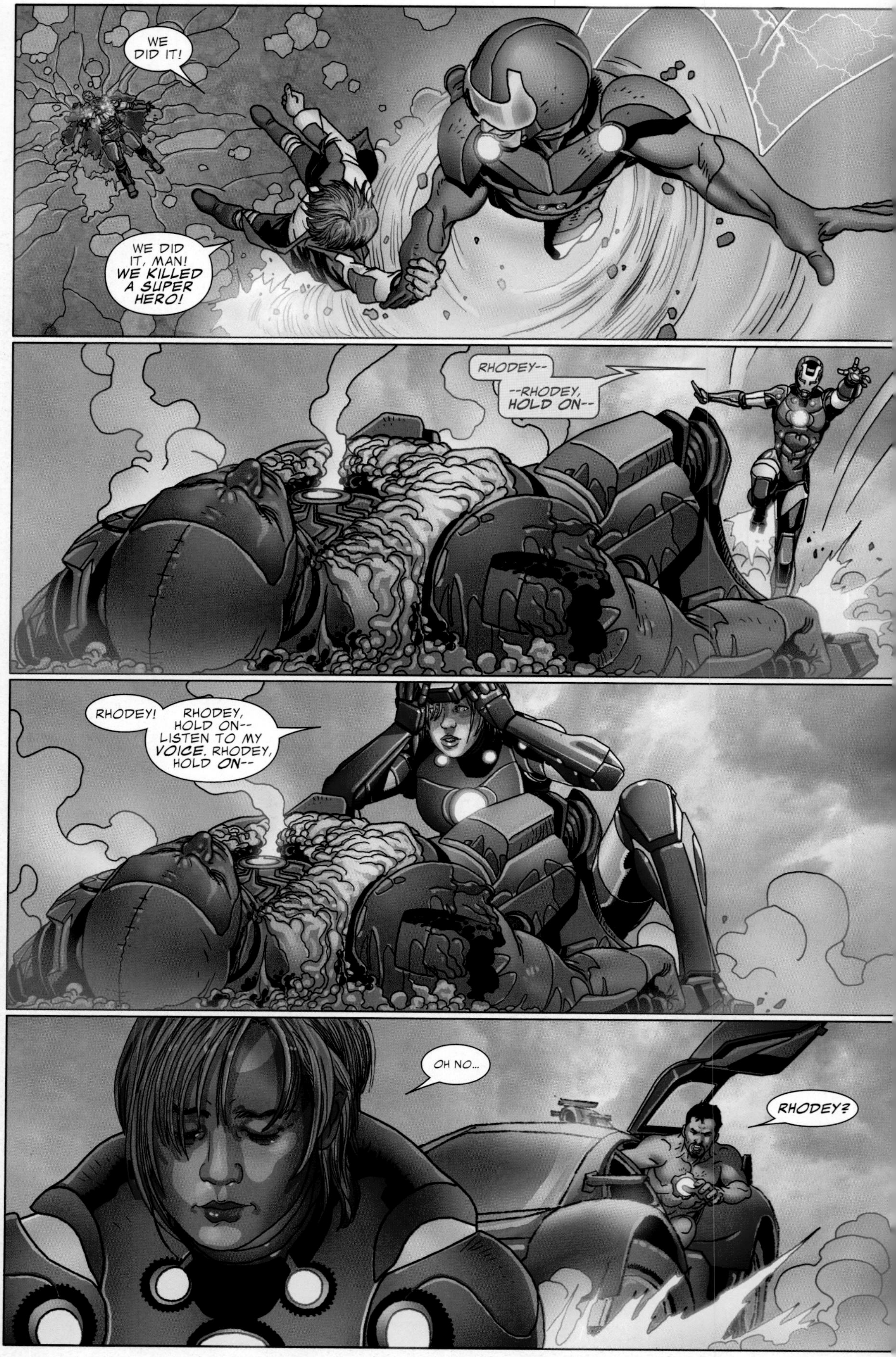
WE DID IT!
WE DID IT, MAN! WE KILLED A SUPER HERO!
RHODEY--
--RHODEY, HOLD ON--
RHODEY!
RHODEY, HOLD ON-- LISTEN TO MY VOICE. RHODEY, HOLD ON--
OH NO...
RHODEY?

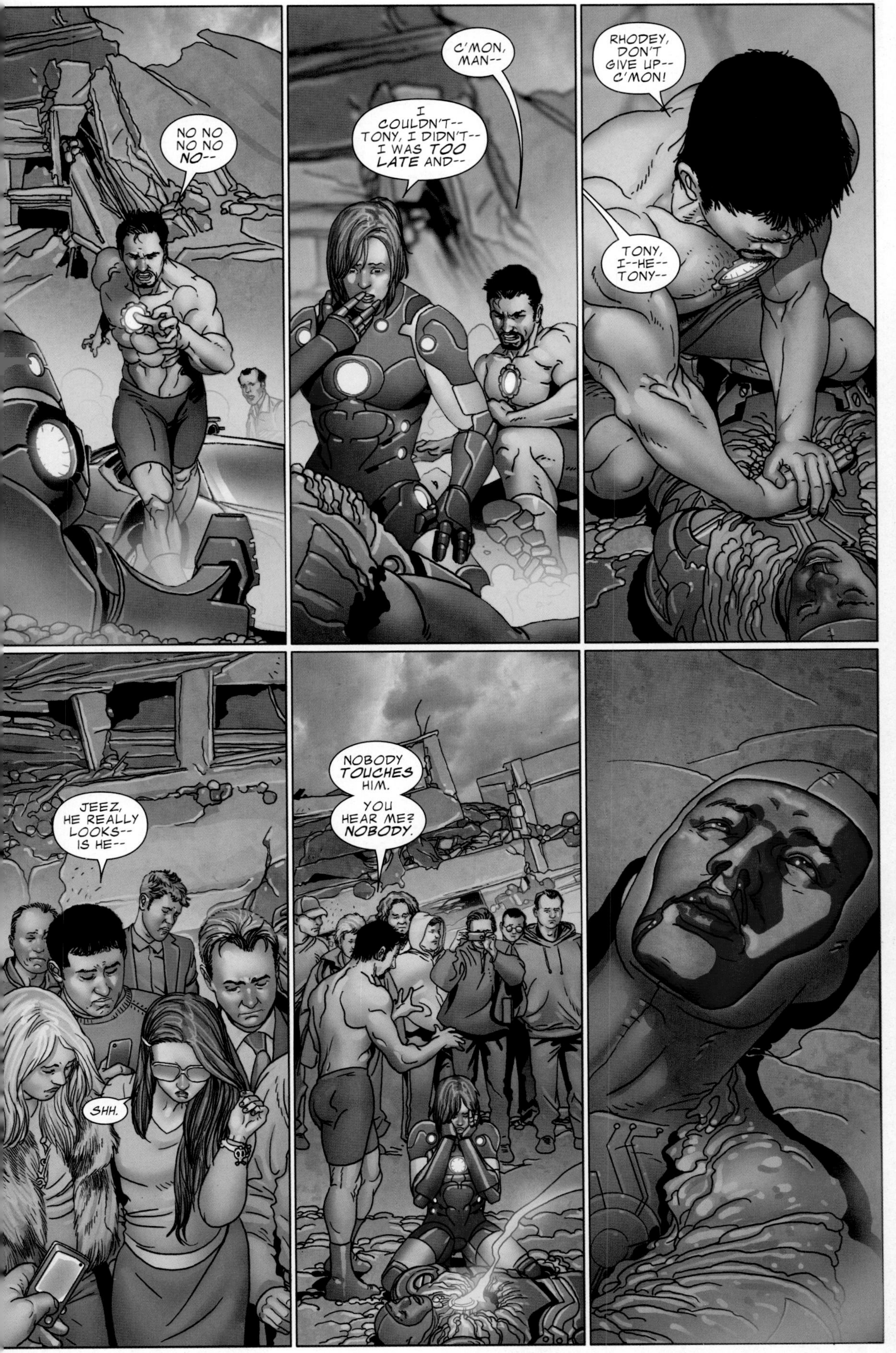
NO NO
NO NO
NO--
C'MON,
MAN--
I
COULDN'T--
TONY, I DIDN'T--
I WAS TOO
LATE AND--
RHODEY,
DON'T
GIVE UP--
C'MON!
TONY,
I--HE--
TONY--
JEEZ,
HE REALLY
LOOKS--
IS HE--
SHH.
NOBODY
TOUCHES
HIM.
YOU
HEAR ME?
NOBODY.

STANE! STANE.

HI. WE DID IT! HI. NOBODY HAD TO GET BLOWN UP OR ANYTHING.

STANE? HELLO?

WE JUST KILLED *WAR MACHINE* AND WRECKED HALF OF DOWNTOWN L.A.

HUH?

OH, RIGHT. RIGHT. YEAH, GOOD, GREAT. I'LL LET *MANDARIN* KNOW...

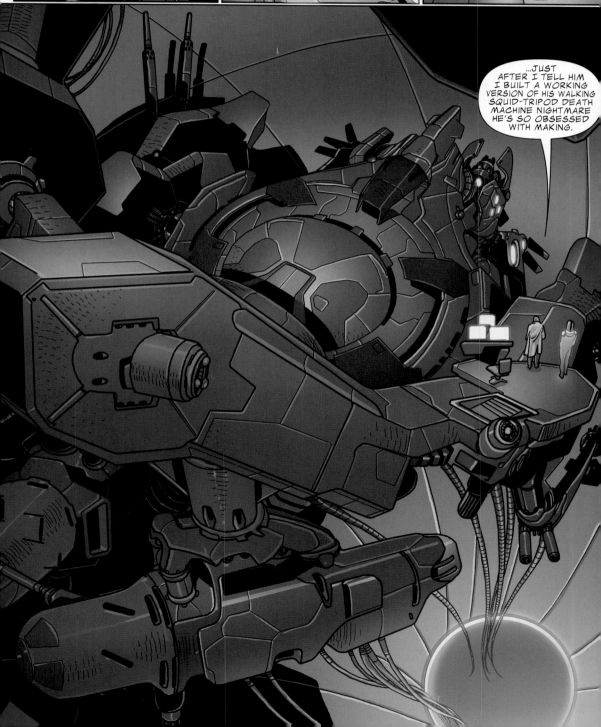

...JUST AFTER I TELL HIM I BUILT A WORKING VERSION OF HIS WALKING SQUID-TRIPOD DEATH MACHINE NIGHTMARE HE'S *SO* OBSESSED WITH MAKING.

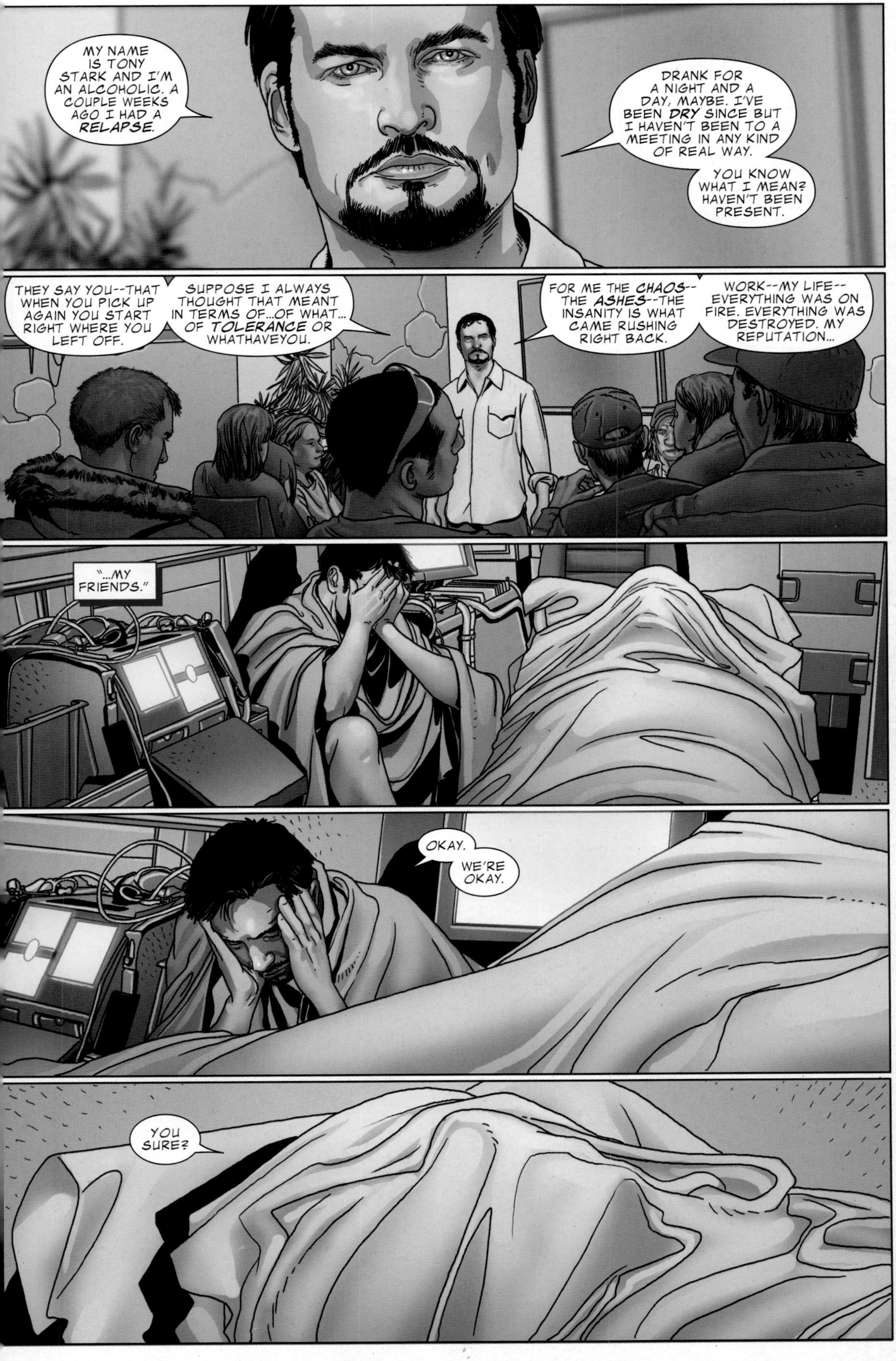
MY NAME IS TONY STARK AND I'M AN ALCOHOLIC. A COUPLE WEEKS AGO I HAD A RELAPSE.
DRANK FOR A NIGHT AND A DAY, MAYBE. I'VE BEEN DRY SINCE BUT I HAVEN'T BEEN TO A MEETING IN ANY KIND OF REAL WAY.
YOU KNOW WHAT I MEAN? HAVEN'T BEEN PRESENT.
THEY SAY YOU--THAT WHEN YOU PICK UP AGAIN YOU START RIGHT WHERE YOU LEFT OFF.
SUPPOSE I ALWAYS THOUGHT THAT MEANT IN TERMS OF...OF WHAT... OF TOLERANCE OR WHATHAVEYOU.
FOR ME THE CHAOS--THE ASHES--THE INSANITY IS WHAT CAME RUSHING RIGHT BACK.
WORK--MY LIFE--EVERYTHING WAS ON FIRE. EVERYTHING WAS DESTROYED. MY REPUTATION...
"...MY FRIENDS."
OKAY.
WE'RE OKAY.
YOU SURE?

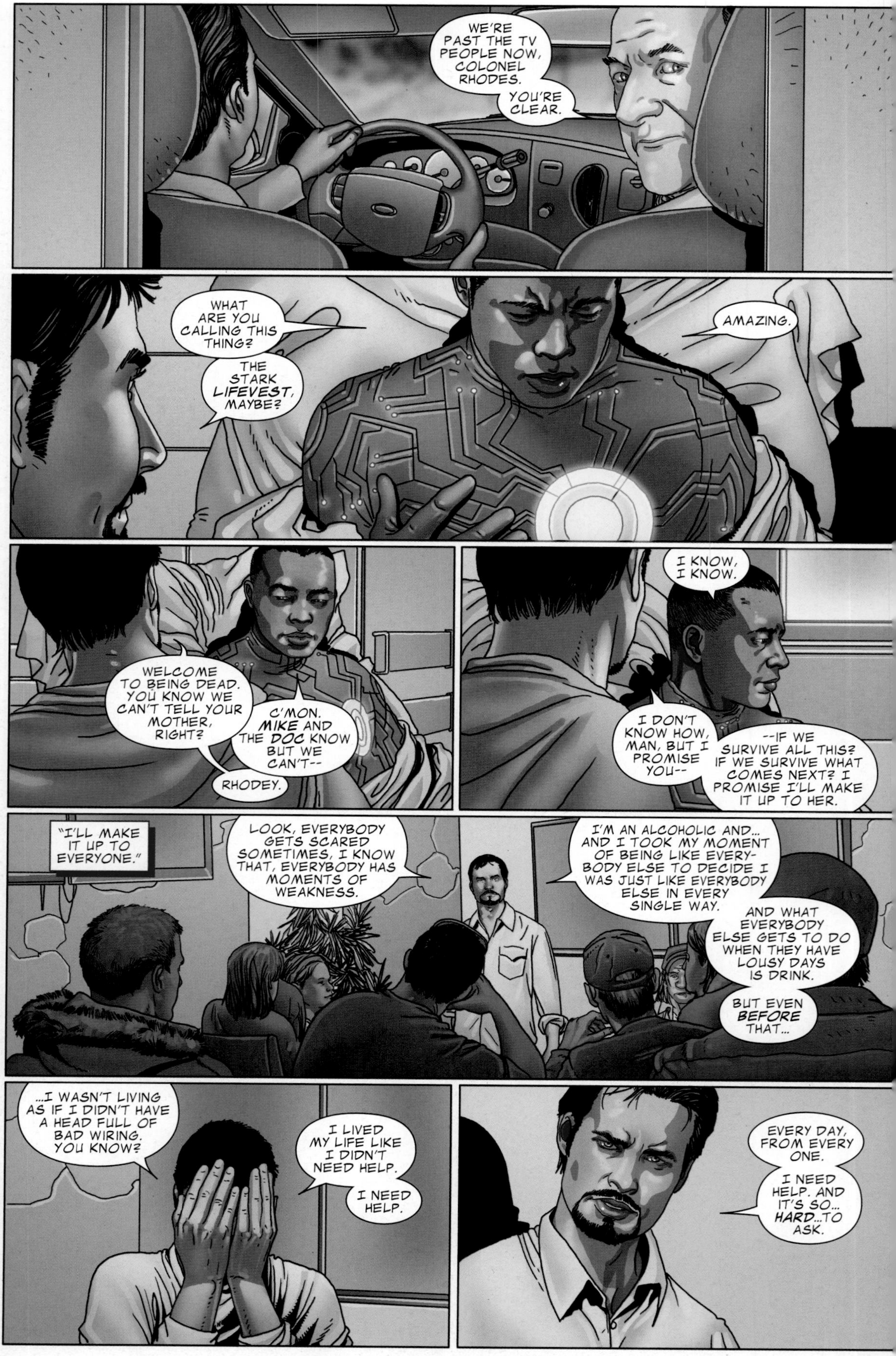
WE'RE PAST THE TV PEOPLE NOW, COLONEL RHODES.
YOU'RE CLEAR.
WHAT ARE YOU CALLING THIS THING?
THE STARK LIFEVEST, MAYBE?
AMAZING.
WELCOME TO BEING DEAD. YOU KNOW WE CAN'T TELL YOUR MOTHER, RIGHT?
C'MON. MIKE AND THE DOC KNOW BUT WE CAN'T--
RHODEY.
I KNOW, I KNOW.
I DON'T KNOW HOW, MAN, BUT I PROMISE YOU--
--IF WE SURVIVE ALL THIS? IF WE SURVIVE WHAT COMES NEXT? I PROMISE I'LL MAKE IT UP TO HER.
"I'LL MAKE IT UP TO EVERYONE."
LOOK, EVERYBODY GETS SCARED SOMETIMES, I KNOW THAT, EVERYBODY HAS MOMENTS OF WEAKNESS.
I'M AN ALCOHOLIC AND... AND I TOOK MY MOMENT OF BEING LIKE EVERY-BODY ELSE TO DECIDE I WAS JUST LIKE EVERYBODY ELSE IN EVERY SINGLE WAY.
AND WHAT EVERYBODY ELSE GETS TO DO WHEN THEY HAVE LOUSY DAYS IS DRINK.
BUT EVEN BEFORE THAT...
...I WASN'T LIVING AS IF I DIDN'T HAVE A HEAD FULL OF BAD WIRING. YOU KNOW?
I LIVED MY LIFE LIKE I DIDN'T NEED HELP.
I NEED HELP.
EVERY DAY, FROM EVERY ONE.
I NEED HELP. AND IT'S SO... HARD...TO ASK.

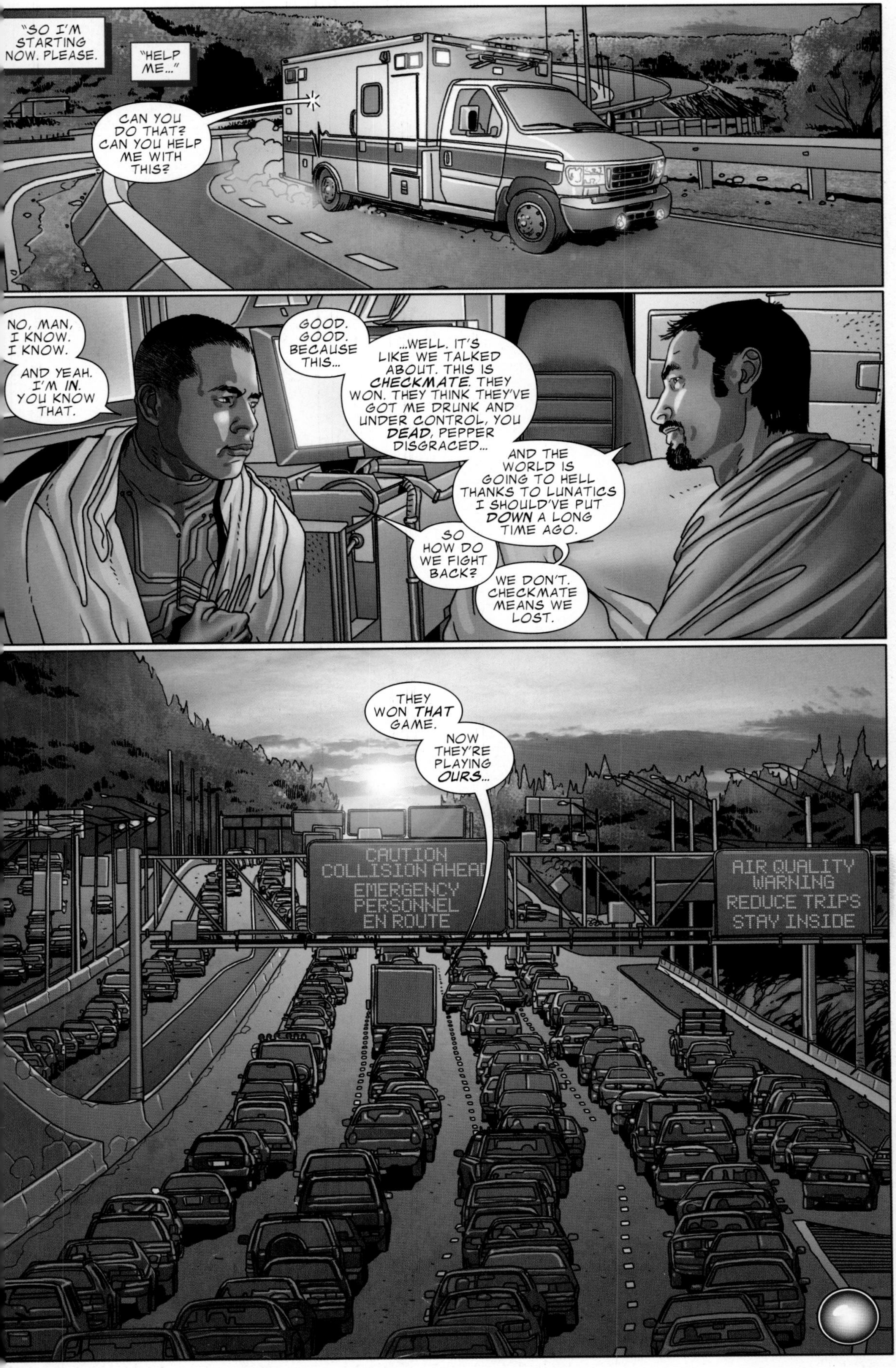
"SO I'M STARTING NOW. PLEASE.
"HELP ME..."
CAN YOU DO THAT? CAN YOU HELP ME WITH THIS?
NO, MAN, I KNOW. I KNOW.
AND YEAH. I'M IN. YOU KNOW THAT.
GOOD. GOOD. BECAUSE THIS...
...WELL. IT'S LIKE WE TALKED ABOUT. THIS IS CHECKMATE. THEY WON. THEY THINK THEY'VE GOT ME DRUNK AND UNDER CONTROL, YOU DEAD, PEPPER DISGRACED...
AND THE WORLD IS GOING TO HELL THANKS TO LUNATICS I SHOULD'VE PUT DOWN A LONG TIME AGO.
SO HOW DO WE FIGHT BACK?
WE DON'T. CHECKMATE MEANS WE LOST.
THEY WON THAT GAME.
NOW THEY'RE PLAYING OURS...
CAUTION COLLISION AHEAD
EMERGENCY PERSONNEL EN ROUTE
AIR QUALITY WARNING
REDUCE TRIPS STAY INSIDE

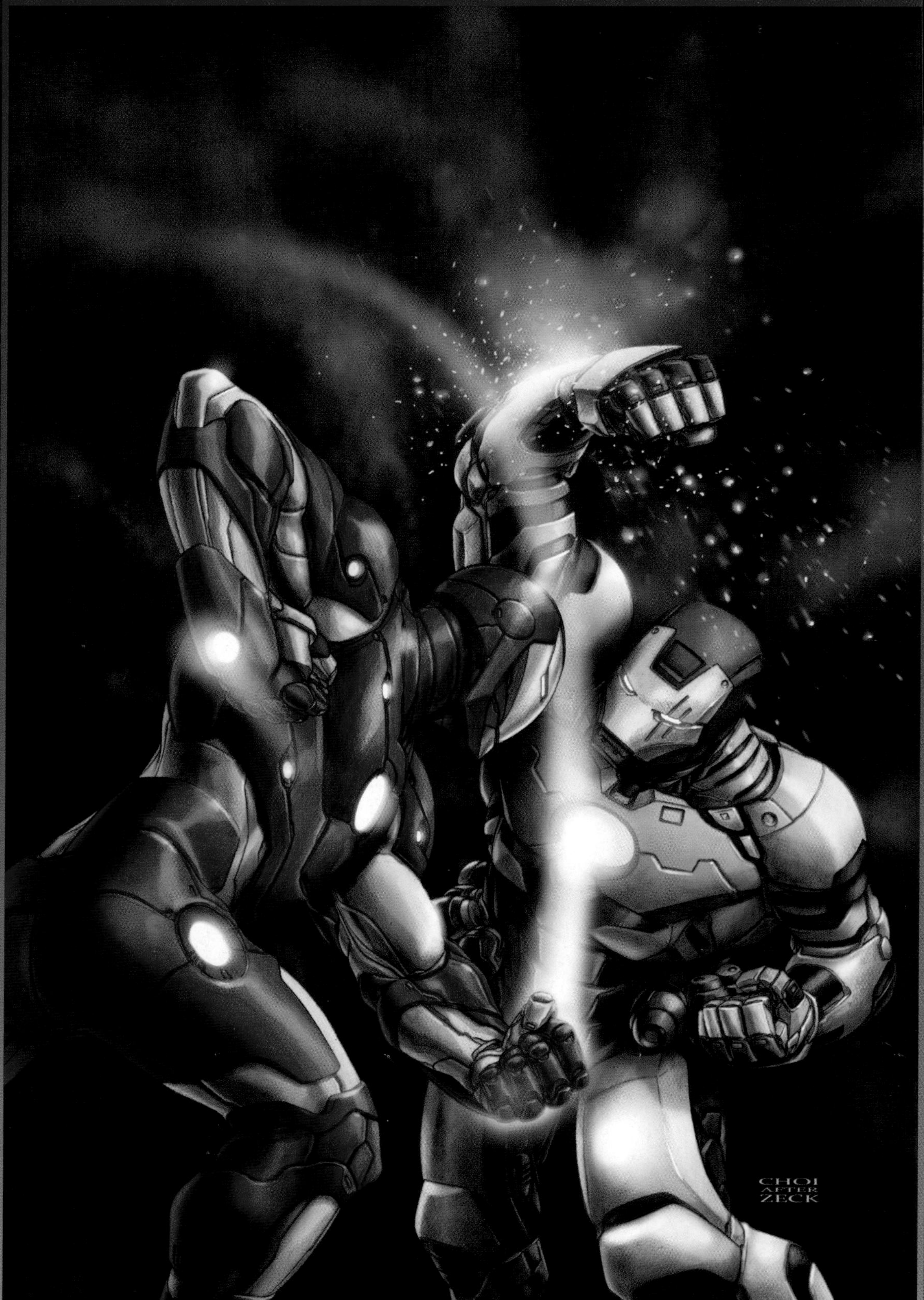
CHOI
AFTER
ZECK

#510 MARVEL 50TH ANNIVERSARY VARIANT
BY MIKE CHOI

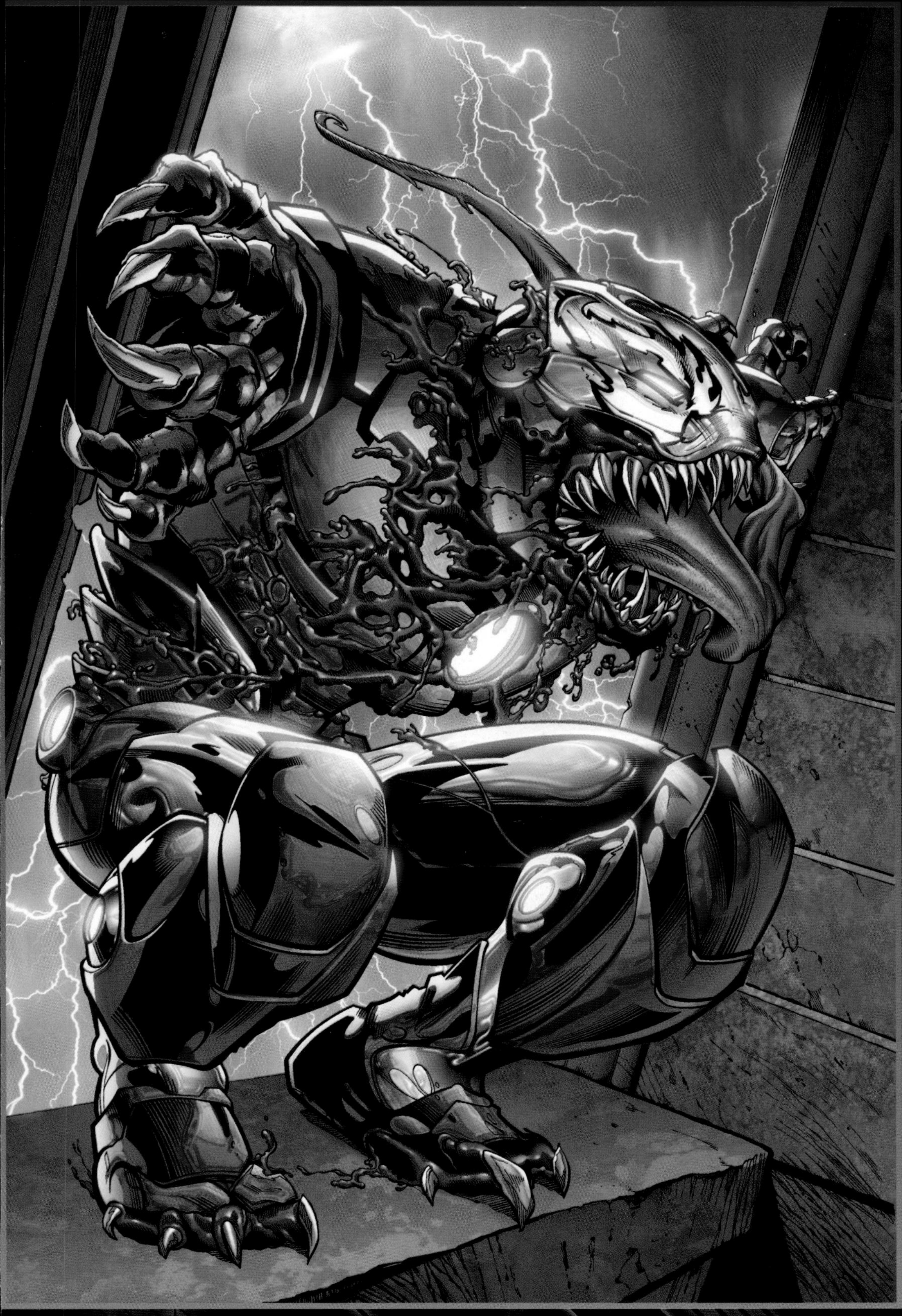

#512 VENOM VARIANT
BY LARRY STROMAN, DAVE MEIKIS & GURU-eFX

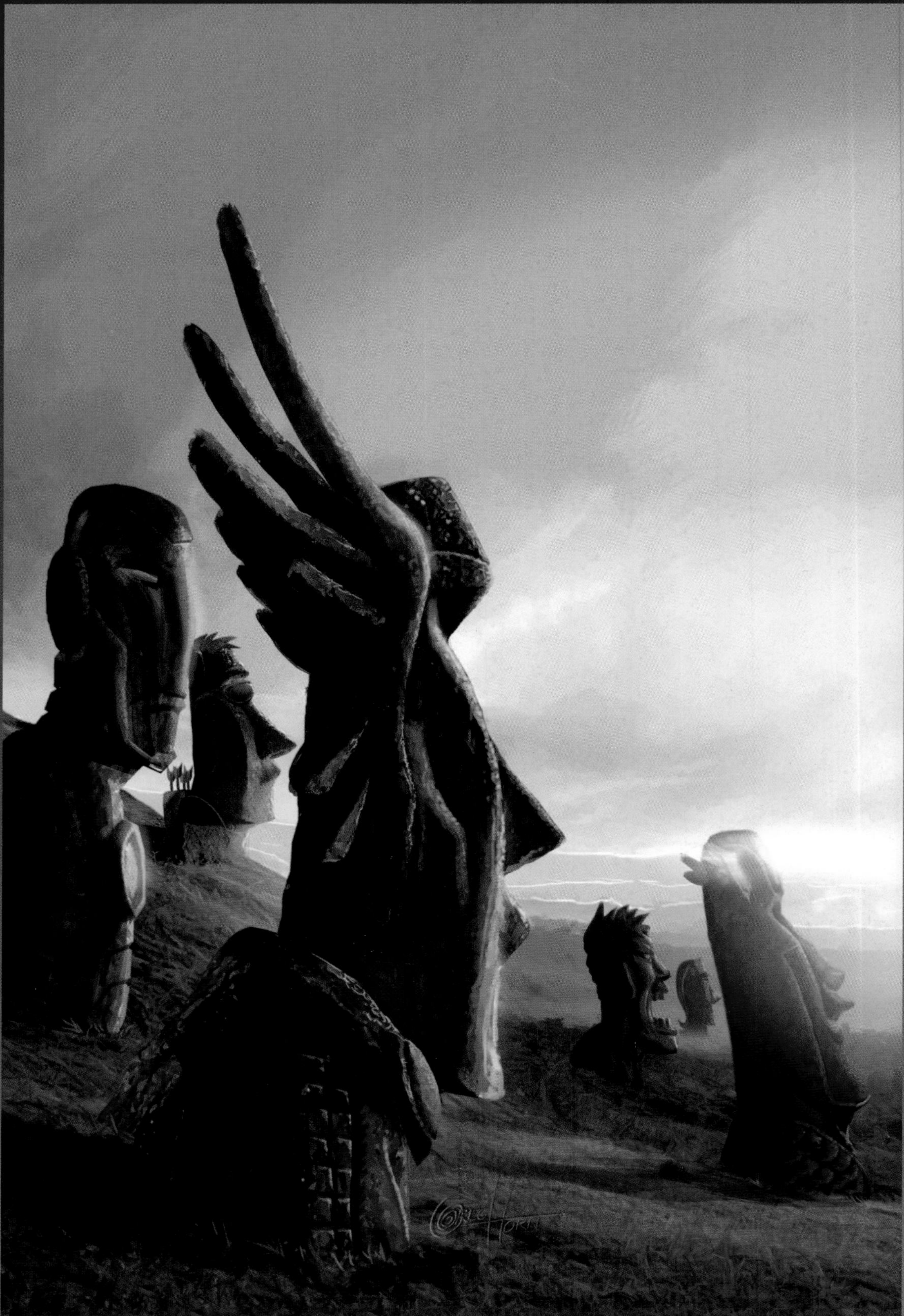
GREG HORN

#515 AVENGERS ART APPRECIATION VARIANT
BY GREG HORN

Pick Up These Classic Adventures of the Invincible Iron Man

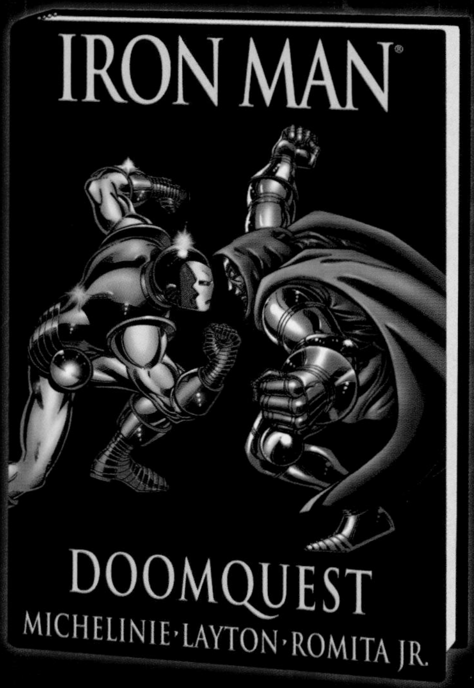
IRON MAN®
DOOMQUEST
MICHELINIE·LAYTON·ROMITA JR.

IRON MAN: DOOMQUEST PREMIERE HC
978-0-7851-2834-2

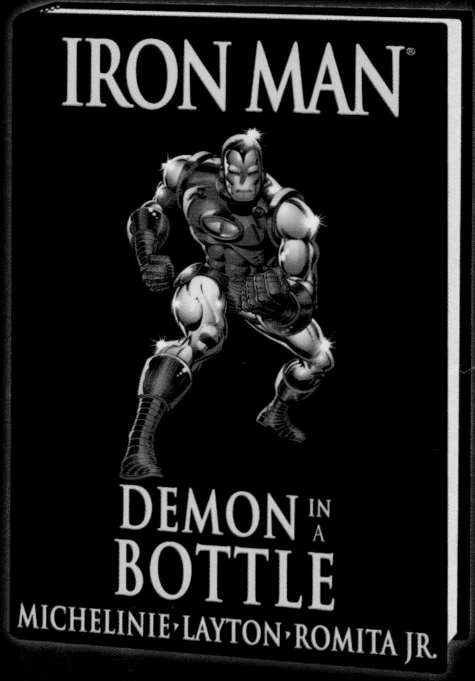
IRON MAN®
DEMON IN A BOTTLE
MICHELINIE·LAYTON·ROMITA JR.

IRON MAN: DEMON IN A BOTTLE PREMIERE HC
978-0-7851-3095-6

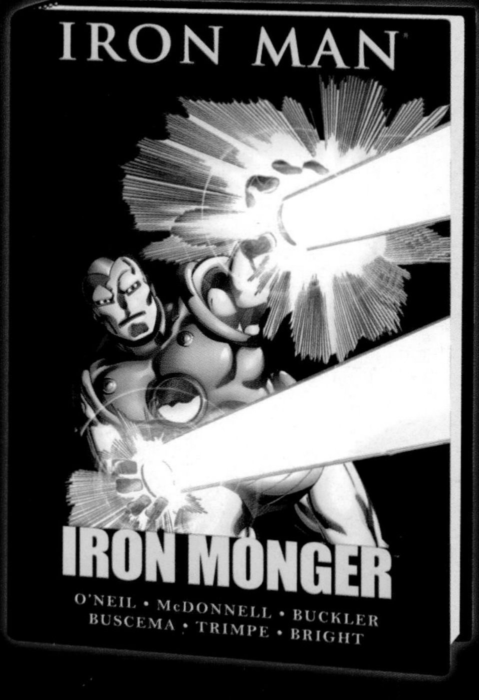
IRON MAN®
IRON MONGER
O'NEIL • McDONNELL • BUCKLER
BUSCEMA • TRIMPE • BRIGHT

IRON MAN: IRON MONGER PREMIERE HC
978-0-7851-4260-7

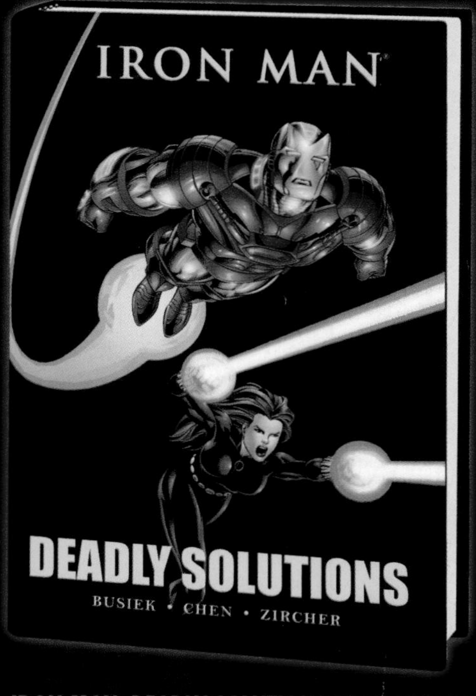
IRON MAN®
DEADLY SOLUTIONS
BUSIEK • CHEN • ZIRCHER

IRON MAN: DEADLY SOLUTIONS PREMIERE HC
978-0-7851-4258-4

On Sale Now

MARVEL